T0374261

Energy Literacy
for Climate Action

Energy Literacy for Climate Action

Technology, Best Practices, and Insights

Francis M. Vanek, PhD

ENERGY LITERACY FOR CLIMATE ACTION
TECHNOLOGY, BEST PRACTICES, AND INSIGHTS

iUniverse books may be ordered through booksellers or by contacting:

iUniverse
1663 Liberty Drive
Bloomington, IN 47403
www.iuniverse.com
844-349-9409

Because of the dynamic nature of the Internet, any web addresses or links contained in this book may have changed since publication and may no longer be valid. The views expressed in this work are solely those of the author and do not necessarily reflect the views of the publisher, and the publisher hereby disclaims any responsibility for them.

Any people depicted in stock imagery provided by Getty Images are models, and such images are being used for illustrative purposes only.
Certain stock imagery © Getty Images.

ISBN: 978-1-6632-5949-3 (sc)
ISBN: 978-1-6632-5950-9 (e)

Library of Congress Control Number: 2023924602

Print information available on the last page.

iUniverse rev. date: 03/14/2024

CONTENTS

LIST OF FIGURES

Chapter 3

Chapter 4

Chapter 5

LIST OF TABLES

Chapter 9

Chapter 10

ACKNOWLEDGMENT

There are many people I would like to thank for their contributions to making this book possible. I would like to thank my partner Catherine Johnson for her ongoing encouragement and for acting as a sounding board along the way. I would also like to thank my parents, for inspiring my interest in renewable energy from the time that I was growing up: my dad Jaroslav Vanek, who passed away in 2017, and my mother Wilda Vanek, who passed away in 2023.

During the production process I received invaluable assistance. Martha Stettinius assisted with editorial review during the manuscript stage and provided many helpful suggestions. Deborah Crowell proofread the manuscript and added many corrections and improvements to the clarity and succinctness of the text. I am grateful to them both. (Disclaimer: while these contributions are warmly acknowledged, responsibility for any and all errors and omissions lies entirely with me.) I also wish to express thanks to Megan Pugh of Blink Digital, who designed the cover. Thanks also to Charissa King-O'Brien of Cornell University for providing the author photograph on the back cover.

The project of writing this book benefitted from work over many years on two textbooks of which I am lead author, *Energy Systems Engineering: Evaluation and Implementation (4th edition)* and *Sustainable Transportation Systems Engineering*. I wish to thank my coauthors Louis Albright, Lars Angenent, James Banks, Ricardo Daziano, David Dillard, Mike Ellis, and Mark Turnquist for their interaction and contribution in these projects. In particular, I would like to remember Louis Albright and Mark Turnquist, who are no longer with us.

Other appreciations go out to the many faculty and staff colleagues at Cornell University where I work, as well as colleagues at other colleges and universities, whose interactions have informed this book. Thanks also to the many students I have taught over the years, mostly at Cornell since 2001 but also earlier at the University of Pennsylvania, Heriot-Watt University, and Ithaca College. These conversations and questions have provided direction and also inspiration for the book. Appreciation also goes out to the Ecovillage at Ithaca intentional community where I have lived since 2002 for the many hands-on lessons I have learned related to energy efficiency and renewable energy along the way. Thanks to the members of Ithaca Community Power, our local sustainable energy nonprofit, for the opportunity to pursue together numerous feasibility studies in and around Ithaca. I wish also to give thanks to the yoga community at Cornell and in Ithaca, and the Kripalu Yoga community further afield, who have helped to keep me centered and at peace during this long process. Lastly, to anyone else I might have overlooked, thank you.

PREFACE

I grew up in the midst of the solar energy movement of the 1970s, living in a family and a community of friends who tinkered with devices that could pump water or heat swimming pools. Our family car was a Volkswagen bus, and on the back was a bumper sticker that read "TRY THE SOLAR SOLUTION TO NUCLEAR POLLUTION." I took it on faith that nuclear power was the enemy and that solar energy was the answer. (We had no idea that within 30 years, growth of large-scale wind turbines, as yet uninvented, would outstrip that of solar systems in the U.S.) We paid no attention to the coal-fired power plant that operated fifteen miles from my home, on the shores of Cayuga Lake (except that it was an excellent place for lake fishing, since the fish congregated in the warmed water by the power plant outlet). It had been there for decades and would always be there. Our nemesis was further away along the Susquehanna River in Pennsylvania, at a place called Three Mile Island.

Later, I came to question many things about that bumper sticker – and about the renewable energy movement. Did nuclear energy really cause pollution? Was solar the solution? Did solar itself cause pollution? What about all the other types of renewable energy? What was their appeal – and limitations? All I had thought about were the solar contraptions I could see working right in front of me. Even though I had exposure to solar energy through high school and on into college, it never occurred to me to look at the vast quantity of energy delivered by non-renewable and nuclear energy sources, or the numbers of solar devices of any given size it would take to displace this energy supply. At a minimum, it seemed that, in hindsight, we had focused on the wrong source: today it turns out that the burning of fossil fuels, including coal-fired power plants, are the most immediate threat to our global environment, because of their leading role as drivers of climate change. Nuclear power plants continue to function and their risks are still present, but society's focus has shifted to greenhouse gas emissions.

Not only that, but the role of different fossil fuels has changed in surprising ways. Electricity from burning coal, which once seemed to have an indomitable position in the energy market, gave way to competition from other sources, notably from combustion of natural gas, which not only delivered more power per unit of carbon dioxide emitted from the smokestack, but also avoided certain types of pollution that accompany the burning of coal. Coal-fired power plants that were not able to repower with natural gas lost economic competitiveness and closed. The plant on Cayuga Lake was one of the facilities that shut down. The ubiquitous coal trains that trundled through Ithaca going to and from the plant disappeared.

My life journey from then until now brought me through years of teaching and research on sustainable energy, alternative transportation, and green building, and eventually to becoming lead author on two textbooks, *Energy Systems Engineering: Evaluation and Implementation* (currently in its 4th edition) and *Sustainable Transportation Systems Engineering*. Coauthored with colleagues Lou Albright, Lars Angenent, Ricardo Daziano, and Mark Turnquist of Cornell University (where I currently work) and Mike Ellis and Dave Dillard of Virginia Tech, and published by McGraw-Hill, these textbooks provide us as a group of authors with an outlet for sharing teaching materials with other colleges and universities. Moreover, with the current strong desire of the community of nations to reduce greenhouse gas emissions to protect global climate, to have sufficient secure energy to support our quality of life, and to expand access to energy in poor countries, energy is a very timely topic.

Naturally, a long engineering textbook tends to be dominated by technical content, such as equations, figures, and tables, which are useful for technical educational purposes. However, for a broader audience, there is interest in the underlying argument for acting on sustainable energy without all the engineering details needed in a textbook. To this end, *Energy Literacy for Climate Action* draws on the same subject matter as *Energy Systems Engineering* and *Sustainable Transportation Systems Engineering* but distills it to the essential information that can be contained in a shorter book. In my day-to-day conversations with friends and acquaintances I would hear questions about energy and climate and think to myself, "I can answer that question with content in our textbooks." Naturally, this led me to want to write a different book, based on the same content but with this other type of reader in mind.

In writing this book, I have been inspired by a number of popular books that make the connection between the environment and the economy, and strive to move us in the direction of sustainable development, including Amory Lovins et al's *Natural Capitalism*, Hazel Henderson's *The Politics of the Solar Age*, Herman Daly's *The Steady-State Economy*, E.F. Schumacher's *Small is Beautiful*, Lester Brown's *Plan B*, Bill McKibben's *Deep* Economy, Van Jones's *The Green-Collar Economy*, and Fred Krupp's *Earth: The Sequel*, among others. One of the strongest common elements of these four books is an emphasis on the need to develop sustainable energy resources. My book is of course entirely in agreement with this view, and I aim to complement these other books by focusing on the fundamental characteristics that underpin sustainable energy solutions, based on my long experience teaching about them.

Lastly, the subject of achieving sustainable energy to protect the global climate is a daunting one, so it is important to find ways to maintain hope. Even in the time since the first edition of *Energy Systems*

Engineering came out in 2008, the challenges have become starker. The calls to accelerate the global energy transition have grown louder, and at the same time, annual CO_2 emissions have grown faster than the community of nations desired, extreme weather impacts have worsened, and the pathway toward limiting temperature rise to 1.5°C has narrowed. At the same time, new technologies have appeared on the stage at a surprisingly rapid rate. The worldwide growth of solar and wind energy has outpaced predictions from 10 or 20 years ago, and electric vehicles have proven a surprising success. In 2004, I visited the Fenner wind farm near Syracuse, NY, with a class trip from Cornell. Looking to the east from the hilltops of that wind farm, I could just see on the distant horizon the spinning blades of the next wind farm over, the Madison wind farm close to Utica, NY. Two years later, our family was returning from a summer vacation and detoured off the New York State Thruway to drive up into the hills and have a look at Fenner. Looking again to the east, I could still see the Madison farm – and also two new wind farms that had been installed on the hilltops between Fenner and Madison.

NOTE ABOUT COMMERCIAL REFERENCES

A note about references to enterprises and products mentioned in this book: these references are made solely for the convenience of the reader to be able to easily find examples in the literature and on the internet. No endorsement of any product or enterprise is expressed or implied. No financial contributions were received in exchange for these references.

A NOTE TO READERS ABOUT ENERGY UNITS IN THIS BOOK

The presentation in the body of this book on energy literacy revolves around quantities of energy large and small. Some readers are already familiar with these units from everyday usage. For others, a refresher on both metric and U.S. standard energy units is provided to make the examples in the book more accessible.

The review of metric energy units begins with the relationship between energy and other units of mass, force, and energy. It is helpful to start with a unit that is tangible and work our way up, so we begin with the kilogram (kg), the metric unit of *mass* that is equivalent to approximately 2.2 U.S. pounds. The unit of *force* is the Newton (N). One Newton is the amount of force required to accelerate a mass of 1 kg by 1 meter per second in the time of one second when applied. In other words, suppose a block of some material weighing 1 kg is standing still. After the force of 1 N is applied for 1 second, the block would be moving at a speed of 1 m/s. One way to define *energy* is that it is equivalent to a force applied over a distance, so that the amount of energy provided is equivalent to the process of force and distance. The unit of energy is the Joule (J), equivalent to 1 Newton multiplied by 1 meter. In this example, if the force of 1 N were applied to the block over a distance of 1 meter, the amount of energy provided would be 1 J. Lastly, *power* is defined as the amount of energy provided per unit of time. The metric unit of power is the Watt (W), and 1 Watt is equivalent to 1 Joule per second. As an alternative to Joules, metric quantities of energy can also be conveniently expressed by multiplying power (energy per unit of time, in units of, e.g., Kilowatts) by units of time (in units of time) to arrive at units of Kilowatt-hours, or kWh. Since there are 3,600 seconds in an hour, 1 kWh is equivalent to 3,600 kJ, or 3.6 MJ. There follows a handy rule for conversion: To convert from watt-hours to Joules, multiply by 3.6 and increase the metric prefix by one, e.g., kilo- to Mega-, Mega- to Giga-, and so on. Table 1 presents the various metric prefixes from kilo- to Exa-.

Prefix	Abbreviation	Value
Kilo-	k	10^3
Mega-	M	10^6
Giga-	G	10^9
Tera-	T	10^12
Peta-	P	10^15
Exa-	E	10^18

Table 1 Prefixes used with metric units

Some examples of the use of the prefixes in Table 1 are in order. Household electricity customers think of measuring electricity consumption around the house in kilowatt-hours or kWh; large electricity producers think in larger terms than a single house and therefore use the price per megawatt-hour or MWh to consider the buying and selling of electric power. A convenient measure for a householder purchasing natural gas in a European country is a gigajoule or GJ. The maximum output of a large power plant might be given in megawatts or MW, but the total rate of energy consumption of the planet can be measure in terawatts or TW. Annual energy consumption of entire countries like the United States is measured in exajoules or EJ.

Energy can be expressed as force exerted over a distance, and it can also be expressed as the capacity to raise the temperature of an object or volume of liquid or gas. The measure of tangible quantities of heat is used to introduce units of energy on the U.S. customary side, also called "standard" units in the United States. The unit of heat in this system is the British thermal unit or Btu. One Btu is defined as the amount of energy required to raise one pound of water at room temperature and ambient temperature by one degree Fahrenheit; it also approximately the amount of energy released by burning a kitchen match. Since Btus are units of energy, it follows that power can be measured in U.S. customary units as energy per unit of time, such as Btus per hour or Btus per second. (U.S. customary units of force are not used in this book.) Table 2 compares units of energy and power in the metric and U.S. customary systems, with metric units further divided into two columns, measures based on Joules and on Watts. A Joule is a measure of energy, so it follows that dividing Joules by a unit of time, such as Joules per second, gives a measure of power, as shown in the table. However, a Joule per second is, by definition, a Watt, so the unit of Joules/second is not generally used, since it is simpler to use the unit of Watts.

Measure	Metric		Standard
Energy:	Joules	Watt-hours	Btu
Power:	Joules/second	Watts	Btu/hour

Table 2 Comparison of metric and standard units of energy and power

The choice of units of Watts for power and Watt-hours for energy can lead to confusion, even in national publications read by millions of readers, where writers routinely confuse the two. Compare the situation to that of distance and speed. If a location is 65 miles away and takes an hour to reach, we easily infer that the speed while traveling there was 65 miles per hour. Or, if we are told that the location is 65 miles away and travel speed will be 65 miles per hour, then we know that the trip will take one hour. However, if someone is asked "how far is it from Binghamton to Syracuse?", they will certainly not respond that "it is 65 miles per hour away." With power and energy, it is not intuitive that if a certain amount of power, say 10 kilowatts, is being provided for an hour, that we could multiply the two units together and create a unit for energy called "kilowatt-hours" and state that the amount of energy delivered is 10 kWh.

Table 3 illustrates the difference between speed/distance and power/energy, all using a time period of one hour. Obviously, traveling at a speed of 100 miles per hour (mph) for one hour leads to a distance of 100 miles, and similarly producing or consuming power at a rate of 100 kW results in an energy amount equivalent to 100 kWh. Alternatively, in U.S. customary units, power provided at a rate of 1 MMBtu/hour (million Btu) for one hour amounts to 1 MMBtu of energy. Furthermore, kWh can be converted to Joules by multiplying by a conversion factor of 3600 kJ per kWh, resulting in a total of 360,000 kJ, which can be more easily written as 360 MJ. In U.S. customary units as well, since kWh are an official unit in the U.S. system, we can multiply by a conversion factor of 0.000293 kWh per Btu, which results in a total amount of 293 kWh of energy.

Desired Quantity:	Examples: Distance	Energy (met.)	Energy (U.S.)
Rate	100 mph	100 kW	1 Million Btu/h
Time	1 hour	1 hour	1 hour
Result	100 miles	100 kWh	1 Million Btu
Conversion	n/a	3600 kJ per kWh	0.000293 kWh/Btu
Result	n/a	360 Megajoule	~293 kWh

Table 3 Comparison of units for energy/power and distance/speed

Lastly, some energy units not connected to the metric or U.S. standard system are instead derived from energy sources themselves. A "barrel" of oil is a volume of oil of 42 gallons – not to be confused with the 55-gallon drum, another barrel-shaped unit used for transporting liquids. A gallon of crude oil has an average energy content of approximately 138,100 Btu, so the energy content of a barrel of oil amounts to 5.8 million Btu. A larger unit related to oil is the "tonne of oil equivalent", which again uses the average energy content of a typical quantity of crude oil. One "toe" has an energy content of about 41.9 GJ, so a quantity of 1,000 GJ is equivalent to approximately 23.9 toe. For larger energy quantities, units of 1,000 toe (ktoe) or million toe (mtoe) are useful; for instance, the total energy consumption of the United States in 2012 of 95 EJ could also be expressed as ~2,269 mtoe. Turning to other units, a unit of 1,000 cubic feet of natural gas at atmospheric pressure has an energy content of about 1.04 million Btu. Coal varies widely in energy content depending on quality, but one tonne of good-quality coal might have an energy content of approximately 25 GJ.

CHAPTER 1

Before All Else, the Power of Human Energy

This book is mostly about what humans do with energy. It considers many sources from which we could sustainably derive energy. It also considers many different applications where we use energy, and ways to transfer energy from where we find it to where we use it.

However, this is also a book about taking action to confront climate change. Because the focus on preventing and reversing climate change is so important, and because the way we use energy has such a critical role, before all other types of energy, the first type to discuss is our own internal human energy to take on this monumental and grand project.

We use our human energy to set a goal and strive to reach it, to persevere against resistance and obstacles, and to fight for a future for our descendants and for all living beings. We will need this internal human energy to persist over the long haul. Up until now climate change has already proven very challenging, and although no one can see the future exactly, this situation is all but certain to continue and to grow more severe, before it eventually begins to subside if our efforts pay off. Here are three reasons why energy to persist will be necessary.

First, as best we know with the technology we have now and that we can predict will emerge in the foreseeable future, transforming our global energy system is a long road. We must be willing to keep going with steps that yield little apparent progress from day to day. Years of hard work will yield slow and begrudging progress. We must be prepared to keep going, and when the time comes, one generation must inspire another to keep going as the torch is passed. For many who are working on this issue now, the challenge of climate change is bound to outlive us.

Secondly, there will be other challenges along the way – poverty, disease, and so on – that will need to be addressed simultaneously. Climate change will exacerbate these challenges. Society will need to continue moving forward to change our energy system, even as we address these vital needs.

Lastly, sometimes climate change itself will be the very force that undercuts our progress toward a sustainable energy system, even as we seek to make changes. All systems in the built environment, including energy systems, are susceptible to damage from fire, flooding, sea level rise, and extreme weather that result from climate change. For example, in September 2017, Hurricane Maria made landfall as a Category 5 hurricane near a windfarm in Humacao, Puerto Rico, and tore all the blades off the turbines erected there to provide carbon-free electricity. A year later, not one turbine had been repaired, and the windfarm stood idle. The equipment needed to fight climate change was prevented from fighting climate change by climate change itself. If we proceed down the path of converting to renewable energy, a global energy system with a massive footprint on the land will need to coexist with a climate system that has become unstable and violent in the meantime. We must not become discouraged, but rather be prepared to make repairs over and over again to drive down carbon emissions.

On a more positive note, in our work to transform our energy system we can draw inspiration and energy from our deep concern for all the communities on whose behalf we are striving. One such community is the community of all non-human living organisms, plants and animals, who are depending on us to not irreversibly change our planetary climate and home. They participate unwillingly in humanity's energy system, so we should not impose a negative outcome on them.

A second are the people living in absolute poverty, often in developing countries in more tropical regions. Due to their lack of disposable income, these people derive relatively little benefit from modern energy, yet they often suffer disproportionately from the negative effects of climate change. Simple fairness demands that the beneficiaries of the modern global energy system work to prevent climate change.

A third are people of limited economic means living in the "developed" world who nevertheless live from paycheck to paycheck and have little breathing room to think about energy transformations to address climate change. Although they may have more access to material goods than people in developing countries, they do not benefit from access to cheap and abundant energy in the same way that wealthier first-world residents do: large houses, powerful cars, exotic vacations, and so on. They are also not well equipped to pay out of pocket for a large increase in their cost of energy or to upgrade their lifestyle to be more energy-efficient, should society begin to push in that direction.

It is already the reality that some people living in impoverished conditions, whether in developing or industrialized countries, are finding a way to become involved in climate activism. Yet it is also certain that many, many others in these two groups will not be able to do so, due to the difficulties in their day to day lives. And so it is imperative that people in the middle and upper classes work even harder to compensate.

And finally, another group from which we can draw motivation is the future generations of people (not to mention animals and plants) that are not present now to participate in the decisions that we make, but who will be affected by them someday, for better or worse. This feature was given the term "intertemporality" by the United Nations: the right (and responsibility) of the current generation to meet its needs without jeopardizing the ability of future generations to do so.

Although the focus in the rest of this book is on tangible energy (electricity, heat, cooling, fuel, and so on), we should always keep in mind that human action also requires human energy: to set out on a course and follow it through to completion, and to regroup after setbacks. By implication, every project and solution starts with the intangible energy of human resolve.

CHAPTER 2
Dimensions of Energy Literacy

Energy literacy to support action on climate change starts with the following claim: A potential solution exists for sustainable global energy that will lead to climate protection. The countries of the world should band together and exert themselves to achieve it with all their collective might. Doing so will not only avoid future suffering by preventing climate change, but also deliver benefits from a cleaner and more just energy system. If we choose to go down the sustainable energy path, we have a chance to achieve this goal.

In the past 30 to 40 years, all of the essential elements of a sustainable energy solution have emerged. These elements include ways to generate renewable energy from diverse sources. They also include applications both stationary and mobile that can harness that energy, and ways to transmit and store it more efficiently. The pace at which these solutions come on the market has accelerated in recent years, even as the impact of climate change grows more pronounced.

Governments and the United Nations may be coming up short so far, but individuals and non-governmental organizations are stepping in to fill the gap. If you look only at global treaties such as the Rio Summit, Kyoto Protocol, or Paris Climate Agreement, you see that global agreements to date have not yet fully addressed climate change. For example, the Paris Agreement includes all the UN member countries but does not include commitments from member countries sufficient to achieve emissions reductions targets.[1] However, if you look at a regional or local level, people everywhere are taking steps with increasing numbers and with ever increasing vigor, notably in the transition to more renewable energy.

Consider the worldwide growth in installed solar photovoltaic capacity since the year 1990. Figure 1 shows how growth was relatively slow through 1997, and how it accelerated thereafter through 2003. However, when this growth is overlaid on the growth from 1990 to 2019, as in Fig. 2, the same growth that appears as a major upturn in the 1997-2003 period is barely visible compared to the year-on-year growth in the years from 2010 onward. Recent installation rates are simply much higher than could have been predicted in the early 2000s. The cumulative installed quantity through 2003 was approximately 3300 Megawatts (MW).[2] The amount installed in either 2018 or 2019 is actually more than ten times as large as this amount, in a single year. Yet, if someone had predicted this level of growth in 2003, they would have been met with great skepticism.

---

[1] To be precise, the Paris Accord included the United States at the time of its signing, then for a time the U.S. was in the process of withdrawing, before rejoining in 2021.
[2] Throughout this book, amounts of energy systems are frequently measured in units of "nameplate capacity", meaning the maximum amount that a device, or quantity of devices, can produce under ideal conditions. For example, 3,300 MW of solar panels can produce 3,300 MW instantaneously when conditions are perfect: clear skies, sunlight shining directly onto the panel, and so on. See Chap.5 on solar energy for details.

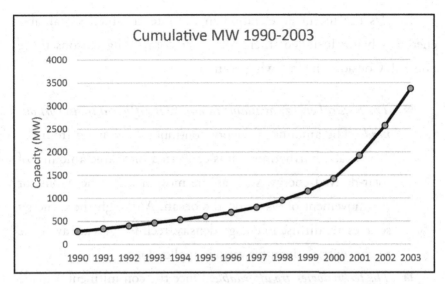

Figure 1 Growth in cumulative world solar PV installed capacity, 1990-2003.
Source: SolarPower Europe.

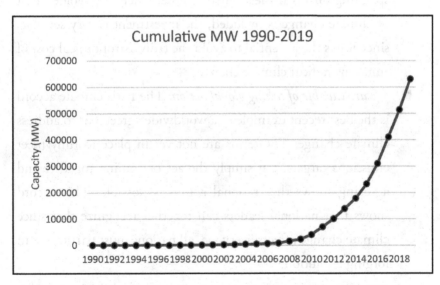

Figure 2 Growth in cumulative world solar PV installations for period 1990-2019.
Source: SolarPower Europe.

Besides the recent acceleration in the rate at which sustainable energy is being installed, there are other compelling reasons to be hopeful. Consider the following points:

- *The physical energy available in nature is sufficient to support our needs:* The amount of energy continuously arriving from the sun is vast. Furthermore, it is converted into large amounts of solar-derived energy, such as the movement of the winds, or the movement of waves on the ocean. Although these energy sources are diffuse in energy density, technologies are available to concentrate them for various applications.

- *The technologies are affordable:* Once the commitment is made to transition to renewable energy sources in a big way, the eventual cost is of the same order of magnitude as continued spending on fossil fuels. Furthermore, when the avoided cost of climate change is included, the investment is very sensible, since it has the potential to avoid the truly astronomical cost of runaway, radical climate change.

- *We are capable of taking global action:* The Paris climate accord is the best recent example of a worldwide agreement to address climate change. The terms are not yet in place to fully meet emissions targets, but simply the act of coming together and agreeing shows that rational action is possible. This accord shows that national leaders can together recognize that since climate change affects everyone, all nations must participate in forging a solution.

Connecting Energy and Climate to Other Major Challenges

As we look around, we see in the United States a country beset by difficult, intractable problems that defy easy, quick solutions. Climate change is only one of them; there are many others. Yet it is important to see climate change in this context because addressing energy and climate has the potential to ease other challenges as well. The economy went through the Great Recession of 2008-2010, then entered a recovery, then experienced the downturn of the Global Pandemic; many citizens do not feel economically secure. Our health care system leaves out a large number of citizens, who cannot afford health insurance and are at the mercy of whatever fortune their health may bring, for good or for ill. Our educational system comes up short, with many students taught inadequately, by teachers who struggle to earn a living and in schools that are falling into disrepair. Our armed forces are deployed overseas year after year; the U.S. military presence in Afghanistan has become the longest war in our history. Tying all of these together, our legislative process seems too partisan, slow, and inefficient, and public confidence in our elected officials is low.

Compared to problems like these – economy, financial system, health care, education, military, government – does solving the energy problem, of which the development of renewable energy is a part, rise to the level of being a top priority? Certainly, energy-related topics such as the price of oil, green-collar jobs, and climate change are regularly in the news, but they are not the most frequently covered item. Furthermore, some of the energy coverage that does take place is in response to disasters, such as the breaching of a coal sludge holding pond belonging to Duke Energy in North Carolina in the aftermath of Hurricane Florence in September 2018. News reports like these get considerable attention for several days or weeks while they are in progress, and then fade from memory. They inform the public about the risks associated with current energy sources, but they do not directly address how system-wide energy problems such as climate change and continuity of supply will be solved going forward. The psychological effect is profoundly depressing: one hears about how problems from climate change continue to fester, but not about efforts to solve them.

Even with other major problems that we face, the energy and climate problem ranks alongside any of the others. Consider the serious effects that the energy problem might bring in the future. One dimension is the volatile price problem: wild spikes in energy prices, like the fluctuations in the price of oil between 2008 and 2018, can permeate all aspects of the economy – as a business and consumer cost, as a component of moving goods and people, or as a raw material for the petrochemical industry. Another dimension is the supply problem: sooner or later, with more and more demand around the world and no way to increase the rate of extraction from traditional energy sources, it becomes physically impossible to deliver people the energy resources they expect, whenever they want them. As a result, supplies of gasoline, natural gas, or electricity could be disrupted, leading to hardship. The final dimension is the accelerating impact of climate change: droughts, floods, changing crop yields, rising sea levels, all predicted to increase as the concentration of CO_2 in the atmosphere increases.

And increase it will. Figure 3 shows average global CO_2 concentration for each year from 1960 to 2020, measured in parts per million (ppm) in the atmosphere. The year 2015 was the first time this measure reached 400 ppm, meaning that for every million molecules in the atmosphere (nitrogen molecules, oxygen molecules, and so on), 400 were CO_2 molecules. By 2020 it had reached around 410 ppm. With total world emissions of CO_2 exceeding the amount that the planet can absorb from year to year, the upward trend will continue in the near term, until our actions to reduce use of fossil fuels are sufficient to "bend the curve" in a different direction.

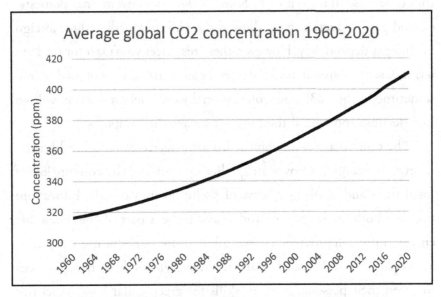

Figure 3 Global average CO_2 concentration in parts per million of volume, 1958-2018.

Data Source: National Oceanic and Atmospheric Administration.

Fortunately for us, *solving the energy problem through renewable energy can play a role in solving many or even all of the other major problems which face us.* Addressing the economy, for example, the transition to renewable energy will create enormous numbers of jobs. These jobs happen in the initial deployment stage, since so many renewable energy systems must be installed, whether large systems like wind farms or small ones like residential photovoltaic (PV) systems. Thereafter, they continue to sustain jobs. A worldwide renewable energy system large enough to meet global demand would be so large that devices would always be reaching the end of their lives and requiring replacement.

Addressing the financial system, renewable energy creates an energy resource in the U.S. to displace imports of foreign energy resources, improving our balance of payments and keeping funds in our economy that otherwise drain out of it. Since 2008, nonconventional domestic oil and gas production have allowed the U.S. to greatly reduce foreign oil and gas dependency. However, these resources won't last for the long term. Based on estimated size of reserves and current rates of production, sometime in the 2030s nonconventional fossil fuel production will go into decline, and with it their impact on avoiding imports.

The other major issues on the list are affected as well. Health care: renewable energy improves air quality by avoiding the combustion of fossil fuels and resulting release of pollution into the air. Education: training both young people and adults to be a part of the renewable energy transition provides a powerful focus for our educational system, as people in all walks of life learn about everything from best practices to green their personal lives, to skills for green-collar jobs, to science and engineering needed to create the next generation of technology. National defense: as we as a nation become permanently self-reliant for energy, we are less dependent on other parts of the world and less entangled in regional political struggles. And yes, along the way, creating the renewable energy society may even enforce a discipline on our legislative process that will make it more responsive and effective.

Energy Consumption Through History

In the year 210 B.C.E., the emperor Qin Shihuang of China, concerned about groups of raiders entering his kingdom from the North, ordered that a wall be built along the northern frontier to keep them out. The ensuing project took some 10 years to complete and at times is estimated to have had as many as 300,000 men working on it.

When it was finished, the wall stretched for more than 3,000 miles and was 15 to 30 feet high and 12 to 16 feet thick at the base. Aptly named the "Great Wall of China," much of it stands to this day.

The Great Wall reflects how much human society has changed in terms of its access to and use of energy sources. With no modern energy resources available (such as electricity and petroleum products) and apparently little use of draft animals, Emperor Qin had no choice but to bring in vast numbers of people using nothing more than basic hand tools in order to complete the project (picks, shovels, and baskets). No one can dispute that the result of their labor was an impressive achievement; however, the maximum power output by any one of the laborers was rather modest, by modern standards. Because maximum exertion (for example, to lift a heavy stone into place in the Great Wall) will quickly tire a laborer, the sustained maximum output, averaged over many hours of work, is not more than the energy input into a 75 watt incandescent lightbulb.[3] A modern freight locomotive might have a maximum output of 8,000 kilowatts, or 8 million watts; if a full length freight train in the U.S. requires five locomotives to pull it, then the group of locomotives has about twice as much power available to it as the entire army of laborers at work on the Great Wall – even though a crew of just three people is needed to operate the train. It is true that the railroad company needs some additional supporting staff in other roles not physically inside the locomotive cab to help it to run (such as mechanics, operations managers, and the like). However, even including this number, the total staff is far, far fewer than a number in the hundreds of thousands.

---

[3] From Lorenzo (1994, p.30). Other authors might dispute the figure of 75 watts per human, but the general point would be upheld even with a different number, since the maximum sustained output of a human being is so small compared to a locomotive.

Put another way, a modern construction engineering company could go back today and build a similar wall with similar dimensions, and also within a ten-year time frame, but employ many fewer people. They would first level the ground for the wall and excavate some sort of foundation, and then use not hewn stones but some modern building material such as reinforced concrete to build the wall up to its designed height. They might require no more than a maximum of 1,000 people working on the project at any one time – and at times they might well need far fewer. To reduce labor needed, they would use modern machinery, such as earth-moving equipment at the site, or trucks and maybe train cars to bring concrete and steel in from a distance. And, of course, they would use energy – lots of it.

For more than 2,000 of the 2,200 years from the building of the Great Wall to the present, not much changed in the amount of energy produced per human being on planet earth, and since the total number of humans grew only slowly, global energy demand did not grow very much either.

Then, starting in about 1850, and especially after 1950, the pace increased, as shown in Fig. 4. Population grew from just over 1 billion in 1850 to over 7.7 billion in the year 2020. Furthermore, the worldwide average amount of energy used per person tripled, so that total human energy use is up more than 20 times from 1850 to 2020. Today, the spread between rich and poor countries in terms of per capita energy use is enormous – the average U.S. citizen uses about 300 million Btu (British thermal units) per year[4], while the average Bangladeshi uses just 6 million Btu, according to the U.S. Energy Information Administration, or EIA. Note that the downturn between 2015 and 2020 does not represent a fundamental change in direction for world energy policy, but rather the economic downturn due to the global COVID-19 pandemic in that year.

---

[4] One Btu is the amount of energy needed to heat one pound of liquid water by one degree Fahrenheit.

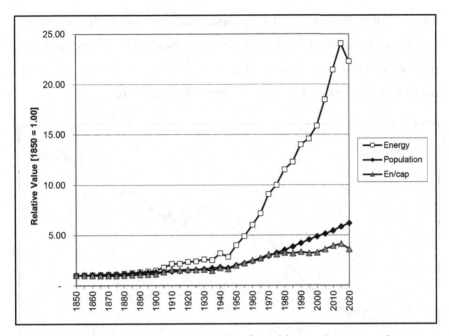

Figure 4 Historic growth of world population, total energy use, and per capita energy use in the industrial age 1850-2020, indexed to a value of 1850 = 1.00. Values in 1800: Population 1.26 billion, energy ~25 quadrillion Btu, energy per capita ~19 million Btu/person.

Data source: U.S. Energy Information Administration.

In a remarkable example of increasing energy demand, from about the year 2000 onward the energy consumption model of the OECD countries (Organization for Economic Cooperation and Development, mainly North America, Europe, and Japan) began to spread to other parts of the world. In the case of China, the result was astonishing (Fig. 5). The U.S. surpassed 40 quadrillion Btus[5], or Quads, of total energy consumption in the year 1955, and then took another 49 years to surpass 100 Quads of consumption. In China, the same 40-to-100 Quad transition took just 11 years. China in the year 2000 had

---

[5] 1 Quadrillion = 1 x 10^{15}; in other words, a "1" with 15 zeroes after it.

a population of over 1 billion people, had available to it the energy technologies that the U.S. and its peer countries had pioneered, and was playing "catch-up" in terms of lifting its population out of poverty. The result was energy development at a breathtaking pace.

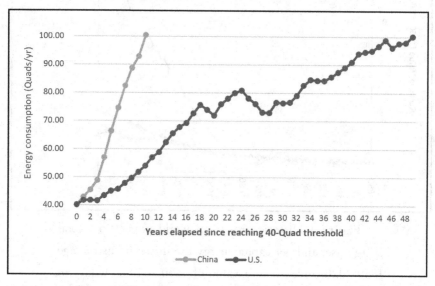

Figure 5 Years elapsed to grow total energy consumption from 40 to 100 Quads: China and USA.

Notes: USA crossed 40-Quad threshold in 1955; China crossed in 1999. Data source: U.S. Energy Information Administration.

The ability to harness and use modern energy sources in large quantities compared to pre-industrial times is a two-edged sword. On the one hand, it is an impressive achievement that we as a society have figured out how to multiply our individual human strength so much that most people in the workforce in a modern, industrialized economy do not work using brute strength. On the other hand, we have created a modern economic system and way of life that requires continued access to massive amounts of energy, by historical standards. Presumably, if we want to maintain our standard of living, then we also need to keep providing energy at something like the rate we do today.

Most of the energy production to meet this demand today comes from fossil fuel resources, whose ultimately recoverable amount is subject to debate, but whose nonrenewable status no one disputes – sooner or later fossil fuels will run out. Briefly explained, these fuels come from a time millions of years ago when biological matter (primarily plant residues but also some animals) became trapped under layers of earth. Over time, and with the help of heat and pressure, they were transformed into the fuels we use today: coal, oil, and gas. In theory, there are places under the earth's surface where they are continuing to form even now, though, of course, not nearly as fast as we are depleting them. So, as human society moves forward into the future and non-renewable energy supplies are gradually exhausted, we must either find other ways to support society with abundant sources of energy – or completely reorganize the way it operates.

Is society then doomed in its pursuit of maintaining the modern way of life? Is the energy bubble of the industrial age a one-time fling, that once finished will never come again? Fortunately, there is an amount of energy even vaster than the world's current energy consumption. Every year, the cumulative amount of solar energy arriving at the edge of the earth's atmosphere is some 9,000 times greater than the amount of worldwide energy consumption shown in Figure 4 for the year 2015.[6] It takes just a few months of the energy gain from the sun to equal all the energy that is stored in all the fossil fuels that have been or ever will be extracted from the earth. Clearly, the amount of energy available from solar and other renewable resources is more than adequate to meet all

---

[6] Calculated using the solar constant of 1,372 watts per square meter, the cross-sectional area of the earth, and converting this amount of energy flow in watt-hours to Btus.

our needs – if we make the necessary investment in infrastructure to capture, distribute, and in some cases store it. There is hope.

Current Energy Consumption: Modern Lifestyle, Massive Amounts

If the amount of energy available in nature is so large, then paradoxically, the amount that the minority of people that have access to modern conveniences is massive in terms of what the rest of the world accesses, and also compared to the average amount consumed per person over the course of human history. We are familiar with the adage that "the U.S. uses a disproportionate amount of the world's resources for only representing a few percent of the global population." But to put that intensive resource use in visual terms is startling.

Think about your own lifestyle. Every day you work, travel, shop, stay warm, stay cool, all using energy. To varying degrees, everyone else in a modern economy like that of the United States does too, and it all adds up to a tremendous amount of energy, on the order of Quadrillion Btus per year. The ups and downs of the economy might make you do more or less of some things – and these changes mean that energy consumption does to some extent "track" the economy. For example, in a downturn, people travel less on long trips by car or plane, leading to reduced energy consumption that shows up in the national energy "budget" (i.e., total amount of energy consumed in a year). Large-scale downturns can be observed in Fig. 3: The Great Depression reduced world energy consumption from 1930 to 1935, the deprivations of World War II did the same from 1940 to 1945 (despite the war effort), and a global pandemic decreased consumption from 2015 to 2020. Even with these fluctuations, however, the massive use of energy continues – and because the overall population and economic wealth of the planet is growing, the general trend is upward. In other words, you, the energy consumer, cannot stop eating, staying warm, or getting where you need to go, so some base level of energy consumption continues, no matter what.

So how do we as Americans manage to consume 300 million Btus per person of energy in a year? Let's start by adopting a different unit from a Btu, one that is more tangible: a barrel of oil equivalent. A barrel of oil is equivalent to 42 U.S. gallons; you could picture a barrel three feet high and nearly two feet in diameter at the base.[7] That barrel full of oil has an energy content of about 6 million Btus, so we could think of ourselves using 50 barrels of oil each year. Imagine filling up a patio 20 feet wide and 10 feet deep with rows of barrels of oil, and then stacking it as many layers high as there are persons living in your household. You would use that up in a year; then start out again the following year with the same amount. Of course, this is only the national average; you might use more or less based on your personal circumstances and choices.

Our personal energy budget can be divided into two segments: that which we control directly when we use modern conveniences that we own, and that which is consumed in the national economy on our behalf. The energy consumption that we control comes in three forms: electricity, "heating fuel" (natural gas, heating oil, propane, or the like, if one does not also heat with electricity), and motor fuel (usually gasoline, sometimes diesel). The energy required to make the electricity that you use might take the equivalent of nine barrels to make, and the gasoline you buy might take another nine barrels. The heating fuel component is what flows into your home not only for heating, but also for cooking

---

[7] The term "barrel of oil" conjures up the image of a 55-gallon drum, but the oil barrel is actually slightly smaller. The smaller 42-gallon barrel was used for a time to transport oil. The modern oil industry no longer uses barrels for transportation (tankers and pipelines are used instead); however, the use of the term "barrel of oil" to mean a unit of 42 gallons remains in use. The number of barrels in the example has been rounded to 50 so as to use a round number and make the explanation more transparent.

or domestic hot water. This part of your "home energy budget" is a little less than the other two, at about 6 barrels per year. That brings us to 24 barrels. Again, your own numbers may be quite different – if you don't own a car, the nine barrels for buying gas does not apply to you.

So where are the other 26 barrels? Much of it is in "production" or "industrial" energy use – everything from farm production, to mines, to factories. You might not personally work in one of these facilities (in our modern service economy, the odds are that you don't), but if we reason that these activities are essential to making our economy function, then it makes sense to spread out their energy use over the entire population. The industrial component works out to about 16 barrels per person. Another seven barrels goes to "commercial" energy use: energy to operate all the offices, retail spaces, and other public facilities that are an essential part of our economy. (Although not strictly commercial, public-sector buildings like government offices and schools are included in this category.) This leaves transportation energy use that does not involve private automobiles: all types of freight transportation, for about four barrels, and commercial passenger transportation (mostly air travel but also some trains, long-distance buses, and urban mass transportation) for three barrels.

There is a risk that, by taking the large fraction of total energy use dedicated to industrial applications and dividing it among the population, it may give the impression that there is a large quantity of personal energy consumption over which the individual has no control. This is, however, not true: by consuming fewer goods, or by making the non-perishable goods (e.g., personal cars, furniture) already in our possession last longer, we reduce the number of barrels of oil equivalent dedicated to industrial inputs. Note also that these inputs are harder to measure: for instance, we can look at a utility bill to see how much energy we took in per month in natural gas purchases for heating and cooking, but we usually cannot look at the packaging for a given product to know its life cycle embodied energy from raw materials to final delivery.

In any case, if we include both energy consumption directly controlled and embedded in our other activities, we arrive at 50 barrels per person annually – year in and year out. In 1949 it was about half of that; it increased rapidly up to the 1970s, drifted upward to a peak of 60 barrels per person in the early 2000s, and has decreased slightly since then.

As individuals and collectively as a society, we are totally capable over time of reducing this amount through concerted effort. We can also develop more environmentally benign forms of energy to lessen the impact of its consumption. But we cannot wake up one morning and abruptly cut our energy use to zero.

Many Types of Energy, But Only Three Primary Sources

Next, we might ask, where does the energy come from? We can start by thinking about "primary sources" of energy as they are found in nature, before any sort of conversion takes place. A primary energy source could be either the raw energy content of a fossil fuel, a biologically derived fuel, or the energy available in a flow of wind or sunlight. Primary energy "conversion" takes place when the energy is converted into a more useful form, such as when a wind energy device converts motion in the moving wind into rotation of a shaft that can pump water, grind grain, or generate electricity.

Since the link between climate change and carbon emissions is so important, we can make the most basic distinction among primary sources of energy between fossil and non-fossil resources. Worldwide,

Francis M. Vanek

fossil fuels provided 84% of the world primary energy supply in 2019, up from 83% in 2000, according to USEIA. Output of renewables grew significantly, but so did total energy supply, so the net impact was fossil fuel dependency actually increasing slightly (Fig. 6). The "Other" energy sources in Fig. 6 can be divided between nuclear and renewable, and renewables can further be divided between "mature" renewables, such as large hydroelectric dams, and "new" renewables, such as rooftop solar photovoltaic arrays or large-scale wind farms. Large hydro produces more energy than any other renewable source worldwide, but it is very limited in its room for additional growth in the U.S. – there simply are not many locations left where we could build a large dam. (There are, however, opportunities for small- and micro-hydropower to be expanded several-fold, since the base level is so low.)

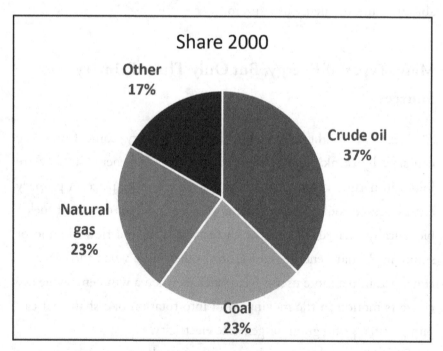

Figure 6a Allocation of world primary energy supply between fossil and non-fossil resources, 2000. Total: 394 Quads. Source: U.S. Energy Information Administration.

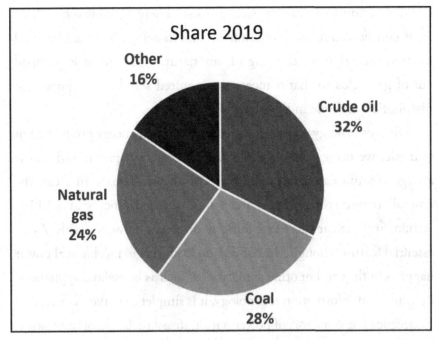

Figure 6b Allocation of world primary energy supply between fossil and non-fossil resources, 2000 and 2019. Totals: 394 Quads for 2000, 605 Quads for 2019. Source: U.S. Energy Information Administration.

If we continue to follow the energy trail from primary source to end user, energy resources undergo varying degrees of conversion. The most obvious one is electricity generation: in the U.S. economy, we convert all nuclear and large-scale hydro, most coal, some natural gas, and a small amount of oil into electricity for distribution to consumers over the electricity transmission and distribution grid. Broadly defined, this electricity grid includes both long-distance power lines that carry electricity at high-voltages, and local distribution networks that carry it at lower voltages to its final destination, such as homes and businesses. We also convert a large fraction of new renewable energy sources to electricity for local use or grid distribution. Besides electricity, other energy products such as gasoline used in cars undergo less radical transformation in the conversion process. There is, however, at least some conversion: refining of crude oil into diesel, gasoline, and jet fuel for transportation, or cleaning of raw natural gas after it is pumped out of gas fields so that it meets the required standards of purity for distribution and sale in the national gas grid.

Different energy applications require different energy products. For example, we use gasoline derived from oil for transportation because a large amount can be stored in a relatively small space in a car, the cost of storage is low, the fuel can be dispensed quickly at a filling station, and the car can travel for long distances between refills. As an essential feature, though, the conversion from fuel to mechanical power happens in the car. For other applications, such as household appliances, lighting, and information technology, it is simpler to make a conversion to electricity at some sort of power station (fossil fuel, hydropower, solar, or the like). Then the electric grid distributes a "carrier", electricity, which can be applied to a wide range of tasks without noxious emissions in the site where the application is carried out.

Use of electricity helps with the diversification of primary energy from many different primary sources. Electricity-using applications have direct access to the full range of primary energy sources, because each source can be converted to electricity. Transportation applications, on the other hand, are almost completely dependent on just one primary source: crude oil. Electrification of vehicles aims to change this situation, but as of 2018 these vehicles number less than 1% of the total on U.S. roads.

How does the breakdown of energy among primary sources and end-use applications affect the development of renewable energy? It is essential to know what the specific requirements of the application are, if you want to make the best possible match with renewable alternatives that are available. For instance, does the energy demand for the application vary by time of day (like lighting), or by season of the year (like heating or cooling)? If so, is there flexibility in adapting the demand to match the proposed renewable resource? For example, could you increase the amount of some activity in seasons when either solar or wind are at their peak, to absorb the increased energy available? Or is the demand a hard constraint, in which case the renewable resource must be adapted? For example, heating in winter in a harsh northern climate in the northern hemisphere is essential if we wish to maintain basic comfort, health, and even life safety.

The problem is that for all these needs that vary all over the world by location, time of day, and season of the year, there are in the end only three primary energy sources. On one level, energy resources and applications are very diverse. For example, you can take crude oil and refine it into gasoline, or diesel, or jet fuel; you can also burn it as fuel oil in a power plant to make electricity, or burn it as heating oil to heat your home. Similarly, you can convert wind energy into electricity for the grid, or you can convert it to mechanical power for local use to pump water, as is still done on many remote farms around the world. But if you reduce them to their essential properties, there are ultimately only three kinds: fossil, nuclear, and renewable.

Even renewable energy, which might appear to be the most diverse, is mostly derived from the sun, either directly or indirectly. The incoming solar energy might power a photovoltaic panel, but it also creates the wind that powers wind turbines. The winds in turn blow across the oceans and generate waves that can power wave energy generators. Solar energy is captured in various plant species large and small, leading to the availability of biomass energy. Solar energy also drives the hydrologic cycle, in which water is lifted into the atmosphere as vapor, forming clouds, and then falls down again as rain; when these rain waters eventually accumulate in the flow of rivers, they are capable of driving turbines in hydroelectric dams. In fact, of all renewable energy types, only tidal energy (caused by the moon's gravitational pull) and deep geothermal energy (derived from the release of thermal energy from the earth's core) is not tied to solar energy – and these two are relatively small contributors to energy production at present.

The three fundamental energy types are actually related to each other. First, all fossil energy originally arrived on the earth as solar energy. Like biomass energy, it was stored in plant matter and then tucked away underground for millions of years. In turn, solar energy comes from the continuous nuclear reaction taking place in our sun. We could therefore think of solar energy as actually a type of nuclear energy taking place in a very large reactor, with a large heat source in the center, heating the planets at various distances. As for nuclear energy, if fusion energy (generating energy from the reaction where two atoms are joined into a single larger one) were to be perfected in the future, and we were able to use the most abundant fuel for fusion on the planet, namely deuterium (an isotope of hydrogen with one neutron), the amount of resource available for this type of energy would be so vast as to be "quasi-renewable"—that is, lasting nearly as long as the projected lifetime of our sun. At that point, the distinction between "renewable" solar energy and "nonrenewable" fusion energy would become blurry.

Not only are fossil, nuclear, and renewable the only types of energy we have, but *they are the only types we will ever have*. In the future we will discover no other fundamental types of energy. In fact, if we look at the time scale of centuries, at current rates of fossil fuel consumption we will in time be left with only two energy types, nuclear and renewable. Also, nuclear energy currently relies on the fission of the Uranium235 isotope[8], whose supply we will use up in the space of several decades at

---

[8] An isotope of Uranium having 92 protons and 143 neutrons in the nucleus, so that the combination of protons and neutrons adds up to 235.

current rates. If we do not develop a safe and cost-effective alternative to U-235 that is more plentiful, then this energy source will be lost, and we will be left with just one type: renewable energy.

Energy Use and Global Greenhouse Gas Emissions

As we enter the decade of the 2020s, potential scarcity of energy sources seems like a challenge that lies further out on the horizon. More immediate is the climate change threat caused by increasing greenhouse gas emissions.

Most nations have joined the Paris Climate Accord to limit global average temperature rise to 1.5 degrees Celsius, and a growing consensus suggests that the community of nations will need to reduce total greenhouse gas (GHG) emissions compared to the baseline year of 2005 by 80% in the year 2050. Even in this ambitious scenario, some severe consequences from global climate change, both before 2050 and after, are almost inevitable, including more extreme weather events and loss of productivity of agriculture in certain regions around the world.

Unfortunately, compared to the 2050 targets, the recent track record of the community of nations points in the wrong direction. Looking at the energy data shown in Fig. 7, the European Union, Japan, and the United States appear to be contained in terms of the growth in energy use, and even declining slightly since approximately 2005. However, the BRIC countries, led by China's eye-popping increase of energy consumption from 40 to 150 EJ between 2000 and 2017, have seen such a surge in energy use that they now constitute a bigger fraction of the world total than either the EU or U.S. Furthermore, much of the growth in BRIC energy use is tied to the increasing amount of their energy extraction and manufacturing, ranging from consumer products from China and energy products from Russia to wind turbine blades from Brazil. As industrial output moves from the EU and U.S. to the BRIC countries and others, industrial energy consumption that was once "on the books" of the rich countries reappears outside of their boundaries.

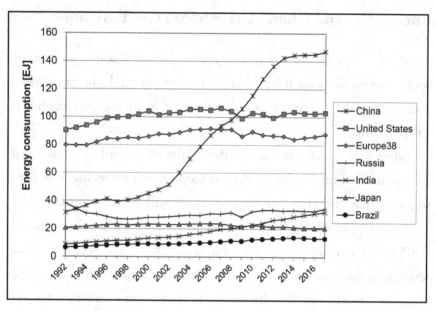

Figure 7 Energy consumption of U.S., European Union, Japan, and BRIC (Brazil/Russia/India/China) countries in Exajoules (EJ), 1992-2017.

Notes: 1 EJ = 10^{18} Joule = 0.948 quadrillion Btu = 0.948 x 10^{15} Btu. To avoid cluttering the figure, other countries' energy consumption is not included; however, the countries shown represent approximately 75% of the world's energy consumption. "Europe38" is a collection of 38 countries in contiguous Europe. Source: U.S. Energy Information Administration.

Since energy consumption is dominated by use of fossil fuels, CO_2 emissions trends in Fig. 8 mirror energy consumption trends in Fig. 7. The largest increase is for the BRIC countries, who after 2002 became the largest emitter. Europe, United States, and Japan appear to be edging downward after approximately 2005.

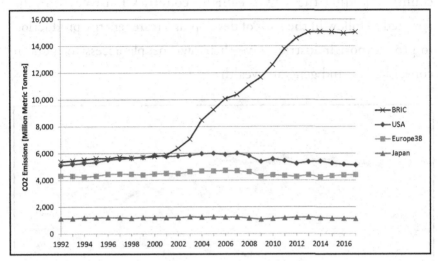

Figure 8 CO_2 emissions for BRIC countries versus USA, Europe, and Japan, 1992-2017 in million metric tonnes[9]. Source: U.S. Energy Information Administration. Notes: Europe38 includes 38 countries in contiguous Europe, BRIC includes Brazil/Russia/India/China.

Despite the concentration of growing energy use and CO_2 emissions in industrializing countries, disparities within industrialized countries in *per capita* energy consumption and CO_2 emissions continue. The BRIC countries, representing four of the nine most populous countries on earth and about 40% of the world's total population, have an average per capita value significantly lower than that of the U.S. or Japan, except for Russia, which has a cold climate and is a large energy producer and exporter (Figs. 9 and 10). In the BRIC countries, energy consumption and CO_2 emissions rates are

---

[9] Throughout this book, the spelling "tonne" is used to indicate a metric tonne, i.e., 1000 kilograms. The spelling "ton" indicates a U.S. customary ton, or 2,000 pounds.

generally rising whereas they are falling for the U.S. and Japan, but the gap is still wide. With the carbon-intensive lifestyle of the richest countries leading the way, the BRIC countries must certainly be tempted to follow in the path of developing greater energy production to grow export industries, give their own people access to modern conveniences, and generate wealth.

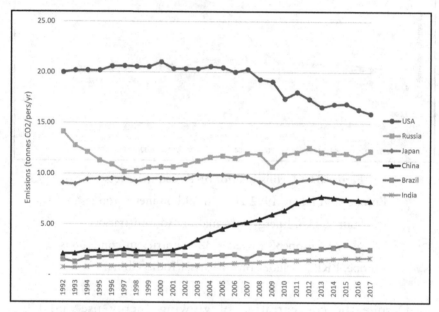

Figure 9 Per-capita energy consumption for the U.S., Japan, and BRIC countries, GJ/person, 1992-2017.
Source: U.S. Energy Information Administration.

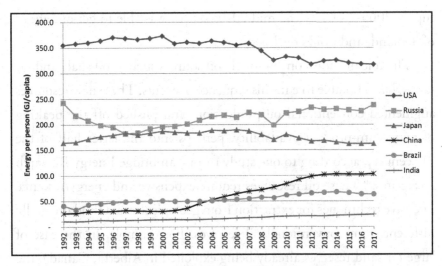

Figure 10 Per-capita CO_2 emissions in metric tonnes
for the U.S., U.K., Japan, and BRIC countries, 1992-2017.
Source: U.S. Energy Information Administration.

Energy Use and the Peaking of World Oil Output

At present, GHG emissions are the dominant concern with our conventional energy supply, and the energy security concern ("will there be enough energy") around nonrenewable fossil fuel resources has receded. However, there was a time in the 2005 to 2009 period when prices were climbing, and a period of prolonged scarcity appeared to be approaching.

Reliance on oil as an energy source requires the ability to pump it at a certain rate for reliable supplies. The total amount left in the ground does not matter: if supply cannot keep up with demand, there will be difficulties. In the recent past, oil companies were able to improve their ability to extract oil from more difficult-to-access fields, and also their ability to extract a greater fraction of the oil available in a field through advanced technology. Compared to the period of constrained supply 2005-2009, by the mid-2010s supply was able to get out ahead of demand, and prices declined.

The role of "non-conventional" oil sources such as oil shale and tar sands, had a notable role in this sequence of events. These new resources augmented conventional oil production, and pushed off the peaking of petroleum-product availability, perhaps into the latter half of the 21st century, according to one study from Cambridge Energy Research Associates.[10] These oil resources require expensive and energy/resource intensive techniques for extraction from geological strata fundamentally different from conventional oil reserves. For example, in the case of large tar-sand reserves already being exploited in Alberta, Canada, the tar must be extracted from the sand using large quantities of water and energy. When the worldwide oil cost is $15 to $30 per barrel, as it was in the 1990s, the additional extraction cost alone makes it uncompetitive to sell oil from tar sands on the world market. However, once the price per barrel surpasses a certain threshold – thought to be about $50 per barrel in the case of tar sands – extracting these resources becomes economically attractive. Prices above $50/barrel have been observed in the 2008-09, 2010-14, and 2017-2020 periods, so for much of the last decade, they have been sufficiently high (Fig. 11).

---

[10] Cambridge Energy Research Associates (2006), study 60907-9, as quoted in Sperling & Gordon (2009), *Two Billion Cars*, p.120.

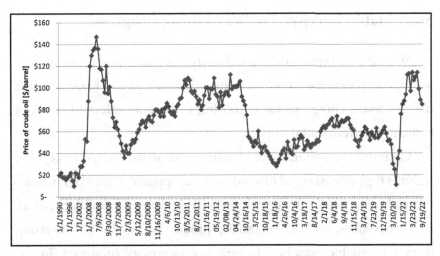

Figure 11 Global oil price in dollars per barrel, 1990-2022
Source: For 1/90 to 1/06, U.S. Energy Information Administration; All other, personal record of reported prices in news media.

Much uncertainty surrounds the global output and price of oil in the future. On the one hand, a growing number of countries with emerging economies, led by the "BRIC" countries of Brazil, Russia, India, and China, may increase demand for oil for transportation and other services. This trend would put upward pressure on oil prices, which might stay at current levels or continue to rise. On the other hand, if electrification of private automobiles takes off, there may be rapid transition to other energy sources for electricity for vehicles, so that the pressure on oil prices and production may no longer increase the way it did in the past.

Francis M. Vanek

Sustainable Energy: Are We Making Progress?

With the carbon emissions and energy consumption challenge laid out before us in these terms, one naturally would like to know whether the renewable energy sector is starting to have an effect in terms of reducing environmental impact.

Consider the performance of utility-scale wind energy (large wind turbines typically arranged in wind farms, as opposed to small household-size turbines), which along with solar PV is the most prominent of all new renewables, on total electricity production in the U.S. Starting from a negligible presence, in terms of electricity produced, in the year 1980, the industry grew on the success of wind farms of 50- to 100-kW machines (small by today's standards) in a few windy passes in California, eventually spreading to other locations. With experience gained from these early installations, the technology advanced, and the turbines increased in size, to 500 kW, 1 MW, and eventually 1.5 MW in size by the end of the 1990s.

The result? In 2000 utility-scale wind produced less than 1% of U.S. electricity production.

From the year 2000 onward, capacity grew much more rapidly, with the wind industry often installing more capacity in a single year than the entire amount that had been installed up to 2000. Large turbines with a capacity of 1.5 MW or larger became the norm, with turbines as large as 2.5 MW appearing in some locations (with as much capacity in a single turbine as 50 of the early 50-kW machines). Wind turbines became part of the rural landscape in New York State, Pennsylvania, Virginia, California, and the Midwest. Moving of oversize loads of turbine blades or turbine tower segments by tractor-trailers on state highways and interstates became a common sight. Wind energy became the fastest growing new renewable energy source, whether measured in

34

absolute amounts or percent increase in installed capacity, growing faster each year than other forms such as solar photovoltaics or geothermal.

The result? In 2007 utility-scale wind still produced less than 1% of U.S. electricity demand.[11]

Finally, from 2008 onward the wind energy sector really began to accelerate. The U.S. industry installed 8,000 MW of turbines in 2008, 10,000 MW in 2009, and, in the record-setting year of 2012, more than 13,000 MW of turbines were installed. This amount was more in a single year than the industry had installed in its entirety from 1980 to the beginning of 2007.

The result? Utility-scale wind finally broke through the 1% barrier. In 2013, wind produced 168 billion kWh, surpassing 4% of total energy production. Trends continued, and in 2017 the amount of 254 billion kWh constituted 6.4% of total net generation. However, output is still less than 10%. The main carbon-free sources – nuclear, hydro, wind, and solar – produced 36% of the net electricity supply. The other 64% of the electricity supply came from fossil fuels, mostly natural gas and coal. Furthermore, the 36% share for renewables is only for the electricity market, not for the entire primary energy supply. A significant portion of the primary energy supply supports the heating and transportation sectors, where renewables have a lower share.

These numbers are presented not to discourage the development of wind energy and other renewables, but rather to encourage honesty

---

[11] Underlying data: the industry grew to approximately 2600 MW of installed capacity in the year 2000, equivalent to about 1700 1.5-MW turbines. Total electricity production in 2000 amounted to 5.6 billion kilowatt-hours, or kWh. By 2007, capacity had increased to nearly 17,000 MW. Output grew more than five-fold, to 32 billion kWh. For 2012, 2.5 MW is a more typical turbine size, so 13,000 MW is equivalent to about 5,200 turbines. Total electricity output for U.S. from all sources was 3,802 billion, 4,159 billion, and 4,014 billion kWh in 2000, 2007, and 2017, respectively.

and candor in assessing what we have achieved relative to the challenge. We should not cut back on the amount invested in wind and other renewables because we fear they are ineffective, but rather radically accelerate them so that they can be effective. For example, let us put our annual investment in wind energy in some context: At an average of $2 million per megawatt of installed capacity, the price tag for the 13,000 MW installed in 2012 was on the order of $26 billion. This seems like a lot of money until you realize that U.S. electricity consumers, ranging from large industries to homeowners, purchased about 4 trillion kWh per year, which at an average price of 10 cents per kWh including generation and delivery would cost $400 billion. It stands to reason that if you want to shift a large percentage of electricity production to renewables like wind, you need to spend big on renewable projects – especially since most of the cost for renewables is the capital cost of the equipment.

If we go down the path of accelerated investment in renewable energy sources, one might ask, "Are there sufficient physical resources available in the U.S. land mass to be harnessed?" Looking specifically at wind energy, one study published by the U.S. Department of Energy predicted that the nation would need 320 GW of installed turbine capacity in order to deliver 20% of all electricity in the year 2030, based on projected growth in electricity demand over the next 20 years and predicted productivity of that number of turbines.[12] However, the same report estimated that there would be room for up to 8,000 GW worth of wind turbines – more than 20 times as much. Furthermore, much of this wind energy potential can be developed in sparsely populated parts of the country where space or aesthetic concerns are not impediments.

[12] USDOE, Office of Energy Efficiency and Renewable Energy, "20% wind by 2030: Increasing wind energy's contribution to U.S. electricity supply." Published July 2008.

To conclude, the physical resource for harnessing wind energy is abundant in nature, as is the case for many other types of renewable energy. However, with the exception of large-scale hydropower, for most renewable energy sources we have only harnessed a small fraction of the available resource. We will need to work much more quickly to develop these resources if we want to see noticeable results soon. To answer the question posed, yes, we are making progress – but not fast enough. This insight leads directly to the subject of the next section: To move faster, we need to scale up the level of activity.

The Scale-Up Problem for Transforming Energy

On October 8, 2018, the Intergovernmental Panel on Climate Change (IPCC) announced that the world urgently needed to keep warming within 1.5 degrees Celsius, and that to do so the community of nations needed to spend 2.5% of world GDP on solutions to prevent climate change (renewable energy, more efficient buildings, and so on). The news coverage did not mention, however, that if the world suddenly shifted this amount of funding (about $2 trillion in 2018) to climate solutions, we would be totally unprepared for this sudden increase in spending. Although everyone from solar panel manufacturers to energy-efficiency contractors might have some slack in their operations to increase business, this capacity would be quickly overwhelmed by the accelerating pace, and the effort would stall until more capacity could come online.

This problem is sometimes called the "scale-up problem." Especially in the case of infrastructure, it is not enough to have invented a technological solution. Several other ingredients are needed, including:

1. *Raw materials:* Depending on the technology in question, it may be necessary to have a way to extract large amounts of raw materials and transport them to where they are either installed or incorporated in some manufacturing process. Some raw materials (such as rare earth metals) have the additional problem that they are scarce, and a sufficient supply must be guaranteed or else a substitute found. However, even for raw materials that are abundant (such as iron ore), there must still be a supply chain in place to extract and convert enough of them.

2. *Locations for installation:* New or refurbished equipment or infrastructure requires a physical location somewhere. For energy efficient retrofits, this may not be a problem, as the same house in the same location is modified to become more efficient. However, for renewable energy sources such as solar and wind, this question is clearly a challenge. By their nature, these energy sources have a large footprint on the land. If they are installed close to population centers, people will tolerate them up to a point, but will oppose them if they threaten to "industrialize the countryside." If they must be installed far away from population centers so as not to be an eyesore, then transmission infrastructure is required, and that too needs a physical location.

3. *Manufacturing facilities:* If you want to increase use of renewable energy or improve energy efficiency, you need enough factories to make all the equipment and materials that you require. To give a concrete example, in 2015 the global wind industry added 63 gigawatts (GW) of wind turbine capacity, and the world solar PV industry added another 59 GW of capacity. To put these numbers in tangible context, if a typical wind turbine has 2.5 megawatts (MW) of capacity, the wind amount

is equivalent to about 25,000 wind turbines installed in one year; 59 GW of solar is the equivalent of 59,000 1-MW solar PV farms, although some fraction of this capacity was installed in distributed locations. Since not every factory would have produced at 100% of capacity in 2015, there was some additional capacity to produce more, and since then the global industry has been adding capacity in response to demand. However, the transition to renewables to prevent climate change requires an *order of magnitude* (i.e., 10 times as much) more annual installations, and enough manufacturing capacity to build it. This installation rate would be maintained over 2-3 decades, or more. Clearly, many new factories and assembly lines would be required, not to mention warehouses, distribution centers, and other types of industrial facilities. The same logic applies to efficiency: For example, if you want to replace refrigerators in hundreds of millions of homes with a new generation of ultra-efficient ones, and to do it in 5-10 years, you need sufficient refrigerator building capacity. This same exercise needs repeating for all major energy-using appliances.

4. *Financing:* For investments in the transformation of our energy system to take place, money needs to change hands. This is especially true of renewable energy sources like solar and wind, where the day-to-day energy supply comes from nature free of charge but the up-front cost is large. A developer may purchase a wind or solar farm without needing to pay cash for the whole cost. However, if they do not, then some kind of financing must be arranged, and there need to be sufficient lenders to support the transaction.

5. *Human resources and expertise:* The fifth and final ingredient is the workforce. Many different types of expertise are needed.

For renewables, workers required include those with technical skills to design and manufacture the equipment, the installers, those responsible for maintenance, and those who manage the finances. The mixture includes both white-collar skills (engineering, science, finance) and blue-collar trades (electrical, mechanical, construction, and so on). Any of these trades can become the bottleneck that slows the rate of construction, if they are not in sufficient supply.

The news in response to the scale-up problem is mixed. On the one hand, it appears that the world economy is responding "rationally" to the demand to do something about climate change, especially in the case of wind and solar energy. Raw-materials resources are being developed. Locations are being scouted for new installations. Manufacturers are adding capacity, anticipating that the market will continue to grow. More and more investors see sustainable energy (both on the supply side and in the investment in new energy sources) as a promising area of investment. Lastly, more people are training, or re-training, to enter the relevant fields.

The question remains as to whether enough raw materials, locations, manufacturing facilities, financial resources, and personnel will be available to carry out the transition at the rate needed. We are a long way from meeting the target for phasing out GHG emissions from energy production, because we are a long way from being at a sufficiently rapid transition rate.

We can look at the energy transition before us through the lens of technology transitions in general that have been observed in the past, as shown in Fig. 12. Suppose we have a product that will eventually take over the market from some other incumbent. At first there are early adopters as the product germinates and prepares to grow rapidly in the market. After a time, sales or installations take off, and the next generation of fast followers join the market. These consumers are much more numerous than the early adopters, and their emergence indicates that the product is likely to grow to maturity and market dominance. At some point the trajectory moves to the rapid buildout phase where the general consumer has joined the early adopters and fast followers. Lastly, as penetration approaches its maximum value (shown as 100% in this case, although the upper bound could be lower), the rate of adoption slows down as the final stragglers join the market, although more slowly as structural obstacles of various kinds prevent them from shifting to the new technology.

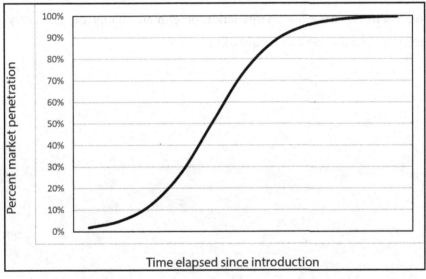

Figure 12 Typical penetration curve for a new product

Many of the most important technologies have followed a path similar to this one. The International Council on Systems Engineering (INCOSE) has compiled the years required for different technologies to reach market saturation in the U.S. – electricity, landline telephones, and automobiles (Fig. 13). In each case there was a 20- to 30-year germination period, where the technology existed but was only adopted in small numbers. Then the technology "took off", and the rest is history, up to the point where the rate of adoption slowed down as the final customer segment became more and more difficult to reach. In the case of automobiles, adoption had only reached 75% because reasons of cost or disability prevented individual ownership. On a world level, in the case of solar and wind energy we appear to be leaving the early adopter phase and moving toward maximum growth. But what will the path look like in the future? Will it look like electrification in the U.S., where penetration went from 2% to 95% in 30 years, aided by strong support from the Rural Electrification Administration in the 1930s and 1940s? Or more like the automobile, where the comparable figure is 2% to 75% in 80 years? Successful action on climate change depends very much on the answer to this question.

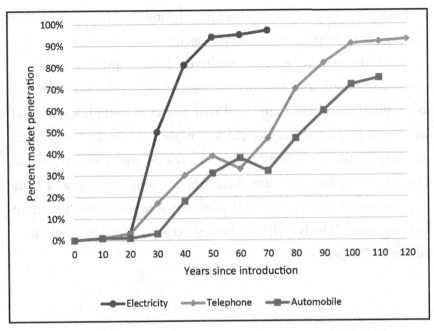

Figure 13 Market penetration in the U.S. market as a function of years elapsed since launch for electric grid connection, radio, landline telephone, and automobile.

Source: International Council on Systems Engineering, *INCOSE Systems Engineering Handbook, Third Edition.*

Knowledge is Power: Using Our Understanding of Energy to Pursue Climate Goals

Scaling up the response to the energy and climate challenge may seem dauting, but fortunately, abundant renewable energy exists in nature to meet global needs if we build a system to extract it. But what more do we need to know, and to do, in order to get there? Over the next several chapters, we will look at ways to make the energy system as efficient as possible, to help lower our resource footprint. We will also encounter large sources like solar and wind, and relatively smaller sources like hydropower and biomass energy.

First, though, we need to understand more about fossil fuels, which are sometimes called "conventional" energy because they are so ubiquitous, and have remained that way even though leaders and activists have been sounding the alarm about climate change since the early 1990s. Fossil fuels are not just the dominant energy source: The way they behave has shaped our whole approach to energy and by extension much of society. It is important not to skip over this step of focusing on fossil fuels at the beginning, so that is why they are the next subject in Chapter 3.

CHAPTER 3

Fossil Fuels – Starting From Where We Are Now

As discussed in Chapter 2, the fraction of world energy still derived from fossil fuels remains stubbornly and surprisingly large. Despite vigorous efforts to develop renewables, between 2000 and 2019 the fraction of world energy derived from fossil fuels actually increased by 1 percentage point. This unfolding of events was partly due to the rapid growth in world demand, which alone amounted to a 54% increase over that 19-year period. Certainly, it would have been easier to increase the fraction of energy from renewables if the total amount of energy used had been constant, instead of growing rapidly. Fossil fuels are, however, well positioned to meet world energy demand when it is growing rapidly. These reasons go back to the fundamental characteristics of fossil fuels, which are essential to understand and the subject of this chapter.

We also need to study fossil fuel characteristics because they are a fundamental part of energy literacy. It is not enough to familiarize ourselves with renewable energy technologies and how they work because of idealistic notions of what renewables might deliver in the long run. It is also necessary to thoroughly understand the characteristics of fossil fuels, given that, at present, fossil fuels remain by far the dominant world energy source and therefore shape the way we use energy now. Understanding how we use energy now will help us find a path to the energy future we want.

Before we start, it is helpful to review the different kinds of fossil fuels available. We use different fossil fuels for different energy applications. Petroleum products (i.e., made from crude oil) are used primarily in transportation, coal is used in electricity generation and industry, and natural gas is used for generating electricity and providing heat and hot water in residential, commercial, and industrial settings.

Table 1 describes major fossil fuel types and their applications. For example, the combination of conventional and non-conventional oil extraction delivers the supply of unrefined crude oil that is then processed into different petroleum products. Among these, gasoline, diesel, jet fuel, and maritime shipping fuel are all complex hydrocarbons, meaning that each molecule of a given fuel contains many atoms of carbon and hydrogen. They differ from each other in their molecular makeup, so that, for instance, an automobile built to combust gasoline cannot combust diesel fuel, and vice versa. Natural gas is quite different from petroleum because its primary component, methane, is a simpler atom, with one carbon molecule and four hydrogen molecules. Coal is a fossil fuel but not a hydrocarbon: its molecular structure consists of carbon atoms with various other impurities interspersed, but without hydrogen. Some of these impurities, such as sulfur or mercury, are harmful and therefore reduce the grade of the coal. Note that both methane and complex hydrocarbons can be created out of biological sources (crops or forest products from the plant world), so that it is possible to displace fossil fuels with bio-energy (Chap. 7). A distinction is drawn between "biofuels," which are replacement fuels for transportation applications including ethanol and biodiesel, and "biomass," which can be combusted for heating or generating electricity.

Energy resource type	Description	Applications
Oil, conventional	Crude oil extracted from either on-shore or off-shore wells. Exists in a liquid form.	Gasoline for cars and light trucks; diesel fuel for heavy trucks, railroads, etc.; jet fuel for aircraft; heavy fuel oil for ocean-going ships.
Oil, non-conventional	Oil resources including tar sands oil extracted from tar sands; shale oil extracted by fracturing oil shale underground, releasing oil that can then be extracted.	Once non-conventional oil has been extracted and refined, it is used the same way as conventional oil.
Natural gas, conventional	Energy source consisting of mostly methane extracted from on- or off-shore fields. Exists in a gaseous form, but can be liquefied at low temperature for ocean-going transport.	Combustion in power plants; use for heating occupied spaces in buildings; cooking and heating hot water for buildings; Industrial uses.
Natural gas, unconventional	Natural gas resource including gas released by hydraulic fracturing, i.e., injecting high-pressure fracturing compounds into shale formations to release gas that can then be extracted.	Once non-conventional natural gas has been extracted, it is used the same way as conventional oil.
Coal	Energy source that can be extracted either in mines open to the surface or deep shaft mines. Available in a range of grades, with higher-grade coal worth a higher price per ton	Combustion in power plants; industrial uses such as input to the steel-making process. Occasionally used for home heating.

Table 1 Characteristics and applications of major fossil fuel types

Energy dense, dispatchable, and transportable

It is not a coincidence that total human use of energy grew relatively slowly until the year 1800, and then faster and faster since. This growth is a direct result of key characteristics of fossil fuels. Fossil fuels are energy dense, meaning that once you find them, you do not need to do as much work to concentrate them to do useful work as you would with most alternative energy sources. They are also dispatchable, meaning you can control the rate at which they do work, from stepping on the accelerator on your car to turning up the thermostat in your home.

They are relatively easy to transport, by barge, pipeline, or other means; their movement is relatively easy to control; and when they are put into storage, they can be stored in one place at length without degrading. Also, the infrastructure they require, such as an internal combustion engine or a power plant, is relatively inexpensive for the amount of power they are capable of producing. This economic feature makes it difficult to justify alternative investments, which tend to require larger upfront investment to deliver returns in the long run.

Consider first the question of energy density, using the example of electricity generated from coal compared to electricity generated directly from the sun using solar PV panels (Table 2). A cubic meter of good quality coal typically contains about 20 Gigajoules (GJ) of energy, which is also about equal to 20 million Btus.[13] The process of converting coal to electricity, including transporting the coal and combustion in a power plant, is about 33% efficient, so the resulting electricity amounts to about 6.7 GJ. Converting this quantity to a more familiar unit for electricity gives 1800 kWh, which can be compared to 5,000 kWh, the annual electricity consumption of a typical U.S. household. Compare the quantity of energy in the coal to the rate at which the U.S. receives energy from the sun. A mid-range value of "solar gain" for U.S. cities such as Atlanta or St. Louis is on the order of 200 W/m². This quantity is not the peak amount of solar energy received on a sunny day – which approaches 1,000 W/m² – but instead the amount taking into account the impact of nighttime, the seasons of the year, and cloudy weather. Furthermore, the solar panel might achieve 15% efficiency, so the rate of electricity production is on the order of 30 W/m² on average. At this rate, the square meter surface produces about 263 kWh per year and

---

[13] To be precise, 1 million Btu = ~1.055 GJ, so 1 Btu is slightly more than 1,000 Joules. However, for simplicity in this book these figures are at times treated as equivalent.

will take about 7 years to make as much electricity as could be generated from the coal.

Item	Quantity
Coal, energy content in 1 m³	20 Gigajoule (GJ)
Efficiency	33%
Energy converted to electricity	~6.7 GJ
In typical electrical units	1800 kWh
Sun shining on 1 m³ in USA	200 W/m2
Efficiency	15%
Average PV panel output	30 W/m2
Output per year	~263 kWh/m2
Years to make equivalent kWh	~7 years

Table 2 Comparison of electricity from 1 cubic meter of coal and 1 square meter of solar gain

This analysis does not discount the fact that the total amount of renewable energy arriving from the sun is vast. Based on the size of the earth as a planet and the fact that the sun is continuously shining on it, energy arrives at a rate *several thousand times* higher than the rate at which humans use energy for all our various purposes. However, this vast amount is arriving in a diffuse way, meaning that it is spread over a huge area – the entire surface of the earth – so that, as Table 1 illustrates, the amount reaching a square meter in a week or a month is small compared to our overall need. If we are going to do work with it, we need to concentrate it; for that, we need to install the necessary infrastructure.

A second key characteristic of fossil fuels is that they are dispatchable, meaning that we control when they are combusted and turned into useful work, and how fast. Whether the fuel is coal, natural gas, or a liquid fuel refined from crude oil, the fuel is moved along its supply chain until it reaches the points where it is used. This could be a coal supply in a power plant, or a fuel tank in a car. Then at this point the size of the system is designed so that the maximum speed at which it can operate is larger than the average, giving the system some "breathing room" to ramp up output if called upon. For example, cars driving at constant speeds on the highway burn fuel at a fraction of the maximum rate, but if drivers need to climb a long hill while maintaining speed, they can press the gas pedal and their engines will respond by drawing more fuel and working harder.

However, most of our available renewable energy supply does not work this way since it is the opposite of dispatchable—namely "intermittent." For resources such as solar and wind, we know the expected amount of energy that will arrive over time for different locations (dry versus wet climates, temperate versus tropical latitudes, etc.), but we can't predict with certainty out into the future how much energy will arrive at any given moment. Some renewable sources are dispatchable, such as biofuels, hydropower, or geothermal power plants based on underground steam resources, but their total potential available on the planet is small relative to total human energy demand. Certain countries are well-endowed with these resources – Iceland for geothermal, or Switzerland for hydropower – but this is geographic good fortune not shared by most other nations. The U.S. is actually the world's largest producer of electricity from geothermal, but even so, the total annual production is small compared to overall U.S. electricity demand, and there are few opportunities to expand this resource (See Chap.7). Even a resource such as hydropower is not always dispatchable: a network of hydropower dams and generating stations may be dispatchable in general, but in a period of extended drought, water reservoir levels may fall, and output may be constrained so that dam and generating stations can no longer be relied upon to generate power at the full range of output levels needed.

Fossil fuels are also advantageous because they are relatively easy to transport. Consider petroleum products: crude oil can be refined near its extraction point or transported long distances before being refined. When there is an oversupply of oil in the world market, it can be stored in oil terminals on land, or even at times, in oil tankers at sea. Refined gasoline, diesel, and aviation fuel are relatively imperishable and can be stored or transported long distances as well. Most major modes of transportation – ship, rail, truck, and especially pipeline – are used to transport crude oil or refined petroleum products, depending on the circumstances. We do not usually transport petroleum products by air because their average "value density," or dollar value per unit of weight or volume, is not large enough to justify the high cost. However, for certain remote locations, air transport can be used as well, when the recipient is willing to pay a premium for delivery.

Even the blending of biofuels into petroleum products can introduce greater problems with storage and combustion. Because they are made from crops and other agricultural raw materials, biofuels such as ethanol and biodiesel are more temperamental: they require more care to avoid clogging of tanks and lines, and they cannot be stored for as long as petroleum products.

The situation with coal and natural gas is similar to that of petroleum. Coal can be moved by ship or rail and stored for a long time before being used. Shippers also use trucks to carry coal over shorter distances, for example to reach a final destination that is not accessible by rail or water. Natural gas can be pressurized for long-distance transmission by pipeline, depressurized for local delivery in an urban network, and stored in on-land terminals. In addition, natural gas can be cooled to very low temperatures, creating liquefied natural gas or LNG, which can then be transported long distances over the ocean in specialized LNG tankers that maintain the low temperature.

To conclude, fossil fuels may be dense, dispatchable, and transportable, but they are obviously not without risks. Risk emerges both from the flammability of fossil fuels in certain contexts and from the risk of contamination. Events ranging from the 2010 Gulf of Mexico oil spill, to the spilling of coal ash at coal-fired power plants into surrounding environments, to periodic explosions and fires at oil refineries are all examples of these risks. Yet because of the advantages of density, dispatchability, and transportability, society has built up a system for supplying and consuming energy around fossil fuels while tolerating a certain level of risk.

The energy production footprint on the land

The idea of an energy production footprint gets at the question of visibility and intrusion into our everyday life. Do we notice the production of energy, and is it an eyesore and a nuisance? Or is it hidden from our view, so that we benefit as users without seeing where it is coming from? Also, when we say "our view" to whom are we referring? Fossil fuel production may occur far from middle- and upper-class communities, but it occurs disproportionately in proximity to poor communities. Or the relationship may be the reverse. Neighborhoods near energy production are undesirable, but it is where the poor can afford a home, so it is where they end up.

Initially, we might think of fossil fuels as having a large negative footprint on the land. Activities such as open-pit mining or mountain-top removal expose acres and acres of ground, destroying forests, threatening water sources, and requiring decades to reclaim land once mining has stopped. More recently, hydraulic fracturing (also known as "hydro-fracking" or "fracking") has allowed for natural gas extraction in rural regions that previously had no such industrial presence. This advance has created tension between the industry and rural residents, especially when air quality is degraded or water supplies polluted.

There are also instances, however, where the footprint of fossil fuels on the surface of the earth is quite low, and where replacing them with solar or wind energy would be quite large. Whenever the energy source is under the earth and only a small orifice is needed to extract it, the amount of energy produced per surface acre can be quite large. Examples include deep shaft coal mines or offshore drilling platforms. Consider that energy arrives from the sun under ideal blue-sky conditions at the rate of approximately 1,000 Watts per square meter. If we measure the cross-sectional area of the pipe in an offshore drilling platform that brings crude oil to the surface, and the fact that oil fields can produce millions of barrels of oil per year, then the density of energy flowing per square meter is much, much larger.

A similar story can be told for coal from an underground coal mine that travels to a power plant. The coal comes out of the ground through an opening that is small relative to the total area of tunnels underground from which it is extracted. It then travels perhaps by train to the power plant, using a rail right-of-way that is 20 feet wide. The footprint of the plant is typically on the order of acres, and since the electricity produced can be transported hundreds of miles at high voltages, it can be sited away from population centers. A 300-Megawatt power plant near Ithaca, NY, produced 1 to 2 billion kWh per year of electricity from coal for decades before market conditions changed and coal-fired electricity became uncompetitive.[14] The plant sits on about 20 acres of land. How many acres of solar panels or wind turbines would

---

[14] As an illustration, if the 300-MW plant were to run at 100% output, it would produce 300 MW x 8760 hours/year = 2,628,000 MWh, or about 2.63 billion kWh per year. The amount of 1 to 2 billion kWh per year therefore represents a capacity factor of between 38% and 76% of this maximum.

be required to replace this one plant? And how many solar panels and turbines total for the whole country, given that there are hundreds of large power plants that need to be phased out? (These questions are revisited in Chap. 4 on solar and Chap. 5 on wind.) As a country we do not yet feel the effect of the big footprint of renewable energy that may be coming in the future because renewables are still only a small percentage of our energy supply.

There are some examples of countries with small populations and an abundance of certain renewable resources that do not have a large footprint on the land, where renewables do provide a substantial fraction of the energy supply. For example, in Iceland (population 380,000 in 2022), geothermal energy exists in the form of steam resources that are near the surface and can be accessed without the high visibility of large solar and wind farms. Similarly, Switzerland (population 8.8 million in 2022) is a mountainous country with disproportionately large hydropower resources thanks to rivers running down from the mountains that can be harnessed to generate electricity. Of course, major world economies (Brazil, China, India, Russia, and the U.S.) should take advantage of geothermal and hydropower for carbon-free energy where this can be done in an ecologically responsible way (see Chap. 7). However, these large-population countries do not have sufficient geothermal or hydro to depend primarily on these resources to meet their significant energy supply needs. In fact, the U.S. is the world's largest generator of geothermal electricity, yet receives less than 1% of its electricity from this source.

Matching Fossil Fuels to the Electricity and Transportation Sectors

The allocation of fossil fuels to different sectors depends on their advantages and disadvantages. Furthermore, in the case of the electricity sector, the breakdown of types of fossil fuels used is undergoing a major shift. Figure 1 shows the breakdown of U.S. primary energy consumption in 2019. Out of 100.1 quads total, all but 20 quads, or ~20%, is obtained from oil, natural gas, or coal. A large fraction of the fossil fuel primary energy supply is converted to electricity, while the remaining fraction that is not converted to electricity is also large.

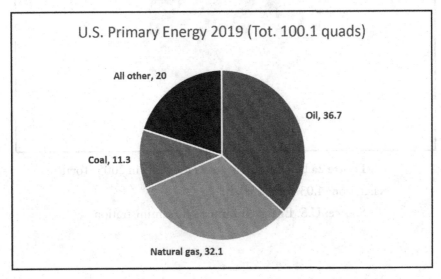

U.S. Primary Energy 2019 (Tot. 100.1 quads)

All other, 20

Oil, 36.7

Coal, 11.3

Natural gas, 32.1

Figure 1 Breakdown of U.S. primary energy consumption by source in 2019, in Quadrillion Btu.
Source: U.S. Energy Information Administration.

Turning first to the electricity sector, a breakdown of the 2005 and 2019 U.S. electricity generation mix from the U.S. Energy Information Administration is illustrative (Fig. 2). In 2005, total production was 4.06 trillion kWh, with about half coming from coal. If the average household in the U.S. consumed 5,000 kWh per year, the 2005 total would be enough for about 800 million homes (of course, much of the electricity goes to uses other than houses which is why the figure is so much higher than the U.S. total number of households). In 2019, the total generation was 4.13 trillion kWh, and by this time, more electricity was produced from natural gas (38%) than from coal (23%).

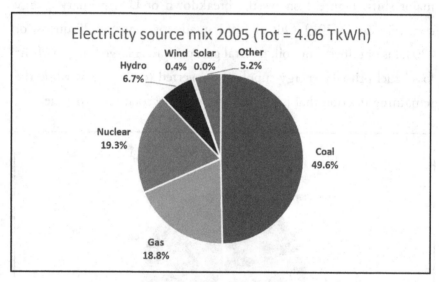

Figure 2a U.S. Electricity generation mix in 2005. Total generation: 4.03 trillion kWh.

Source: U.S. Energy Information Administration

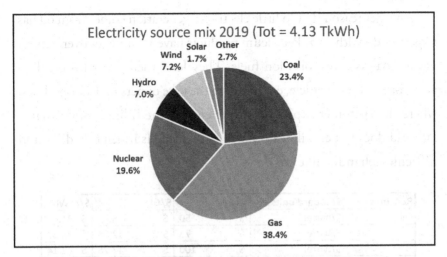

Figure 2b U.S. Electricity generation mix in 2019. Total generation: 4.13 trillion kWh.

Source: U.S. Energy Information Administration

About 62% of the electricity in 2019 came from fossil fuels, and almost all of this came from natural gas and coal. The "Other" category includes electricity generated from oil, as well as other renewables besides solar/wind/hydro that are not broken out. Thus, since the total for "Other" is only 2.4%, by implication, generation from oil is rare: typically, it only occurs in a facility that for historical or geographic reasons (such as being on a remote island that is difficult to reach with other fuels) uses some type of petroleum product. As for the non-fossil electricity generation, around 20% comes from nuclear, a figure that has stayed roughly constant for many years. Hydropower was the largest renewable contributor in 2004, but wind energy has risen rapidly since then, and because the potential resource is so large, wind had by 2019 surpassed hydro as the largest renewable resource by kWh generated. The remaining renewables include solar, biomass, geothermal, and tidal energy.

Another reason that so little electricity generation comes from oil has largely to do with cost. Petroleum products have advantages over natural gas or coal as transportation fuels. They lend themselves to refueling and storage in the vehicle, especially in the case of personal automobiles, where the customer expects an experience at the filling station that is safe and does not entail dealing with a fuel that is inherently dirty and difficult to handle, like coal.

Resource:	Standard units	$/unit		$/GJ		$/MWh	
Oil	$/barrel	$	50	$	8.63	$	31.07
	$/barrel	$	75	$	12.95	$	46.60
	$/barrel	$	100	$	17.26	$	62.14
Natural gas	$/million Btu	$	3	$	2.84	$	10.24
Coal	$/tonne	$	50	$	2.00	$	7.20

Table 3 Cost of oil, natural gas, and coal by unit and by unit of energy, in wholesale or raw form.

As shown in Table 3, the prices of oil, natural gas, and coal at the bulk or wholesale level are reported in standard units of $/barrel, $/million Btu, and $/metric tonne. These are wholesale prices on the world market not including processing or transportation. For example, since oil prices have fluctuated over the last several years, three different values from $50 to $100 per barrel are reported. When values are converted to dollars per unit of energy (whether GJ or MWh, i.e., Megawatt-hours) it becomes clear that the value of crude oil is substantially higher than natural gas or coal, even at $50 per barrel. Values in Table 4 for the price of gasoline, heating fuel, and retail electricity in standard units and in cost per unit of energy tell a similar story. Retail prices of gasoline have been volatile in recent years, but at a price of $3/gallon, the consumer is paying nearly $90 per MWh of energy content (including all taxes and fees), compared to just $14 per MWh for electricity. Thus the electrical grid takes coal at $50 per metric tonne, or approximately $7 per MWh, and although the value added by combusting coal, generating electricity, and distributing it to the customer is substantial, the final value per unit of energy is small compared to what is paid for motor fuels. Put another way, consumers of transportation fuels are willing to pay a premium for these fuels, so it does not make economic sense to sell them to the electrical or heating sectors when the latter are able to buy other fuels at much lower prices per unit of energy content.

Product	Standard units	$/unit	$/GJ	$/MWh
Gasoline	$/gal	$ 3.00	$ 24.64	$ 88.71
Heating fuel	$/million Btu	$ 9.00	$ 8.53	$ 30.71
Electricity	$/kWh	$ 0.14	$ 3.89	$ 14.00

Table 4 Cost of oil, natural gas, and coal by unit and by unit of energy, as final product sold to individual or residential customer.

In the short run, the division of fossil fuels between petroleum products for transportation applications and a mixture of coal and natural gas for non-transportation applications is likely to continue. Pushed by concern about climate change, consumers in both markets will continue to shift to carbon-free alternatives. It is possible that some changes in how fossil fuels are used may take place. For instance, some vendors advocate for the distribution of natural gas for use in vehicles in either a compressed or liquefied form (CNG or LNG). This option might be especially attractive for long-distance trucking, since these vehicles typically refuel in large quantities at a limited number of truck stops around the country, unlike private automobiles that refuel at the much more numerous and ubiquitous gas stations. The challenge for creating a new infrastructure for natural gas fueling of heavy trucks is whether the industry should instead transition directly to carbon-free fuel, as discussed in the next section.

Coal versus natural gas: CO_2 and other greenhouse gas emissions

Energy experts, political leaders, and environmental activists have vigorously debated whether or not we should use natural gas as a "bridge fuel." These arguments revolve around whether or not to consider greenhouse gases (GHGs) besides CO_2, and if so, how to evaluate them, and also whether or not it is appropriate at this time to pursue an energy source that has potentially reduced GHG emissions, but for which emissions are not zero. Initially, it is useful to point out that natural gas has lower CO_2 emissions per unit of energy than petroleum and especially coal (for example, for generating electricity), and to explain why that is. Table 5 shows energy, CO_2, and mass data for the three fuels. The key determinant is the number of hydrogen-to-carbon bonds in the molecules of the fuel per unit of total mass. Natural gas has the chemical formula CH_4. Therefore, it has the minimum amount of total mass possible to possess four bonds since each hydrogen atom forms a single bond to the carbon atom at the core of the molecule, and because hydrogen is so light. If we take gasoline as a representative petroleum product for evaluating the CO_2-to-energy ratio, there are relatively more carbon atoms for the number of hydrogen atoms (the molecular formula is C_8H_{18}), but there are still a large number of carbon-hydrogen bonds. Finally, if we take coal, effectively all energy in coal is stored in carbon bonds, and all remaining compounds in a quantity of coal that is combusted are impurities that are not part of the molecular structure of coal. Therefore, considering that coal provides 30 MJ per kg of fuel combusted (depending on the grade), that oil and natural gas each provide 50 MJ/kg, and that different fuels produce different amounts of CO_2 per mass combusted, the best performance is achieved by natural gas, followed by oil, followed by coal.

Fuel	Energy per mass (MJ/kg fuel)	CO2 per mass (kgCO2/kgfuel)	CO2 per energy (GramCO2/MJ)
Coal	30	3.67	122
Oil	50	3.11	62
Natural gas	50	2.75	55

Table 5 Relative energy and carbon content of coal, oil, and natural gas.

In earlier decades, when there seemed to be more time for phasing out fossil fuels in response to climate change, the natural gas bridge had more appeal. The ratio of more than two to one of emissions intensity per unit of energy for coal compared to natural gas suggested that emissions could be first reduced using gas, and then phased out entirely as carbon-free energy sources gradually developed. Gas also has the advantage of avoiding various contaminants that are released when coal is combusted in a power plant, including heavy metals and sulfur dioxide. These contaminants must either be filtered out, adding cost, or released into the atmosphere and environment, where they are harmful to life and add cost indirectly.

Recently, however, as the effects of climate change have become more urgent, there has been increasing pressure to bypass natural gas and move directly to renewables. Based on the figure of 22% of world energy coming from natural gas as presented in Chap. 1, CO_2 emissions from global natural gas use are already so large that, even if our economy could totally phase out the use of coal and crude oil, the remaining emissions would be larger than the natural environment could absorb. Also, with non-conventional drilling techniques, the total amount of natural gas available is so large that the emissions, if this resource were fully exploited, would place an unsustainable burden on the planet. Advertising in recent years from Shell Energy makes the point: Shell predicted a 250-year supply of natural gas and also pointed out that emissions are half of those of coal (per Table 5). Ironically, this means that they anticipate the emissions equivalent of 125 years of burning coal, which is hardly any comfort at all.

Natural gas has the further problem of fugitive methane emissions, the release of methane when leaks occur at all stages of the supply chain from the point of extraction at the well pad to points along the transmission and distribution network. Fugitive methane emissions significantly undercut the emissions reduction benefit of switching from coal because methane is such a potent greenhouse gas on a per-molecule basis compared to carbon dioxide. The burden is measured in Global Warming Potential, or GWP, which is the number of CO_2 molecules that have the same impact as one methane molecule. Published values range between 32 and 100, depending on assumptions about how long methane stays in the atmosphere. The emissions burden of natural gas compared to coal has been hotly debated. Some research shows that when fugitive methane is considered, natural gas is actually worse than coal; other research disagrees. In any case, even if the "worse than coal" claim is not true, the presence of fugitive emissions significantly reduces the benefit shown in Table 5, making a direct shift to non-carbon sources all the more urgent.

Setting aside the ecological implications or policy debate, the facts on the ground are that natural gas is indeed replacing coal, at a rate much faster than renewables are penetrating the market. Comparing it to wind, which increased by 220 billion kWh in the period 2007-2017 and is the fastest growing renewable in the U.S., natural gas increased by 400 billion kWh in terms of the increase in kWh generated each year (Table 6). As of 2017, the U.S. generated about five times as much electricity from natural gas as from wind. Also, this comparison does not include all the residential and industrial uses of natural gas, separate from the electricity market. Use of wind energy for purposes other than electricity is negligible. In an ideal world, to fight climate change in the decade 2010-2020 we would have had a much faster rollout of solar and wind production, with a supporting role for natural gas. In actuality we had the opposite: a rapid rollout of natural gas production, with solar and wind in a supporting role.

Source	Natural Gas	Wind
	Bil.kWh	Bil.kWh
Output 2007	896.6	34.5
Output 2017	1296.4	254.3
Growth	399.8	219.8

Table 6 Comparison of U.S. electricity production from natural gas and wind 2007-2017, in billion kWh.
Source: U.S. Energy Information Administration

Fossil fuel resources and reserves

Since fossil fuels are nonrenewable, it is important to understand how to measure their future availability. Here the difference between a fossil fuel "resource" and "reserve" is important. The quantity of the resource is the estimated total amount available, including both those whose location and quantity is well understood and those whose extent is known only approximately. A reserve is an amount that is known accurately and can be relied upon for future extraction. Over time, as geologic exploration allows experts to quantify the amount of fossil fuels available in a particular location with confidence, the quantity identified is added to the total reserves for that location or country.

Table 7 shows fossil fuel reserves in 2004 and 2014 for four major energy-producing countries, namely China, Russia, Saudi Arabia, and the United States, as well as a "Rest of World" category. Because the four named countries are all major economies, they are also significant consumers of energy, so some fraction of the reserves present in 2004 will be consumed during the period 2004-2014. However, because the exploration process adds to the size of the reserve even as consumption decreases it, in some case the size of the reserve is actually larger in 2014. For example, thanks to the introduction of nonconventional extraction techniques, the size of the U.S. natural gas reserve increased from 5.4 to 9.6 trillion cubic meters over this period.

Country:	Gas	Oil	Coal
Year 2004	[tril m3]	[bill. Bbl]	[bill. Tonne]
China	1.5	18.2	110.0
Russia	47.6	60.0	250.0
Saudi Arabia	6.5	262.0	-
United States	5.4	21.9	270.0
Rest of World	111.0	902.9	370.0
TOTAL	172.0	1,265.0	1,000.0
Year 2014			
China	4.4	24.4	126.2
Russia	47.8	80.0	173.1
Saudi Arabia	8.2	268.4	-
United States	9.6	36.5	258.6
Rest of World	127.5	1,246.3	421.9
TOTAL	197.5	1,655.6	979.8

Table 7 Fossil fuel reserves in volume and energy units for select countries and overall world in 2004 and 2014.
Source: U.S. Energy Information Administration.
Conversions: 1 trillion m³ gas = 36.4 exajoule (EJ), 1 billion barrel oil = 5.24 EJ, 1 billion tonne coal = 25 EJ.

As for resource size, the values are not known as precisely, but in general can be much larger than the size of reserves. The size of the world coal resource might be on the order of 250,000 EJ, or ten times as much as the reserve value shown in the table. The size of the world crude oil is also not precisely known, but might be on the order of 8 trillion barrels including both conventional and non-conventional resources.

Fossil fuel resource life cycle and "peak oil" phenomenon

Fossil fuel resources in the ground, and notably crude oil resources, have a standard life cycle in which they produce oil slowly in the early years of the life of the oil field, are most productive during the middle of the field life, and then have dwindling production toward the end of their lives. Since the total production of a country is simply the sum of all individual oil fields, eventually if there are enough fields going into decline and not enough new ones to replace them, the overall output of the country will go into decline. This phenomenon of the production peaking years in advance of the end of the availability of the resource is known as "peak oil." Peak oil applies to both conventional U.S. production currently and, in time, will apply to nonconventional production using hydraulic fracturing and other technologies.

The rise, peaking, and decline of U.S. conventional oil production in the period 1900-2008 can be seen in both the annual production of U.S. oil (Fig. 3) or the cumulative production (Fig. 4). The cumulative production is simply the total production of all years up to that year, so that, for example, the cumulative production in 1901 is the production in 1900 plus that of 1901, the cumulative production in 1902 is the cumulative value in 1901 plus the annual production in 1902, and so on. Compared to cumulative production, annual production is relatively uneven, and is affected by factors such as the addition or subtraction of fields contributing to output or the performance of the economy and its impact on oil demand. As an illustration, output declines in the mid-1970s up to the year 1976 but then stabilizes and grows slightly for the next 10 years, due to the inauguration of the Alaska pipeline. By contrast, the cumulative oil production curve has a relatively smooth s-curve shape, similar to the s-curve introduced in Chapter 1 to describe the life cycle of new technologies entering the market. Events such as the inauguration of the Alaska pipeline do not perceptibly change its shape, and from about 1985 onward the curve begins to bend toward some eventual upper limit.

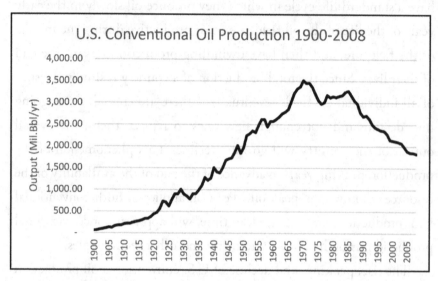

Figure 3 Annual output of conventional oil production from all U.S. fields including Alaska, 1900-2008, in million barrels.

Source: U.S. Energy Information Administration.

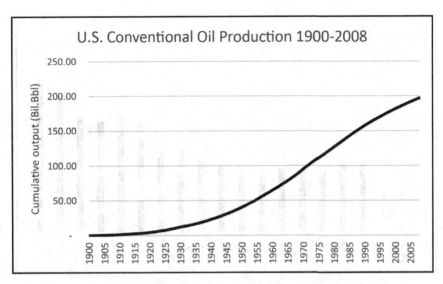

Figure 4 Cumulative output of conventional oil production from all U.S. fields including Alaska, 1900-2008, in billion barrels.

Source: U.S. Energy Information Administration.

The impact of nonconventional oil starting in 2008 was to reverse the decline in U.S. domestic oil production (Fig. 5). Spurred both by rising oil prices and pressure due to anticipated peaking of conventional oil output, the industry invested in developing new techniques, including both hydraulic fracturing that could release oil in locations such as the Bakken Field in North Dakota, and tar sands extraction used in the Athabascan Field in Alberta, Canada. By 2019, output had grown to 4.5 billion barrels per year, surpassing the 1970 peak of conventional oil of 3.5 billion barrels per year.

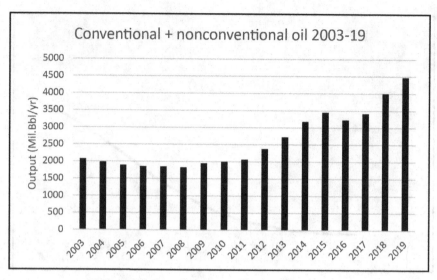

Figure 5 Impact of non-conventional oil development
on total U.S. oil production 2003-2019.
Source: U.S. Energy Information Administration.

The emergence of shale oil and the resurgence of U.S. oil production does not, however, disprove the phenomenon of peak oil. Non-conventional oil can be treated as a separate resource from conventional oil, and its path will ultimately follow the path of rising, peaking, and falling, as that of conventional oil, barring some major disruption. Figure 6 shows a possible pathway under the assumption that eventually 69 billion barrels of nonconventional oil will be recovered. This pathway shows a decline already in the decade of the 2020s. If the amount eventually recovered is larger than 69 billion barrels, the decline would begin later. However, in general, the path is certain to follow the pattern of rise and decline.

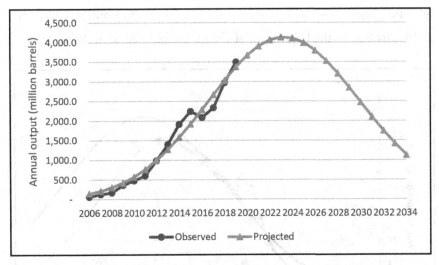

Figure 6 Projected pathway for U.S. non-conventional oil production using observed production 2006-2019 and under assumption of ultimate recovery of 69 billion barrels.

Source for historical observed output: U.S. Energy Information Administration.

Peak oil applied to the world oil supply

The peak oil phenomenon illustrated using U.S. oil production in the previous section can be applied to world oil consumption on the whole. Figure 7 shows historical world oil production from 1900 to 2019, along with two possible smooth pathways for future oil production based on Estimated Ultimate Recovery (EUR) values of either 3.25 or 4 trillion barrels of oil. The historical trend up to 2019 appears to show production in a rapid growth phase from approximately 1950 to 1980, followed by a phase of approaching a historical peak from 1980 to 2019. Output grew by 17 billion barrels per year between 1950 and 1980, and by an additional 8 billion barrels per year from 1980 to 2019. As of 2018-2019, output was continuing to grow: at 30.4 billion barrels, the 2018 output was the largest in history, with a slight decline to 30.3 billion barrels in 2019, just before the beginning of the global pandemic in 2020.

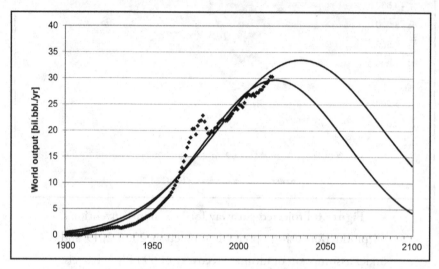

Figure 7 World oil historical production data 1900-2019 and projections for future pathways based on possible EUR values.

Note: Historical production values are individual data points, and projections for future pathway as a function of estimated ultimate recovery values of 3 trillion or 4 trillion barrels are solid lines. Source for historical data: U.S. Energy Information Administration.

Looking to the future, many different pathways are possible. As both world population and GDP continue to grow, annual output may continue to grow for some time beyond 2019. As of that year, cumulative world output had reached 1.41 trillion, so an eventual outcome of 3 or 4 trillion barrels produced is possible at this point. Just like in the case of the U.S. annual production curve, the exact pathway has not followed the smooth projected pathways in Fig. 7 in the past, nor will it in the future. The upper solid curve (EUR = 4T) peaks in the year 2034, so perhaps the actual curve might peak in that year but decline more slowly to arrive at 4 trillion total produced. To reiterate, this projection assumes that oil production is not affected by climate mitigation policies, or that emissions from oil production are offset in some other way.

Here it is important to consider the potential role of non-conventional petroleum resources. Conventional resources might constitute an EUR of 4 trillion barrels, and non-conventional resources might constitute an additional 4 trillion barrels, in the form of oil extracted from shale and tar sands. Figure 8 shows a possible pathway to the year 2070 in which non-conventional resources make up the difference as world demand continues to grow until 2050 and conventional production cannot keep up. Conventional output eventual peaks at around 35 billion barrels/ year in 2040, but combined output peaks at 44 billion barrels/year in 2050, due to the contribution of nonconventional resources.

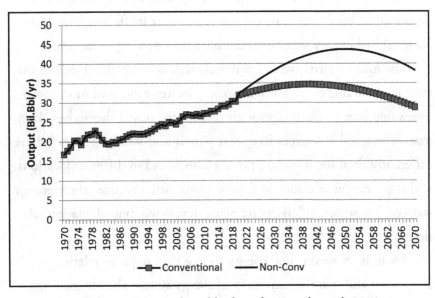

Figure 8 Projected world oil production through 2070, including both conventional and nonconventional sources. Sources for data: U.S. Energy Information Administration, Cambridge Energy Resource Associates.

Francis M. Vanek

Moving Away from Fossil Fuels: What is the First Step?

Fossil fuels have profoundly shaped the world we live in today. They are versatile and easy to use. Although prices are volatile at times, there have also been periods of relatively stable, low prices in many parts of the world. Their availability around the world has made it difficult until recently to justify investments in alternatives.

As we have seen in this chapter, there are two main forces that appear poised to push out fossil fuels. The more urgent at this time is climate change, and the need to reduce greenhouse gas emissions from the burning of fossil fuels to generate energy. The other force is the potential for output to peak and constraints to emerge on the amount of fossil fuels available. In the recent past, this phenomenon of peak output appeared more urgent than climate change. It appears not to be as urgent now, but if efforts to proactively shift to energy sources that do not contribute to climate change are slow or ineffective, constraints on fossil fuel energy supplies could become a driving factor again.

The main alternative to fossil fuels that is being developed at this time is renewable energy. But as society moves more and more toward renewable energy, challenges with this source reveal themselves. Even mature renewable sources like solar panels and wind turbines behave differently than fossil fuels. They are also found in different locations, and require new solutions to deploy, transport, and store these energy sources. These new solutions are being developed, but adaptation takes time.

There is, however, one energy source that requires relatively little adaptation and that the conventional energy system already encourages: energy efficiency. The energy system today incentivizes improving efficiency: if you can offer a technology that pays for its upfront cost by reducing the cost of fossil fuels over time, the economic marketplace will happily adopt it. Efficiency can be applied at all stages. At the generation end, if a power plant can be made more energy efficient, it will deliver electricity the same way, but use less resource. At the consumption end, a more efficient car or appliance uses the same gasoline or electricity but requires less of it. Furthermore, by improving the energy efficiency of the system, we set ourselves up to need fewer solar panels and wind turbines in the future to meet energy demand, as we shift to renewables. For this reason, energy efficiency is seen as the first step, and is the subject of the next chapter.

CHAPTER 4
Efficiency – The Foundation for Sustainable Energy

Suppose you are in a cold climate in winter, and there is significant snowfall on the ground. You notice two kinds of houses: ones where the snow has melted off the roof, and others where the snow remains piled up on the roof. Perhaps on the ones where the snow has melted, you notice lines of snow running in the direction that the roof rises, at regular intervals a few feet apart. Between these lines, the snow has melted away, and you can see the dark surface of the roof itself.

This image provides a visual example of the benefit of investing in efficiency. The house with an intact layer of snow is insulated well, so heat travels through the insulation in the roof only slowly, and the snow stays in place. The homeowner has invested some up-front cost in better insulation, and in return, the ongoing cost for heating in the winter is lower. Also, carbon emissions are reduced: the owner is purchasing less fuel (be it natural gas, heating oil, or propane) and less is being burned. In the house where only lines of unmelted snow are left, the boards that support the roof from below are actually providing insulation that prevents the snow from melting, but everywhere else, the heat readily passes from house to attic, exits through the roof, and melts the snow. Investment in insulation is lower, but heating bill spending and CO_2 emissions are both higher.

From a climate protection point of view, improving efficiency has two benefits. First, it slows the rate of greenhouse gas emissions in the short to medium term. Second, it reduces the quantity of carbon-free energy generation devices, like solar arrays or wind farms, that must eventually be installed to meet society's demand for energy without increasing the concentration of greenhouse gases in the atmosphere. Efficiency and alternative energy are coupled investments: if the starting level of efficiency is low, it makes sense to invest the first increment of energy spending in efficiency and the rest on alternative energy supply because it may not be cost effective to cover the entire starting load from alternative energy sources.

Improving Efficiency: Conversion Devices versus End-use Devices

At the outset it is useful to distinguish between *conversion devices* and *end-use devices*. As energy makes its way from primary energy to final use, conversion devices transform it from a less to more convenient form. Primary energy includes not only fossil fuels but also the original form in which renewables such as wind or solar are captured. End-use devices include all manner of large and small powered objects that consume energy and provide services.

Conversion devices include all manner of systems that generate electricity, which is perhaps the most ubiquitous "carrier" of energy that can be widely transported and used. The largest of these devices are major power plants that use energy from fossil fuels, nuclear reaction, or the movement of water through turbines to first generate mechanical energy (a spinning shaft) and then electricity from a generator. The same principle can be applied on a much smaller scale in a single building, such as a microturbine that burns fuel and generates electricity. A refinery is also a conversion device: It takes crude oil and converts it to various transportation fuels such as gasoline, diesel, or jet fuel that can be transported, stored, and eventually sold for final consumption. Even a boiler in a house or institutional building is a form of conversion device that takes natural gas or heating oil as an input and heats water to be circulated to radiators or radiant floor heating for indoor heat.

End-use devices are even more diverse. Many end-use devices use electricity for heat, from a space heater, to an induction cooktop, to a hair dryer. Other devices use electricity for electronic purposes, such as a sound system, computer, or smart phone. Other devices use it for lighting or cooling, such as a lamp, refrigerator, or air conditioner. Another group of devices use electricity for mechanical purposes, such as dishwashers, washing machines and other appliances, as well as all manner of power tools for individual and industrial use. A visit to a modern home improvement and building center in the U.S. might reveal hundreds or even thousands of different makes and models of end-use devices that consume electricity. Beyond these are the myriad "end-use devices" that use liquid fuels for transportation, from a riding lawnmower to a railroad locomotive.

Every end-use device provides an opportunity to invest in efficiency. Sometimes a new opportunity exists to invest in a device for the first time, for example when a residential or commercial building is constructed on a site where none existed previously. At other times, there may be an opportunity to replace an existing device, in which case one can ask how efficient the current device is, how much more efficient a replacement would be, and how much life is left in the existing device – whether it makes sense to replace it now or to continue to get more life out of it before replacement. In either situation, we can decide whether or not to spend more to get a more efficient option.

Francis M. Vanek

Efficiency versus Conservation and Eco-efficiency versus Eco-sufficiency

Although closely related to one another, "conservation" and "efficiency" are two different things. Conservation is the act of using an existing device or system more efficiently through individual action. For example, remembering to turn off the light when you leave the room or to turn down the thermostat when you will be away from your house for an extended period of time, is conservation. Efficiency is the energy savings gained from the reduced use of energy that is designed into a device. For instance, unlike with the person turning off the light when they leave the room, the energy reduction that comes from a compact fluorescent or LED lightbulb compared to an incandescent bulb is achieved whenever the bulb is drawing energy.

Both conservation and efficiency are important. Although much sustainable energy work is focused on advancing efficiency, any individual, business, or organization that invests in efficiency will likely also pursue conservation because of their interest in climate protection. Furthermore, they can enhance their contribution to climate protection by applying conservation best practices to their investment in efficiency. Such conservation best practices might include signage to remind building occupants to turn off lights when they are not in use or regularly checking tire pressure on a car to make sure tires are inflated correctly.

The distinction between efficiency and conservation can also be compared to the distinction between two other related terms, namely "eco-efficiency" and "eco-sufficiency." Eco-efficiency is the pursuit of technologies or practices that reduce the ecological impact per unit of output of goods or services so that they fall within some maximum allowable amount. For example, a vehicle that drives farther per unit of energy consumed so that it achieves the government's fuel economy standard would be eco-efficient. Eco-sufficiency is the pursuit of the combination of technologies and their amount of use that achieves some overall target for total impact, such as the total annual CO_2 emissions of a country. For example, a region might determine a maximum sustainable amount of CO_2 emissions from driving and then find the combination of more efficient vehicles and programs to reduce kilometers driven to achieve this overall goal.

In general, eco-sufficient solutions are also eco-efficient, but eco-efficient solutions may or may not be eco-sufficient. An example of an eco-efficient solution that is not also eco-sufficient is an enormous private home with many thousands of square feet of space that uses all state-of-the-art energy-efficient technology. All of the lights and appliances are the state of the art in terms of efficiency, all of the windows are triple-paned and tightly sealed, and the overall insulation level of the house is outstanding. However, because the house is so large, the total demand for lighting, heating, cooling, and electronic services offsets the efficiency of each individual component, and the total impact of the house is worse than that of an average-sized house with basic fixtures.

An Illustrative Example: Energy Efficiency and Residential-Scale Solar PV

Consider some homeowners who want to produce 100% of their own electricity from an onsite, residential solar PV system that is connected to the grid and can take advantage of net metering. Net metering is discussed in more depth in Chap. 5, but briefly described, it is an arrangement where each unit of solar electricity not consumed by a household and pushed onto the grid accumulates credit to offset purchases from the grid at times when solar output is insufficient or non-existent (e.g., at night). For simplicity's sake, further assume that the house has an old, inefficient refrigerator and lighting with energy-intensive incandescent lightbulbs, and that the rest of the electricity loads (such as the washing machine or television) in the house will remain unchanged regardless of what happens to the refrigerator and lighting. There are assumed to be 32 light fixtures with an average of a 60-Watt bulb in use 3 hours per day, for a total of about 2,100 kWh per year for all of the fixtures. The refrigerator consumes 1,000 kWh per year, and the remaining consumption in the house amounts to about 4,900 kWh per year. Electricity costs 14 cents per kWh, and since the total consumption is 8,000 kWh/yr, the total cost is $1,120 per year.

As a starting point, the homeowners might install a PV system, also called a PV "array," sized to make approximately the amount of electricity consumed each year. Productivity for their region is found to be 1,400 kWh produced per year for every 1 kW of panel capacity installed, a median value for the U.S. Each 1 kW of capacity costs $3,000 to install. Therefore, the total amount required is about 5.7 kW, at a cost of $17,100. Note that the final installed cost varies widely around the U.S., depending on the level of rebates and tax credits available, and that a lower installed cost as low as $2,300/kW may be possible. However, the value of $3,000/kW in this example has been chosen to make the calculation conservative.

Now suppose that the homeowners still wish to meet 100% of their annual electricity demand across the year with carbon-free electricity purchases by installing a solar PV array, but they are intimidated by the high initial cost.[15] On closer inspection, they realize that they can replace the combined fixtures and incandescent bulbs with integrated LED fixtures for $40 each that use 15 instead of 60 Watts on average. Also, the refrigerator can be replaced with a modern unit that consumes 400 kWh per year for $500. Table 1 compares the resulting energy consumption and electricity cost per year for the base case with the improved case, where the lighting and refrigeration have been upgraded, and the balance of the house is unchanged. The investment in efficiency saves 2,175 kWh and $305 per year.

Item:	Base case		Efficient case	
	kWh	Cost	kWh	Cost
Lighting	2100	$ 294	525	$ 74
Refrigerator	1000	$ 140	400	$ 56
Balance	4900	$ 686	4900	$ 686
TOTAL	8000	$ 1,120	5825	$ 816

Table 1 Electricity consumption for base and improved cases for 8,000 kWh per year example home.

Since the predicted annual electricity production is now 5,825 kWh/year, the size of the array can be reduced as well. The required size is now 4.2 kW, for a cost of $12,600. Even with the investment in lighting and refrigeration, the alternative saves thousands of dollars (Table 2).

---

[15] In practical terms, 100% carbon-free electricity in this case means the household makes more electricity than it consumes in the summer and falls short in the winter, but there are sufficient credits for extra kWh in the summer to offset the winter shortfall. See Chap.5.

Item	Base Case	Improved Case
Solar panels	$ 17,100.00	$ 12,600.00
Refrigerator	$ -	$ 500.00
Lighting	$ -	$ 1,280.00
TOTAL	$ 17,100.00	$ 14,380.00

Table 2 Initial outlay for base and improved cases for example home

Another way to look at the situation is to consider how long the lighting and refrigeration take to pay for themselves, and to compare payback time to that of the solar array. Since the solar array has a constant cost per kW, the payback is calculated on the basis of 1 kW of capacity. The lighting and refrigerator pay for themselves on the basis of the number of kWh saved compared to the equipment that has been replaced. The solar PV pays for itself on the basis of avoided purchases of grid electricity in the first place. As shown in Table 3, the payback for investing in efficiency is on the order of 6 years, whereas the investment in generating renewable electricity pays for itself in 15 years.

Item	Initial cost	Ann. savings	Payback (yrs)
Lighting	$ 1,280	$ 221	5.8
Refrigerator	$ 500	$ 84	6.0
Solar PV, 1 kW	$ 3,000	$ 196	15.3

Table 3 Payback time in years for investments in efficiency or solar PV.

The outcome of this comparison supports the adage in renewable energy that "the first investment in renewables is in the efficiency of the equipment that the system will power." However, the cost comparison does not always work this way: for example, if the house is already very energy efficient in terms of lighting and appliances, there may not be "low hanging fruit" as there was in this case. Instead the investment may be entirely in solar PV. In any case, the possibility of reducing demand should always be examined. Even in cases where the financing of solar PV is out of reach, the homeowners may be able to afford the smaller investment required for reducing consumption, as a first step toward adding solar later when they can afford it.

Another Illustrative Example: An Electricity Market

In the residential-scale solar PV example explained in the previous section, we discussed the tradeoff between choosing energy loads with high energy consumption and the need to meet that demand, versus spending some amount up-front in reduced-consumption energy loads and thereby requiring less energy consumption. In the next example, we scale up the application to an electricity market. Although the scale of the example is much larger, namely an entire region, the same principles apply. Electricity is generated in centralized power stations. Investments in more efficient power plants incur a higher initial cost, but they reduce operating cost through the purchase less fuel or other energy input. The example presented in this section will show how savings over time can pay back the initial cost. The investment also reduces ongoing emissions since each unit of fuel saved also avoids generating a unit of CO_2. This example focuses on generating electricity from fossil fuels, so it has a more short- to medium-term horizon, but the same principles apply to choosing between more or less energy-efficient renewable energy power plants.

The example revolves around a specific type of electric generation plant called a *combined cycle* plant. Originally, power was generated in *single cycle* plants. Some plants burned coal to generate steam for a steam turbine. In others, gas was burned to generate a hot gas-air mixture to drive a gas turbine. The spinning turbine then turned a generator. The combined cycle plant burns gas at high temperature and pressure to turn a gas turbine in one cycle, and then the exhaust heat is used to boil water and generate steam that turns a steam turbine in a second cycle, hence the name. The advantage of the combined cycle plant is higher efficiency values in the 55-60% range, compared to 40% for a single-cycle plant. However, the combined cycle plant is more complex due to the two stages and must be operated for a large enough number of hours per year to justify the higher investment cost. Combined cycle is different from *combined heat and power* (also known as *cogeneration*), where the heat source is used to both generate electricity and for other heat applications, such as space heating or industrial processes that require thermal input. Combined heat and power is discussed in a later section.

The single- and combined-cycle plants are compared in Table 4. The value in the capital cost column is the cost per megawatt per year to own the plant regardless of how much electricity it makes. These cost values assume that the plant is built on a large scale; a small plant would cost significantly more per MW. Values are given on an actual basis but would actually be calculated based on the initial cost of the project, the expected life of the investment, and the amount that would be expected each year to repay the initial cost. The cost per kWh in the table includes all other non-capital cost and is added to the capital cost to give the total expenditure on the plant each year. The combined cycle plant is more complicated to build, and therefore costs *more* per MW, but it is also more efficient, and therefore costs *less* per kWh produced in terms of non-capital cost. In addition, the combined cycle plant consumes less fuel per kWh because it is more efficient, so the amount of CO_2 per kWh is also reduced.

Resource	Fixed cost ($1000/MW/y)	Variable cost ($/kWh)	Emissions (kgCO2/kWh)
Single	$90	$0.065	0.495
Combined	$120	$0.04	0.330

Table 4 Unit fixed cost, variable cost, and emissions for
single- and combined-cycle plants.
Source: Representative values based on own calculations.

Next, we introduce a hypothetical electricity market into which these two kinds of plants will sell electricity in some combination, so that we can examine the impact of choices made. This exercise is carried out using a *load duration curve*, where all the average hourly demand values for a recent yearly period (such as the previous calendar year) are put into a data table and then arranged in decreasing order (Fig. 1). The result is a uniformly decreasing curve that shows the value in the highest value hour of the year (Hour 1 in the figure) and in the lowest value hour (Hour 8760 in the figure, ignoring leap years). Note that the values in this figure are quite large: they are measured in gigawatts or 1,000 MW. If we take 10 GW to be approximately the average value in the figure, and the system maintained this value constantly for all 8,760 hours per year, the output would be 87.6 billion kWh per year. If average homes consume between 5,000 and 10,000 kWh per year, this output would be enough to power nearly 9 to 18 million homes, or 7 to 14 percent of the estimated number of U.S. households in 2019[16]

---

[16] According to the U.S. Bureau of the Census, there were about 129 million households in the U.S. in 2019.

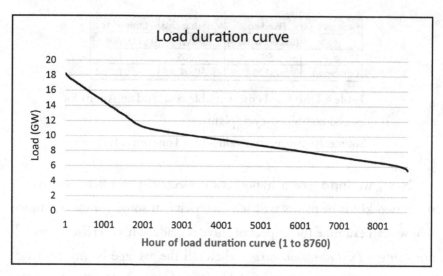

Figure 1 Load duration curve for electricity demand in a hypothetical region (gigawatts of load).

Then, for clarity, suppose we smooth the load duration curve so that it consists of just two lines: One at high levels where demand drops rapidly from left to right and another where it drops more slowly (Fig. 2). We see that now, in the highest-demand hour of the year, the system requires 18 GW of supply, and at the lowest demand hour of the year, it requires 6 GW. This graph means that, continuously for all hours of the year, the system requires at least 6 GW. Also, for 2,000 hours per year, the system requires at least 11 GW of power.

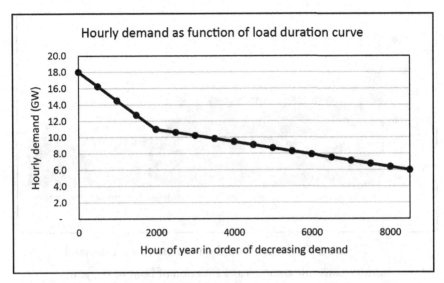

Figure 2 Streamlined load duration curve with demand as a linear function of hour of the year.

Finally, to make the load duration curve even simpler for purposes of calculating quantities of electricity generation and consumption, we will convert the demand into three constant "chunks" in Fig. 3. The first 500 hours at 18 GW represent the peak period of the year (for example, hot hours in the summer when air-conditioning load is large). There are 5,000 hours per year when load is in the middle, at 11 GW. Finally, as discussed above, there is a minimum demand of 6 GW for every hour of the year, so the block in the figure with 6 GW of demand extends for the entire 8,760 hours shown. Totaling kWh of electricity production at 6 GW base load for all hours, then 5 GW of incremental load for 5,000 hours, and finally 7 GW of peak load for 500 hours equals 81.06 billion kWh per year.

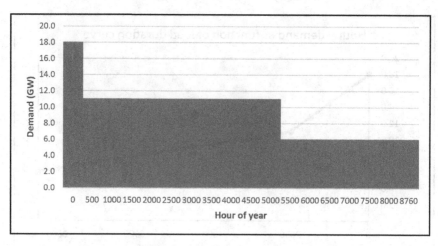

Figure 3 Simplified load duration curve with demand in three constant amounts as a function of hour of the year: high demand (18 GW), midrange demand (11 GW), and low demand (6 GW).

Suppose we set out to meet the electricity demand in Fig. 3 using exclusively single-cycle plants. Historically, this might have been the case if we were meeting demand before 1948 when only single-cycle technology was available, as combined cycle was first introduced to commercial use in the United States in that year. Since the most power required is 18 GW, we would install this capacity at a cost of $90,000 per MW per year or a total of $1.62 billion (Table 5). We would then generate the ~81 billion kWh with this capacity at 6.5 cents per kWh for a total variable cost of ~$5.269 billion. Combining capacities results in a total cost per year of about $6.89 billion per year, or 8.5 cents per kWh to produce. At 490 grams of CO_2 per kWh, the total CO_2 emissions are 40.1 million tons per year.

Load type	Base	Mid	Hi	TOTAL
Capacity (GW)	6	5	7	18
Fixed cost ($M)	540	450	630	1620
Hours/yr	8760	5000	500	(n/a)
Output (BkWh)	52.6	25.0	3.5	81.1
Var.Cost ($M)	3416.4	1625	227.5	5268.9
Total cost ($M)	3956.4	2075	857.5	6888.9
Emissions (MTCO2)	26.0	12.4	1.7	40.1

Table 5 Cost and emissions in all-single-cycle scenario.

The *capacity factor* is a useful concept for understanding how the investment in generating capacity translates to overall operating cost and cost per kWh. The capacity factor is defined as the ratio of the actual production to the ideal production that would have occurred if the electric generating stations in the example had produced at 100% all the time. This would be optimal from a business point of view, since the $1.62 billion per year invested in the operating equipment would result in the maximum number of kWh produced. Of course, in the real world this is not possible. The total capacity is designed for the peak periods, meaning that in the off-peak periods, not all of the capacity will be in use. Since in this case the actual output is ~81 billion kWh per year, and the ideal would be about 158 billion kWh/y, the capacity factor is the ratio of the two, or 51%.

Both the average cost of generating the electricity and the total CO_2 in this case are high, so when the combined-cycle technology comes along, we can take advantage of it. For the baseload 6-GW demand for 8,760 hours per year and incremental 5-GW demand for 5,000 hours per year, shifting to combined cycle is financially justified because the savings in variable cost pay for the additional capital cost (Table 6). All but 3.5 billion of the total 81 billion kWh are generated in the combined-cycle plants. Total annual cost is reduced to $5.49 billion, and total emissions are reduced to 27.3 billion tons CO_2, a 29%

reduction. The average cost of production across the system is reduced to 6.8 cents per kWh.

Load type	Base	Mid	Hi	TOTAL
Capacity (GW)	6	5	7	18
Fixed cost ($M)	720	600	630	1950
Hours/yr	8760	5000	500	(n/a)
Output (BkWh)	52.6	25	3.5	81.1
Var.Cost ($M)	2102.4	1000	227.5	3329.9
Total cost ($M)	2822.4	1600	857.5	5279.9
Emissions (MTCO2)	17.3	8.3	1.7	27.3

Table 6 Cost and emissions for scenario with mixture of combined-cycle for base and incremental load, and single-cycle for peak load.

This example illustrates the potential to reduce both cost and emissions with better technology. Higher initial investment reduces variable cost sufficiently to pay for itself. Note that for the last increment of electricity production (the "peak" load), however, the investment was not cost effective. As shown in both Tables 5 and 6, the combined fixed and variable cost for this increment of 3.5 billion kWh is $858 million per year, for a cost of 24.5 cents per kWh. Not only is this cost much higher than the overall average from Table 6, but the cost would be higher still if combined cycle had been used. The combined cost would have been $1.068 billion, or 30.5 cents per kWh. We will return later in this chapter to the question of what to do about situations such as this one where investment in efficiency is not cost-effective.

To conclude, the broader principle of paying for investing in efficiency is relevant to the overall economic function of energy markets, be they for conventional or renewable electricity. For any energy technology, including solar PV panels and wind turbines, the investor can pay extra to make the device more efficient, and then the device will in turn generate more revenue because it is more productive.

Combined Heat and Power (CHP) and Cogeneration

Unlike combined cycle, which seeks to improve efficiency by converting more useful energy from the energy source into electricity, *combined heat and power* (also known as *CHP* or *cogeneration*) improves efficiency by performing two tasks with the same source. First, CHP generates electricity, and then the byproduct heat (which is no longer hot enough to generate electricity efficiently) is used for some thermal purpose. Possible applications include space heating, industrial processes that need heat as an input (such as certain food processing procedures), and as a heat source for absorption chillers that provide air conditioning. A number of universities such as the Massachusetts Institute of Technology and Cornell University, use CHP to generate a combination of electricity and heat from natural gas. In an interesting variation on this arrangement, the Burrstone Energy Center in Utica, NY, generates heat, power, and chilled water as an independent enterprise and then sells it to the adjacent Utica College and St. Luke's Hospital and Nursing Home.

In the short- to medium-term, conventional sources such as natural gas can provide the primary energy source. However, over time, an existing combined heat and power system might replace the fuel combustion and electricity generation component with power from renewable sources to make it carbon free. Renewable electricity would then provide heat to the existing heat distribution system in whatever form fits best. For example, a large electricity generation station might currently heat a *district energy system* that provides heat and hot water to thousands of homes in the district in its immediate vicinity. Even if the coal or gas combustion is eventually replaced to eliminate CO_2 emissions, the district energy system can continue to be used. Also, although the majority of solar electricity is currently generated using solar PV, some is generated by concentrating sunlight to generate high-pressure, high-temperature steam. CHP could be applied here as well, by developing solar thermal power plants that distribute byproduct heat for other uses.

The CHP process can be brought down to a much smaller scale as well. A 30-kW microturbine installed in a small manufacturing facility with sufficient electric load might produce 250,000 kWh per year and an additional 530,000 kWh/year in byproduct heat, based on an electricity conversion efficiency of 25% and byproduct heating efficiency of 55%. Whether the system is large or small, the advantage of CHP is that, if using fossil fuels is the starting point, the total CO_2 generated is less if the electricity and heat demands are met in combination than if they are met in separate, unconnected processes.

Alternatives When Investment in Efficiency is Not Cost-effective

We now return to the example from above of the electricity supply for a hypothetical regional electric grid. Recall that for the peak-period demand for the highest-demand 500 hours of the year, the up-front cost for the more efficient system, namely the combined-cycle plant, could not be justified by savings over time. This example represents a general category of equipment that is used sporadically, so that the equipment must be purchased as cheaply as possible. The good news here is that sporadic use means the excess pollution is small against the backdrop of total emissions: in the example, the single-cycle plant was used for 500 hours a year, but the unit that ran all 8,760 hours was the more efficient combined-cycle plant, which significantly reduced pollution.

Even if investing in more efficient technology is ruled out, we can explore other options to avoid inefficient "peaking" units. One option is to have users pay the real-time cost of purchasing electricity during periods of peak demand, which will encourage consumers to make different choices since the costs are so high. In this example, the peak-period electricity costs 24.5 cents to produce, plus the transmission cost. If the customer sees this price, they might make choices to conserve energy instead of consuming electricity during peak times. Suppose such a real-time pricing regime is implemented and demand is reduced by 1 GW for the peak 500 hours per year. The demand is now 17 GW instead of 18 GW for that period. Only 6 GW of the production from the single-cycle technology is needed, saving 500 million kWh and about 250,000 metric tonnes of CO_2.

Single-cycle peaking plants might also be replaced by large-scale battery systems or other electricity storage systems. Electricity could be generated by a more efficient source, such as a combined-cycle plant or renewable plant, stored in the battery system, and then discharged during peak demand periods. Depending on the "round-trip efficiency" (total efficiency of putting electricity into storage and taking it out again), this option may be more efficient than generation at low efficiency. In the hypothetical region example, the 5 GW of capacity that is used for 5,000 hours but idle for 3,760 hours, represent an opportunity to generate and store electricity in such a way that emissions decline.

Pushing Greater Efficiency by Putting a Price on Carbon

Another way to encourage efficiency is to put a price on carbon emissions so that the more carbon-intensive the activity, the higher the additional charge. This strategy may be implemented by (1) using a cap-and-trade system, where players must bid for a finite number of emissions permits that declines year after year; (2) a renewable portfolio standard requiring a minimum energy fraction to be generated from renewables, which gradually forces the energy market to shift; or (3) a carbon tax that sets a price for each unit of emissions. Here we focus on the carbon tax as a means to reward efficiency.

In the hypothetical electricity market example, both the single- and combined-cycle plants would pay the tax, since they both combust natural gas. However, the single-cycle plant would pay more, leveling the playing field. Since the combined-cycle plant is currently uncompetitive for the 500-hour peak period, suppose we seek the carbon tax value that would make the two options equal, i.e., allow the combined-cycle plant to break even. It turns out that this value is quite high: since the total cost for the combined-cycle plant to meet the peak demand is $210 million higher than with the single-cycle plant, a tax of $364 per metric tonne of CO_2 is required so that the total cost per year for either option comes out to $1.49 billion per year (Table 7). A robust value for a carbon tax that would broadly influence energy choices, but to which consumers could adapt if it were phased in gradually over time, is on the order of $100 per tonne.[17] If this value were instituted instead, the combined-cycle plant would fall well short of breaking even. This example illustrates how not all carbon-intensive activities can be changed using a carbon tax. Nevertheless, for many other activities, the carbon tax can make the difference in terms of making a more efficient option, or possibly a carbon-free option, cost-competitive.

Option:	Single-cycle	Combined-cycle
Generating cost, $M	$ 857.5	$ 1,067.5
CO2 tax @ $364/t, $M	$ 630.0	$ 420.0
TOTAL	$ 1,487.5	$ 1,487.5

Table 7 Comparison of cost impact of $364/tonne CO_2 tax on regional production cost.

---

[17] For example, a $100/tonne carbon tax was advocated by climate scientist James Hansen at the 2010 Annual Iscol Lecture on the Environment at Cornell University, April 19, 2010.

Many Ways to Pursue Energy Efficiency

New, more energy efficient technologies and products can enter into the market in a number of ways. In one case, an all-new item is introduced. Suppose someone is building a house where none existed previously, or a new driver is buying a car when they did not previously own one. By investing in a more efficient house, or spending more for an energy-efficient car, the individual can reduce ongoing cost and greenhouse emissions at the same time. In other situations, the owner may possess an obsolete car or appliance, which if replaced at present rather than in the future can avoid emissions. Lastly, for some long-lived items such as a house or other structure, the energy efficiency can be upgraded at the present time to avoid future cost and emissions.

More broadly, spending on efficiency represents a partnership between consumers and producers to invest in a more sustainable future. Both sides must commit to taking steps: the consumer to spend extra on efficiency, and the producer on offering more efficient products that typically are priced higher because they cost more to manufacture. Over the longer term, everyone wins: the consumer not only reduces cost, but often improves quality of life; the producer creates new markets for products, and both sides benefit from a healthier global ecosystem. In this way, the push for efficiency protects the environment, creates jobs, and sets up a transition to carbon-free energy in the future. The next chapter shifts the focus from reducing energy demand to increasing the supply of sustainable energy, starting with solar energy.

CHAPTER 5

Solar Energy – The Largest Renewable Source

As discussed in the previous chapter, improving efficiency is a good step in the right direction but does not by itself achieve climate protection. The next step is to develop renewable energy resources, and in this chapter and the next, we focus on solar and wind as the two resources that have massive potential and wide distribution globally.

The first part of this chapter focuses on making electricity from solar energy using the photovoltaic effect, also called "solar PV." In certain materials, when a solar photon, or individual particle of sunlight, strikes the molecular structure in a certain way, it can break loose an electron. By designing the structure of a photovoltaic cell so that large numbers of electrons are broken free and then channeled away from the cell and into surrounding wires, electrical charge can be accumulated for all of the usual electrical applications (lighting, electronics, and so on). Later parts of the chapter consider other solar applications where the heat of the sun itself is put to work without generating electricity, such as heating water and air, or cooking and baking with the sun. The discussion of solar includes overall global potential, impact of variability, and economics of system investment.

Francis M. Vanek

The scope of the solar resource

As was shown for the example of the U.S. in Fig.1 in Chapter 2, the investment in solar infrastructure to date is modest, compared to total energy demand. At the same time, the total amount of solar energy available is vast. As a visual illustration, consider the following example from the town of Springerville in eastern Arizona. The situation occurred in the mid-2000s, when utility-scale solar farms were just starting out, and the electricity market was dominated by coal-fired power plants.

Springerville, population 2,000, lies about 200 miles east of Phoenix and 200 miles west of Albuquerque, New Mexico. It is home to the Springerville solar power station, which is situated several miles north of the center of the town. At the time it was deployed, its 25,000 solar photovoltaic (PV) panels covered about 44 acres and had a capacity of 4 megawatts. At that scale, the facility can make 6 million kilowatt-hours of electricity a year, enough for 1,000 typical homes. If you crunch the numbers, you find that the density of the PV panels at Springerville is about 2.1 Watts per square foot, so about 91,000 Watts of panels fit on an acre (1 acre = 43,560 square feet). Also, the capacity factor[18] (CF) is roughly 17%, which is relatively high compared to other parts of the U.S., thanks to the strong sun in Arizona.

Just to the east of the Springerville solar station is the towering smokestack of the Springerville thermal power plant, which generates electricity from coal. On a similar amount of land area, the thermal plant can call on up to 1,560 megawatts of maximum power output to make 9 *billion* kilowatt-hours of electricity in a year (Capacity Factor = ~66%)—1500 times as much as the solar power plant. Never mind 1,000 homes—the thermal plant can power a whole city.

---

[18] Capacity factor = (6,000 MWh) / (4 MW x 8,760h/year) = ~0.17. Source for Springerville Solar Plant data: Moore and Post (2007).

Springerville thermal may dwarf Springerville solar, but the thermal plant is in turn dwarfed by the astonishing solar energy potential of Arizona's vast, unpopulated reaches. The coal-fired power station's maximum output is nothing compared to Arizona's potential. An area of 67,000 acres covered with solar panels – one thousandths of the area of the entire state – could make as much power as the power station.[19] Taken to another level, 40% of the state covered with solar panels *could meet all the electricity demands for the whole country*, around 4 trillion kWh per year (Table 1).

Type of plant	Area (Acres)	Capacity (MW)	Output (GWh/yr)
Solar PV plant	44	4	6
Plant equivalent	67,000	6,090	9,000
Whole USA supply	29,100,000	2,640,000	3,970,000

Table 1 Examples of solar PV installations in Arizona. Underlying assumptions: Area requirement of 2.09 Watts of nameplate capacity per ft^2, capacity factor 17.1% (1,500 kWh/kW/year).

There are of course some caveats that must be added to the analysis. A solar PV system to generate 4 trillion kWh of electricity per year would require a significant additional investment in storage because of the intermittent nature of solar energy. Even in Arizona, with its low rainfall and many days of sunshine per year, the rate of electricity production would at times get ahead of demand and at times fall behind, so that massive amounts of storage capacity would be required to balance delivery of electricity with load. Furthermore, a major investment in new transmission capacity would be required to move solar electricity around the country. In fact, any realistic plan for solarizing the U.S.

---

[19] Total area of state is ~72.7 million acres, the 6th largest state in the U.S. by land area.

economy would see solar installations in unpopulated areas both in sunny western states and in other cloudier parts of the country, as well as distributed installations at the sites of residences and businesses. Although densely populated urban areas in Arizona are few, much of the land is currently used for agriculture, and at some point covering the land with solar panels would come into competition with growing crops.

The other catch is cost. According to the U.S. Solar Energy Industries Association, or SEIA, utility-scale solar PV achieved an installed cost value of $1 per Watt in 2017, including all materials and labor.[20] At that price, the plan to cover Arizona with solar panels to supply electricity for the country would cost 2.6 trillion dollars – more than the entire annual U.S. budget for all energy costs, and this does not include investments in storage and distribution grid upgrades.

Increasingly, the U.S. and other countries around the world are taking on this challenge to invest in solar PV. The size of solar farms has grown from the 4 MW in this example to hundreds of megawatts per farm in locations being developed today. Financial challenges for generating electricity from coal have helped to create an opportunity for solar PV, and more and more large coal-fired plants like the Springerville Station are having a difficult time generating power at a competitive price. Figure 1 shows how cumulative world capacity has grown from under 10 GW in 2005 to nearly 800 GW in 2020. Figure 2 shows the breakdown by country of where solar PV was deployed in 2018. The list of major users is not limited to industrialized countries like Japan, Germany, and the United States: emerging economies like India and China are in the mix as well, and China in fact has the largest market share at 34%.

---

[20] Solar Energy Industries Association, 2017.

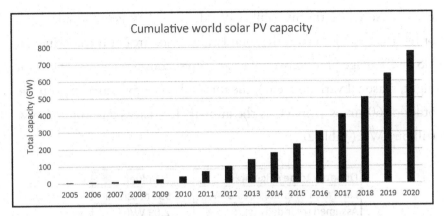

Figure 1 Growth in world cumulative solar PV capacity in GW, 2005-2020.
Source: International Energy Agency.

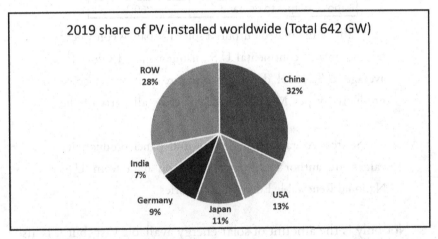

Figure 2 Share of capacity of solar PV installed worldwide, 2019.
Source: SolarPower Europe.

As suggested by the size of the resource available in Arizona, solar energy is a good place to start a discussion of the role of renewable energy in the future because of the sheer size of the solar resource available in nature. Solar energy is the largest renewable resource available to us in nature, exceeding the availability of tidal, biomass, geothermal, wind, or hydropower. Based on the total land surface area of the continental US and average productivity of solar arrays (considering lack of gain at night, seasonal variation, etc.), the total solar energy available is on the order of 60 times as much as the annual electricity consumption of 4 trillion kWh (Table 2).

Quantity to be calculated:	Value:
Land area of contiguous USA	2.959 mil.sq.mi
Assumed solar density	2.09 W/ft2
	58.27 MW/mi2
Productivity of solar panels	1400 MWh/MW/y
Output per sq mi per year	81,577 MWh
Total output per year	241 tril.kWh
Approximate annual demand	4 tril. kWh
Ratio of output to demand	~60:1

Table 2 Estimated output of solar PV panels equivalent to land area of continental U.S., using assumed values for average U.S. panel density per square foot and average productivity per MW of capacity across all parts of the country.

Source: Average solar density and panel productivity values are author's estimates based on data from U.S. National Renewable Energy Laboratories.

Not only is the amount of solar energy available vast, but it is also widely distributed, another advantage. Parts of the U.S., such as the southwest (as shown in the Springerville example), are particularly suited to solar energy, and a solar energy device will be especially productive in these areas. You can, however, install a solar panel in almost any part of the country and produce meaningful amounts of solar energy. As an investment, the solar device may not be as attractive in the northeast or northwest as it is in Arizona. But as a means of providing a measurable fraction of the personal energy needs, it can do the job almost anywhere there is a good exposure to the south that is not blocked by obstacles or shading. *A solar array installed under ideal conditions in western New York State produces about 65-70% of what the same array also installed ideally would produce in Arizona.*[21] It is well known that Arizona has many sunny days per year, and the U.S. northeast is subject to more cloudy weather and rain. However, as an investment, solar PV in the southwest may be more productive, but at the same time, it is not the case that it is ten or twenty times better, as one might assume since the region is so much sunnier.

In terms of latitudes on the planet, any location within the tropics will have especially strong sun, which is also relatively consistent from month to month since short winter days are not a factor. The temperate zones between 23- and 45-degrees latitude in both hemispheres are also fairly productive. Above 45 degrees latitude in either direction, the total amount of available solar energy decreases from the large part of the year when the days are short, and the sun is low in the sky. Still, much of the earth's population lives between 45 degrees latitude north and south, and in the case of the U.S., most of it does. (For reference, the 45th parallel runs across the country approximately through Portland Oregon, Minneapolis, and Portland Maine.)

Although solar energy is a distributed energy source that is available almost everywhere, there are certain regions that are suited to becoming solar energy production and export centers. Around the world, examples of such regions include western China, the Sahara Desert, and the Australian outback; in the U.S., swaths of land that provide this type

---

[21] Example: Output for Arizona taken from Springerville data from previous source: 1700 kWh per year per kW of capacity. A 51.6-kW array facing due south and tilted at 42 degrees in Ithaca, NY, produced 1174 kWh/kW in 2012-2013, or 69% of the Springerville figure.

of resource stretch from western Texas to the deserts of California and up into the great basin in eastern Oregon and Washington. These areas have abundant sunshine and are largely unpopulated outside of the major cities. They can also serve major energy markets on their periphery, such as the state of California with a population of 35 million, or the San Antonio-Houston-Dallas market in Texas. In fact, western Texas is not quite as sunny as Arizona or New Mexico, but it can make up for this shortfall by being closer to the Texas population centers because transmission is more efficient and cheaper. Any such scheme entails major technological challenges, including how to maintain solar energy generating capacity in a harsh environment, how to transmit energy efficiently over long distances, and how to develop solar while protecting sufficient habitat for the various native flora and fauna to thrive. However, these are precisely the kind of infrastructure challenges that we face across the board for generating sustainable energy from renewable sources in the future.

Comparing solar output in different parts of the U.S.

So far, we have considered a solar farm in Arizona with a reported productivity of 1500 kWh per kW of capacity per year, and an estimate of total U.S. potential based on an assumed national average of 1400 kWh/kW/year. Thanks to the PV-Watts solar output estimator from the U.S. Department of Energy's National Renewable Energy Laboratories, it is possible to predict array output in many different parts of the country using PV equipment characteristics combined with long-term meteorological data.

Table 3 compares predicted annual output for a representative residential array in four parts of the country using output measures in San Diego (CA) in the southwest, Atlanta (GA) in the southeast,

Binghamton (NY) in the northeast, and Burns (OR) in the northwest. The conditions input into the simulator are: the array is 5 kW in size, it faces due south, and it is tilted toward the south at the angle equivalent to the degrees of latitude of the location. The first column in the table gives the raw output from the array before considering any losses. The predicted 15% of losses include dust or snow covering the panels that might reduce the penetration of sunlight. It also includes line losses in the wiring from the panels to the house since wiring does not transfer 100% of the entering energy from one end to the other, as some small amount leaks out as heat into the insulation. Lastly, conversion losses occur in the inverter, the device that converts direct current (DC) coming from the panels into alternating current (AC). Figures in Table 3 suggest that, on an annual basis, solar arrays in locations around the country can produce viable amounts of power. The increase going from Binghamton to San Diego is significant, but since the array in San Diego is 35% more productive (and not two or three times), it is clear that the array in Binghamton can also produce viable amounts of solar-generated electricity. Furthermore, although coastal regions of the Pacific northwest are known for cloudy weather (and therefore reduced productivity of solar arrays), the productivity of the Burns array shows that in eastern Oregon and Washington States in the interior basin, a large area of sunny territory (with low population density) is available to provide electricity to population centers in Seattle or Portland.

Location	Raw output	w/ 15% loss
Binghamton, NY	1,445	1,228
Burns, OR	1,727	1,468
Atlanta, GA	1,751	1,488
San Diego, CA	1,948	1,656

Table 3 Predicted annual output for a 5-kW residential array from PV Watts estimator for representative cities in

four regions of U.S., output before and after 15% losses, in kWh/year.

Source: National Renewable Energy Laboratories, PV-Watts simulator. Note: NREL periodically updates their output database, so current predictions from PV-Watts may be slightly different from values in this table.

Along with annual productivity, the seasonal pattern (which provides the total kWh per year in Table 3) is of interest as well because it is important to know how well demand can be met across the year. Figure 3 shows how, as each city passes from winter to spring, output rises with the longer days and more hours of sunshine per day. Atlanta and San Diego, at 34- and 33-degrees north latitude, respectively, do not experience as much of a drop-off in output in November and December as Binghamton and Burns, which lie further north. Furthermore, Atlanta and San Diego have a longer summer air-conditioning season than the other two cities, so the shape of the monthly solar curve is reasonably well-matched to the seasonal rise and fall of electricity consumption. On the other hand, Burns has a drier summer climate than Atlanta; therefore, the Burns array is more productive between May and September than the array in Atlanta. The comparison of the four cities illustrates some key factors in solar PV productivity: latitude of location, average aridity or humidity, and amount of rainfall.

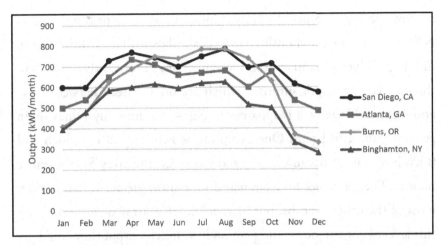

Figure 3 Variation in PV-Watts predicted monthly output for four representative U.S. cities in kWh per month for a representative 5-kW residential array.

Source: National Renewable Energy Laboratories, PV-Watts simulator.

Consistency of solar PV arrays over multiple years

The previous discussion comparing different U.S. locations and data in Fig. 3 used examples that could be generated from PV Watts since this tool is a convenient and efficient way to explore the impact of geography on solar energy. In this section we switch from simulated PV-Watts data to actual historical data from an existing solar array, so we can explore not just the average or predicted behavior but the year-on-year variation and consistency of solar over time.

The PV array in question was installed in 2002 in Ithaca, NY, and was permitted to begin operation by the local utility in 2003. It consists of 16 140-Watt panels, for a total capacity of 2,240 Watts. From 2006 onward, annual output data have been kept for this array, and from 2012 onward monthly data have been kept as well. The monthly production is shown in Fig. 4. Since the array is located not far from Binghamton, NY, the shape of the monthly curve is similar to that of Binghamton in Fig. 3: values in January and December are significantly lower than those of late spring or summer, which are on a plateau between May and August. Visually, it is apparent in Fig. 4 that monthly values are in general quite consistent. One exception is February 2015, which had 0 kWh of output because heavy snow covered the array for the entire month. The six values for March and June show greater variation than most of the other months, but in general, a PV array owner expecting this level of consistency could plan on how much output they could get each month of the year.

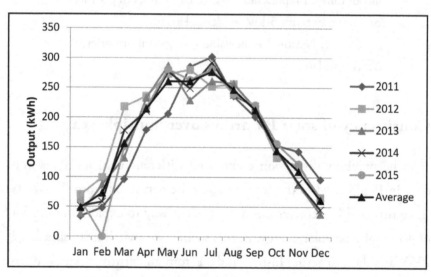

Figure 4 Monthly output from a 2.24-kW solar array
in Ithaca, NY, in kWh, 2012-2017.
Source: Data gathered by the author.

Although the risk from disrupted output due to snow cover in winter might seem worrisome, the economic impact of the February 2015 "no-hitter" was only modest. The array averages 74 kWh/month for all 6 February values compared to 270 kWh/month for May, which is the month with the highest average. Indeed, most of the economic value of the array comes in the spring, summer, and fall, and since this particular array is installed on a rooftop and difficult to access, it was not worth the trouble to clear off the snow.

This assessment might change in the future, however. Someday solar PV may become the largest single source of electricity nationally, perhaps providing a greater fraction than any other source. At that point, the reliability of solar PV in the winter months, even with relatively low capacity factor, might become critical to the economy and national security. Americans might then need to rethink its commitment to keeping snow off solar panels in the winter.

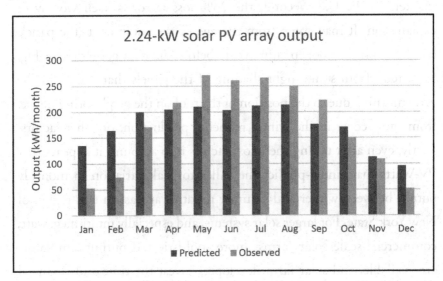

Figure 5 Comparison of 6-year average output from 2.24-kW array (2012-2017) to predicted value from PV-Watts with due south, 25-degree tilt, 23% loss assumption.

Next, we compare the average performance of the array from 2012 to 2017 with the predicted values generated by PV-Watts. For the prediction, we input the physical characteristics of the array, such as the due south orientation and 25-degree tilt of the roof. Based on observation of the solar array, we also assume that 23% of the energy generated by the panels is lost on the way through the system as it is converted to AC and delivered to the energy supply of the house.

Several observations are in order. First, for the purposes of a homeowner wanting a general idea of how much electricity an array will produce, the PV-Watts model provides a reasonable first estimate. The 23% loss factor is on the high side, and if one were to assume 15% loss (the default value in the simulator), then the PV-Watts model would overpredict the economic value of the array, and the owner might be disappointed. However, the error would not be catastrophic, as the value of the overprediction would be less than $50/year for most electricity markets in the U.S. Second, the 23% loss factor is itself worthy of explanation. It may come from the age of the equipment (the panels had been on the roof for nine years before the data gathering in Fig. 5 started), from some slight shading of the panels that occurs in the early morning due to the position of the roof on the neighboring house, from snow cover in the winter reducing production, or other factors. Lastly, even after taking these loss factors into account, it appears that PV-Watts may under-predict the valley-to-peak variation in monthly output between winter and summer months, at least in this region of New York State. For larger solar systems, and especially multi-megawatt, commercial-scale solar farms, more sophisticated output simulators are available, and solar farm developers invest the time and financial resources to run more accurate models before deciding whether to invest or not.

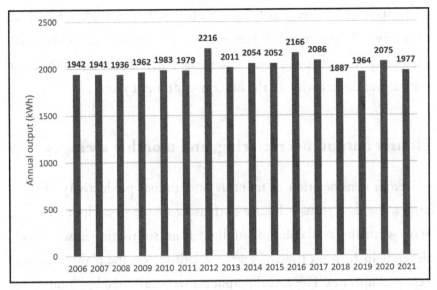

Figure 6 Average annual output from 2.24-kW array
in Ithaca, NY, 2006-2021. Statistics: Average = 2,014 kWh,
Standard Deviation = 88 kWh, Coefficient of variation =
88 / 2014 = 4.4%.

Compared to monthly production data, which was gathered
beginning only in mid-2011, annual production data for the array
being studied are available for a longer period (Fig. 6). For the 16 years
shown in the figure, the coefficient of variation is only 4.4%, meaning
that annual output is very consistent from year to year. Although it is
impossible to predict more than a few days ahead what the daily output
from the array will be in the future, the number of sunny and cloudy
days tends to balance out over the long term, so that annual output is
reliable. Note that in mid-2011 the array inverter malfunctioned and
was replaced. It appears that the replacement inverter is more efficient
than the original because the average value from 2012-21 is higher
than the value from 2006-11 (2050 kWh versus 1957 kWh). Also,
the top two values, in 2012 and 2016, coincide with droughts in the
region, so in the summer months with almost no rainfall, the array was

111

particularly productive. Lastly, we can observe that the 0-kWh month of February 2015 (from Fig. 4) does not have a visible effect on the annual performance for that year compared to the others: Fig. 6 shows the 2015 output was on par with all the other non-drought years.

Hourly output, net metering, and monthly averages

From consideration of monthly and annual productivity of solar arrays, we now turn to hourly output across the day. Hourly output starts with the availability of sunlight from sunrise to sunset, which depends in turn on time of year and latitude on the planet (tropical versus temperate). The actual output is further affected by cloud cover, humidity, and air temperature, all of which affect the amount of sunlight reaching the solar PV panel and the productivity of conversion of sunlight to electricity.

The angle of the sun is important for at least two reasons: first, the sun passing through the atmosphere at a high angle is stronger, and second, at a high angle close to the middle of the day, the sun is likely to strike the panel closer to straight on, increasing output. Starting with the effect of latitude, Fig. 7 compares the angle of the sun above the horizon (also known as "solar altitude") by hour of day for the solstices and equinoxes for a location at 5 degrees latitude versus one at 52 degrees latitude. (Cities in these locations in the northern hemisphere are Abidjan, Ivory Coast; and Rotterdam, The Netherlands, respectively. The solstices are the days of the year when the length of daylight is either the shortest or the longest, and the equinoxes are the two days when day and night are equally long.) The tropical figure at 5 degrees north shows relatively little variation in the height of the sun in the sky by hour of day between the shortest and longest day of the year. On the other hand, the temperate curve at 52 degrees north shows large variation, with the sun above the horizon for 16 hours on the summer solstice but only 8 hours on the winter solstice. This comparison explains why, all other things equal, tropical locations receive more energy directly from arriving sunlight and why they have higher average temperatures across the year. Although a tropical location may not experience long summer days, the length of day is consistent all year round; furthermore, the sun is rising high in the sky across the middle hours of the day all year long (typically 10 a.m. to 2 p.m., as seen in the figure). Since they do not need to contend with the limited solar energy available in winter at higher latitudes, due to short days, tropical locations are better suited for the development of solar energy as a primary energy source in the future.

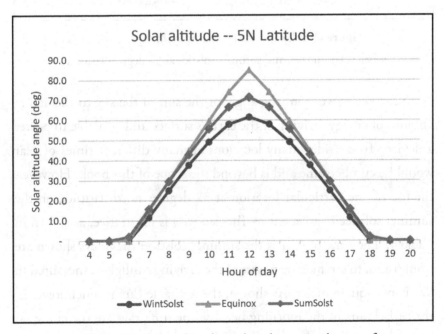

Figure 7a Solar altitude and pathway, in degrees, for winter solstice, equinoxes, and summer solstice at 5 degrees latitude.

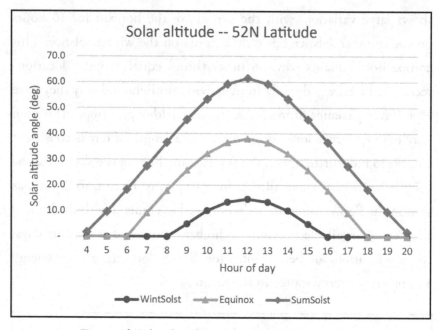

Figure 7b Solar altitude and pathway, in degrees, for winter solstice, equinoxes, and summer solstice at 52 degrees latitude.

Next, we move from the angle of the sun in the sky to the actual amount of energy arriving at the earth's surface and available to power a device. To consider many locations at many different times of year would be cumbersome and is beyond the scope of this book. However, the use of one particular location at 32 degrees north latitude on the summer solstice (equivalent to Tucson, AZ) is illustrative, as shown in Table 4. The time of year is the summer solstice; the hours shown are from 6 a.m. to 6 p.m. The power of the arriving sunlight is measured in Watts per square meter. As shown, the available flux is much lower in the early hours of the morning because the sun's rays are travelling on a long, oblique path through the atmosphere and therefore are diffused more. As in Fig. 7, the solar altitude is the number of degrees that the sun is above the horizon, and the solar azimuth is the angle of the sun away from due south. Negative azimuth values mean that the sun is east of due south, and positive values west. At solar noon, the azimuth is exactly 0 degrees. Since the panel is at a fixed angle facing due south and the sun is moving across the sky as the day progresses, the angle at which the sun strikes the panel (known as the "incident angle") changes from almost sideways in the early morning and late afternoon, to close to straight on at solar noon. Accordingly, the fraction of energy actually delivered to the panel varies between 0.28 and 0.96 (e.g., at 7 AM, dividing 166 Watts actual by 662 Watts available gives a fraction of 0.28, etc.). This type of reduction in available solar energy due to the time of day and the angle of the sun is called *cosine loss*. The problem of cosine loss can be addressed with various types of *tracking*, as discussed in the next section.

Hour	Available (W/m2)	Solar Alt. (degrees)	Solar Azim. (degrees)	Inc. Angle (degrees)	Actual (W/m2)
6*	412	12.2	-110.2	87.2	0
7	662	24.3	-103.4	73.5	188
8	773	36.9	-96.8	59.7	389
9	831	49.6	-89.4	46.2	575
10	863	62.2	-79.7	33.2	722
11	879	74.2	-60.9	21.9	816
12	884	81.5	0	16.5	848
13	879	74.2	60.9	21.9	816
14	863	62.2	79.7	33.2	722
15	831	49.6	89.4	46.2	575
16	773	36.9	96.8	59.7	389
17	662	24.3	103.4	73.5	188
18*	412	12.2	110.2	87.2	0

Table 4 Available solar energy intensity and actual energy received by a fixed-angle solar PV array from 6 a.m. to 6 p.m. at 32 degrees north latitude on the summer solstice. Note that values assume solar array is facing due south and raised to a 32-degree angle.

*Note: at 6 a.m. and 6 p.m., the light strikes the back of the panel so output is reduced to zero. Source for available flux data in 2nd column: American Society of Heating, Refrigeration, and Air-conditioning Engineers (ASHRAE), 2001.

Observed hourly output from the 2.24-kW test-case array on a home in Ithaca, NY, are used to illustrate the impact of changing flux and incident angle on actual output for a sampled day on June 15, 2011 (Fig. 8). This day was chosen in advance for test measurement because the weather was forecast to be sunny all day. With the exception of a period around 3 p.m., where it appears there may have been some slight cloud cover, the values for "PV output" show an almost perfect bell-curve shape, as would be predicted from the "actual flux" column in Table 4. As a result, the array produced a total of 12.0 kWh between 8 a.m. and 9 p.m. The household's electricity consumption (labelled "Res. Load" in the figure) from 8 a.m. to 11 p.m. totals 7.6 kWh.

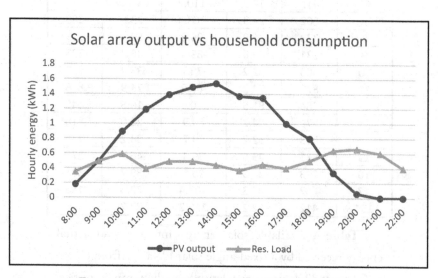

Figure 8 Comparison of daily 2.24-kW PV system output and residential load on June 15, 2011, for household with grid-connected array in Ithaca, NY.

The one-day output from the array in Fig. 8 can be compared to the long-term average for the same solar array for a day in June shown in Fig. 4. The output for the month of June varied from 229 kWh in 2013 to 298 kWh in 2016, for an average value of 261 kWh. This value in turn translates to 8.7 kWh/day for a 30-day month, or 3.5 kWh less than the example day in June. Thus, several factors affect how the long-term average day in June is less productive than the day shown in Fig. 8: there must be many days with partial or complete cloud cover to reduce daily productivity, and also the fact that June 15 is very close to the solstice on June 20 or 21 means that a slightly higher than average amount of solar energy arrives on June 15 than the average day in June.

The PV system in Fig. 8 is connected to the utility grid using a "net metering" system. The connection between the residence and the grid passes through a two-way electric current meter that measures current flowing into the residence like a normal meter, but also current flowing out at the times that the PV array is producing more than the residence is consuming. This arrangement allows the owner to earn financial credit for the excess current, which counts against purchases from the grid.

The benefit of net metering is illustrated by comparing production in Fig. 8 to the residential load over the 14 hours in the figure. The total load is 7.6 kWh, so with net metering in place, the system accumulates a surplus of 6.8 kWh. Some of this amount is used before 10 a.m. and after 6 p.m., when the array is falling short against the load. After taking these amounts into account, the remaining credit is 4.7 kWh, to be used against the electricity bill on a different day when production falls short of load. The benefit of net metering is significant: if no credit were given for hours when the array produces more than the load, so that the array provides benefit only to the extent that it eliminates purchases from the grid, the value would be only 5.2 kWh of electricity. The calculations are illustrated in Table 5, which shows PV output and load for each of the hours of the day. Whenever load exceeds PV output, an amount appears in the "purchase" column. Conversely, if PV output exceeds load, an amount appears in the "credit" column. However, if there were no net metering, the system would get no monetary credit for production beyond the load amount. The value of the solar PV output in a certain time period would be limited to the amount of its output used by the household in that same time period. This value, the minimum of the solar PV and load amounts, appears in the right-most column.

Hour	Solar PV	Load	Purchase	Credit	W/o net mtr
8	0.2	0.35	0.15	0	0.2
9	0.5	0.5	0	0	0.5
10	0.9	0.6	0	0.3	0.6
11	1.2	0.4	0	0.8	0.4
12	1.4	0.5	0	0.9	0.5
13	1.5	0.5	0	1	0.5
14	1.5	0.4	0	1.1	0.4
15	1.3	0.4	0	0.9	0.4
16	1.3	0.4	0	0.9	0.4
17	1	0.4	0	0.6	0.4
18	0.8	0.5	0	0.3	0.5
19	0.3	0.65	0.35	0	0.3
20	0.1	0.65	0.55	0	0.1
21	0	0.65	0.65	0	0
22	0	0.65	0.65	0	0
Daily	12.0	7.6	2.4	6.8	5.2

Table 5 Hour-by-hour comparison of benefit of solar production with and without net metering for example, 2.24-kW array on a home in Ithaca, NY.

Notes: *in case where net metering exists, credit is equal to PV production + purchase – load. For example, in this case, for daily totals: 12.0 kWh + 2.4 kWh – 7.6 kWh = 6.8 kWh. **If there is no net metering (right column "w/o net mtr"), the value of the PV production is the lesser of either the array output or the household load. See text.

Production, consumption, and net metering across 12 months

The process of reviewing solar PV output and electricity load for a single day can be applied to monthly values from an entire year to show the electricity production value of the system. Output for the example array for the year 2017 is used as an illustration (Fig. 9). As shown, the "Solar PV" curve gives the same value of monthly production as was shown in Fig. 4. The curve labeled "Utility Out" shows monthly kWh that were extra beyond the load needed for the house and exported onto the grid. Conversely, "Utility In" shows the kWh where the solar PV current was not sufficient to meet the load, and therefore current flowed in from the grid (for example, at night). Finally, "Net Cons," or net consumption, equals the net kWh of electricity consumed, which is the kWh going out to the grid subtracted from the sum of kWh coming from the solar PV and the grid. For example, in January, the array produced 58 kWh, the grid provided 248 kWh, and 29 kWh flowed out to the grid, so the net consumption was 58 + 248 − 29 = 277 kWh. (As an aside, some readers may find it surprising that at times there was net outflow to the grid in the middle of winter. However, if there are a few hours in the middle of a sunny January day when the lights and refrigerator are not working hard and the array is generating, it is possible for the net flow to be outward from the house.)

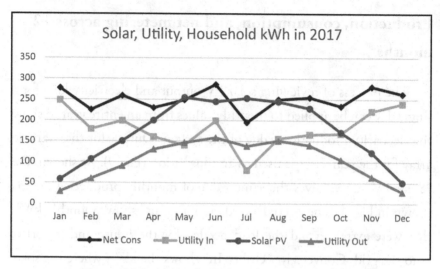

Figure 9 Monthly solar PV production, exports to grid, imports from grid, and net consumption for 2.24-kW array in 2017 on a home in Ithaca, NY, in kWh.

The curves in Fig. 9 show the importance of having access to a net metering agreement with the utility company. The house consumes 3,004 kWh in one year. Of these, 2,086 kWh, or 69%, are produced by the solar array. However, 1,239 kWh are exported onto the grid at times when the array is producing more than the house is consuming. Without net metering, the electric utility account owner would not be able to accumulate credits for this portion of the solar PV production, credits that offset purchases from the grid currently. Only 847 kWh (2086 kWh – 1239 kWh) are produced by the array and consumed by the house, without going out on the grid. Also, although the majority of annual electricity consumption in this household comes from solar, panels could be added to the array to cover closer to 100% of the demand, assuming there is room on the roof.

Increasing productivity with PV tracking

The preceding examples used the case of fixed-angle PV arrays, where the panels are bolted permanently in place, typically facing in a southerly direction but unable to adjust orientation to time of day or time of year. This solution is the least costly but is also subject to the largest cosine losses.

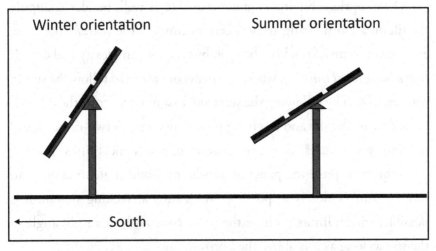

Figure 10 Example of seasonal adjustment of solar array angle for winter and summer conditions.
Note: Diagram assumes location is in the northern hemisphere, in the temperate latitudes (i.e., not in the tropics). For southern hemisphere temperate latitudes, array would be tilted to the north.

Solar arrays that are ground mounted on a single mounting shaft with a pivoting joint (as seen in Fig. 10) allow the possibility of changing the tilt angle with the season. The orientation of the panel is still due south and does not change with time of day. However, the angle can be adjusted periodically so that the tilt is shallow in summer and steep in winter. The array in Fig. 10 can be large enough to meet the entire needs of a household. Compared to a rigid array, the additional cost of adding the capability of changing the tilt angle is modest. The required operational input may be as simple as changing the angle a few times per year. Although the overall weight of so many panels is large, the array is supported from the middle, so its weight is approximately in balance when it is stationary making it possible for the owner to unlock the array and change its angle without great physical strain.

Other options for tracking are available as well, besides changing the tilt on a south-facing array at certain times of the year. At the other extreme in terms of tracking benefit, but also of complexity and cost, is *two-dimensional tracking*, where the panel or array can follow the sun in real time, both by following the sun from east to west across the day as it moves across the sky and by changing the tilt angle. A two-dimensional tracking system uses some combination of mechanical links, pistons, and motors to push the panel or panels from one angle to another to face the sun as closely as possible. With such a tracking system, it is possible, within limits, to have the panel constantly at a right angle to the sun as long as it is above the horizon.

As an illustration, a simulation was run using the PV-Watts online estimator to compare output for three simulated scenarios: (1) a fixed array (such as an array bolted to a south-facing roof), (2) an array facing due south but capable of periodic seasonal adjustment (as in Fig. 10), and (3) an array with two-dimensional tracking. Table 6 shows the results. The site chosen for the PV-Watts test is in Ithaca, NY, (42° N latitude), consistent with the empirical data in Fig.7. For the fixed-angle simulation (Option 1), the array is tilted at 42 degrees. For the seasonally tilted array (Option 2), positions at 20, 42, and 64 degrees were chosen. Then, for each of the 12 months, the angle with the highest productivity was chosen, and the annual output tallied. Table 6 shows the optimal angle for each month in Scenario 2, with the array starting in January at 64 degrees, changing in March to 42, April to 20, September to 42, and November back to 64. Finally, the results are shown for the two-dimensional tracking simulation (Option 3) as estimated by PV-Watts. The difference in results is modest for seasonal tracking and significant for two-dimensional tracking: seasonal tracking increases output by 5% from 1,202 to 1,256 kWh/year, but two-dimensional tracking increases it by 34% to 1,606 kWh.

Month	Fixed 42 (kWh)	Seasonal tilt (kWh)	Tracking Angle, deg.	Tracking (kWh)
January	73	77	64	88
February	89	90	64	107
March	112	112	42	136
April	118	121	20	163
May	123	134	20	179
June	116	128	20	168
July	123	135	20	188
August	121	125	20	167
September	109	109	42	143
October	88	88	42	110
November	70	73	64	85
December	60	64	64	72
TOTAL	1202	1256	n/a	1606

Table 6 Comparison of tracking options for 1-kW array in Ithaca, NY.

The use of tracking panels is beginning to penetrate the market for multi-MW industrial solar power plants. Early solar plants have all been fixed-angle systems, such as the 10-MW plant in Muehlhausen, Germany, which opened in 2006, or the 80-MW plant in Sarnia, Canada, which opened in 2010. More recently, the 266-MW Mount Signal Phase 1 plant in southern California, which went online in 2014, was the first large U.S. solar plant to use tracking. One challenge is that tracking plants must allow more space between racks of panels;

otherwise, the panels shade each other when the sun is at low angles in the sky. Shading should be minimized, but some shading may be acceptable to allow a greater concentration of nameplate capacity per acre or hectare.

Economics of electricity from solar PV

What is the cost of energy produced from solar PV – the cost to produce one kWh of electricity? For one thing, it depends on the scale of production. A large industrial producer pays less per kW of panels than a homeowner with a home-size array, and therefore achieves lower production cost. Furthermore, it depends on how much sun your location receives, because a PV system in a sunnier location will produce more electricity per year and therefore pay back its initial cost faster.

As an example from the southwest, Table 3 above gave a value of 1,656 kWh/year after losses for San Diego. Therefore, suppose a rounded value of 1,650 kWh/year per kW of capacity is used to represent productivity in that part of the country. A 5-kW residential system might produce 8,000 kWh of electricity in a year. The combination of Arizona, California, Colorado, Nevada, New Mexico, and Utah had a total population of roughly 61 million in 2019, or about one-fifth of the U.S. total, with similar amounts of sunshine, so a substantial fraction of the U.S. population has access to this level of productivity from solar PV.

When the analysis is expanded to consider the U.S. as a whole and not just its sunniest part, the average output is somewhat lower than the value for the southwest, but the reduction is not as significant as might be predicted. Based on the values in Table 3, from the output of 1,468 kWh/kW in Oregon and 1,488 kWh/kW in Georgia, we might infer a value of 1,450 kWh/kW in the southeast or northwest. Similarly, with a value of 1,228 kWh/kW in New York State, we might infer a value of 1,250 kWh/kW in the northeast. Output from a 5-kW residential array would then range between 6,000 and 7,000 kWh per year.

Average cost per Watt for all types of solar PV has been declining over many years. Figure 11 shows how, especially since 2009 as the installation rate greatly accelerated, the average cost declined from over $7.00 to under $2.00 per Watt. Note that these figures are the cost per installed watt, including the panels, all other hardware and materials, all labor, and all supply chain and overhead costs. Furthermore, the figures are an average among residential systems (typically the smallest and therefore the most expensive per Watt), commercial systems (for businesses and other users with larger demand than a single residence), and utility-scale systems (the largest, multi-MW systems). Average prices within these categories in 2017 ranged from $2.75/W for residential to $1.50/W for commercial to $1/W for utility-scale PV with a fixed angle (i.e., the panels are installed on a rigid structure and do not track the sun at all).

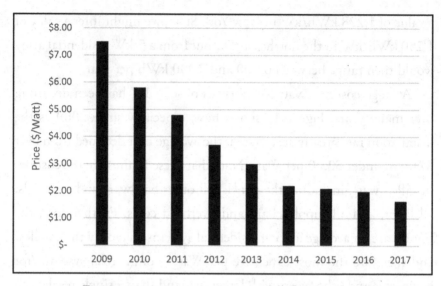

Figure 11 Average cost per installed Watt for solar PV in U.S. across residential, commercial, and utility-scale systems, 2009-2017.

Source: Solar Energy Industries Association.

Table 7 provides the breakdown of the $2.75 cost per Watt for residential PV in 2017. For residential systems, the proportion of cost dedicated to the supply chain, including all the steps from manufacturers to wholesalers to retailers, as well as overhead and profit margins, is a relatively large fraction and constitutes the single largest part of the cost at $1.40/Watt. Of all the physical elements of the array, the panels are the most expensive at $0.35/W. If all of the physical elements of the array are combined, including panels, inverter, electrical balance of systems[22], and all non-electric structure elements, they together comprise $0.90/W of the total cost. The labor required to design and install the system are

---

[22] "Balance of system", sometimes abbreviated BOS, refers to the remaining components of the system that are not specifically broken out in the cost listing. In this case, BOS includes all wiring and electrical components other than the panels and the inverter.

then the remaining $0.45/W. As shown in Table 7, a 5-kW array with these cost per Watt values would cost $13,750 total.

Element	Cost/Watt	5-kW array cost
Panels	$ 0.35	$ 1,750
Inverter	$ 0.25	$ 1,250
Electric BOS*	$ 0.20	$ 1,000
Structure	$ 0.10	$ 500
Labor	$ 0.30	$ 1,500
Design	$ 0.15	$ 750
Supply Chain**	$ 1.40	$ 7,000
TOTAL	$ 2.75	$ 13,750

Table 7 Cost breakdown for residential PV system on a 1-Watt and 5-kW array basis.
Notes: *BOS = Balance of System; **Includes supply chain costs, overhead, profit margin. Source: Solar Energy Industries Association.

Suppose we use the average price before any rebates, tax credits, or other incentive programs of $13,750 for a 5-kW array. To spread this investment out over a long period, we might choose a 20-year economic planning horizon. This length is shorter than the expected lifetime of the array: panels are warranted for 25 years and could be expected to last even longer. However, this choice makes the analysis conservative in the sense that the system is likely to last at least as long as 20 years.

If we simply divide the initial cost into 20 annual portions, the array must repay $687.50 per year over the time horizon to return the initial investment. The purchaser of the array might be content to earn back their $13,750 over 20 years in the interest of protecting the environment. However, as an investment, the purchaser might instead apply *discounting* to the payback on the investment in the same way that a bank when it agrees to lend to a homebuyer recovers a mortgage with interest, not just the principle. Table 8 shows the effect of discounting in the form of different discount rates on the amount that must be repaid for each increment borrowed or invested. The middle column shows the annualized value—i.e., with simple payback or no discounting, the value is $500, or 1/20 of the amount invested. From there, the amount repaid each year increases as interest rates grow from 3% to 7%. Then, the right column then shows the ratio of the amount repaid to the case of simple discounting, so that, for example, the value at 3% is 1.34 times the simple payback value, and so on. Some readers may be more familiar with mortgages that are repaid monthly rather than in a single payment per year. Therefore, as an illustration, consider a $100,000 mortgage borrowed at 4% for 30 years with monthly payments. There will be 12 payments per year for 30 years, for a total of 360 payments. Based on the interest rate, the monthly payment is $477.42, and the face value of all the payments over the lifetime of the mortgage (i.e., $477.42 times 360) is $171,869.51. Therefore, the ratio for this mortgage equivalent to the values in Table 8 is about 1.72.

Rate	Annual pmt.	Total pmts.	Ratio
Simple PB	$ 500	$ 10,000	1
3%	$ 672	$ 13,400	1.34
5%	$ 802	$ 16,040	1.6
7%	$ 944	$ 18,900	1.89

Table 8 Single annual repayment required for investment of $10,000 at present, discounted over 20 years at different discount rates. The face value of repayments is the sum of all the annual payments, and the ratio is the sum of the payments divided by the initial $10,000.

The benefit of investing in a 5-kW residential array can then be assessed by choosing a discount rate, namely 5% in this case, as a typical rate used by the U.S. federal government, and then calculating the resulting cost of generating electricity in different parts of the country

(Table 9). For comparison, simple discounting is also shown. At the 5% rate, the system must recover about $1,100 each year, compared to ~$690/year using simple payback. The cost of producing electricity then depends on the productivity of the array and ranges from ~13 cents/kWh in the southwest to ~18 cents/kWh in the northeast. Production with residential solar PV also avoids distribution charges that must be paid when electricity is generated in a remote location and carried long distance over the transmission grid to the consumer. Distribution charges may be on the order of 5-6 cents/kWh on top of the cost of generation. Therefore, the figures in the southwest are especially competitive with what ratepayers might pay for conventional electricity including both generation and distribution charges. If the charge for residential customers in this region is 7-8 cents/kWh or more for generation plus 5-6 cents/kWh for distribution, rooftop solar is actually cheaper.

Location	kWh/year	@5%	@5%	Simple PB	Simple PB
		$/year	$/kWh	$/year	$/kWh
Northeast	6250	$1,103.34	$0.18	$687.50	$0.11
SE/NW	7250	$1,103.34	$0.15	$687.50	$0.10
Southwest	8250	$1,103.34	$0.13	$687.50	$0.08

Table 9 Productivity, repayment per year, and cost per kWh for a 5-kW array with 20-year investment horizon in different regions of the U.S.

If there is a higher net cost for solar PV, rebates and tax credits from state and federal government may be able to make up the difference. Also, a price on CO_2 emissions in the future (assuming there is not already one in place) might help the investment break even. PV emits no CO_2 in end use, but conventional sources of electricity may produce, as a rough number, 500 grams of CO_2 with each kWh. Suppose the rate for solar is $0.18/kWh (as in the northeast in Table 9), and conventional electricity costs $0.14/kWh including delivery. The resulting savings of 500 grams costs 4 cents per kWh, which works out to $80 per metric tonne of avoided CO_2. Lastly, some homeowners may be willing to pitch in any premium for solar as a charitable contribution on behalf of the environment, similar to donating to an environmental non-governmental organization that promotes climate-friendly policies or wildlife protection.

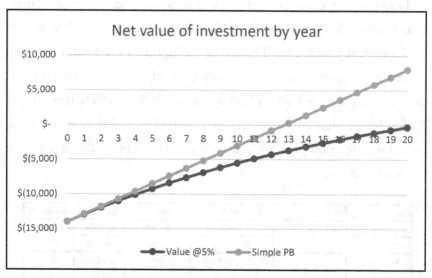

Figure 12 Net present value of 5-kW solar array investment using 5% discount rate or simple payback.
Note: array produces 7,250 kWh/year of electricity. (See text for details about inputs to calculations.)

Another way to look at the residential investment is to look at the *payback period* rather than the value per year of the electricity output shown in Table 9. As an example, suppose we use the output from a representative array in the southeast (e.g., Georgia, Alabama, South Carolina) or northwest (e.g., Oregon, Idaho), in a location where electricity costs $0.15/kWh delivered to the residential customer, including generation and delivery charge. We can then compare the payback timeline of the investment for the case of simple payback versus a 5% discount rate. As shown in Fig. 12, the upfront cost of the array is considered to be incurred in "Year Zero" of the project life, so at first, the net value is -$13,750.

Thereafter, each year, the output has a return value equivalent to the avoided cost of buying 7,250 kWh of electricity at the $0.15/kWh rate, or ~$1,088 per year. If the simple payback principle is applied, the value of the debt for the project is reduced linearly year after year, and the project breaks even in approximately 12.6 years. However, if the 5% discount rate is applied, the value of avoiding purchases of electricity from the grid diminishes with each passing year, bending the net present value curve so that breakeven occurs approximately in Year 20.

Reductions in cost per installed Watt have benefitted multi-megawatt solar power plants as well. Figure 11 shows the average cost for all types of solar arrays, from residential to utility-scale falling to $1.63/Watt in 2017. Part of this mix is the $1.00/Watt price for fixed-angle (i.e., without the additional cost to mechanically track the sun), large-scale solar. Using the 20-year and 5% assumptions from above, each $1,000 spent per kW of capacity must return $80.24 per year to pay for itself in 20 years. For a location with the median productivity value from Table 9 of 1,450 kWh/kW/year (representative of the southeastern or northwestern U.S.), the resulting cost of electricity is 5.5 cents per kWh. For the higher productivity of the southwest (1,650 kWh/kW/year), where many new, larger solar facilities are concentrated, the equivalent value is 4.9c/kWh. Of course, transmission costs would need to be added to this charge, on the order of 5-6 cents per kWh in most parts of the country for residential customers. Therefore, the delivered cost might be more or less equal to the customer building the solar array on their own roof, if conditions allow it. Either way, however, the upshot is that within some margin of error, *distributed or centralized electricity from solar PV has become competitive with conventional sources.*

Solar energy for thermal applications

Along with using the photoelectric effect to generate electric current from solar rays, the thermal energy from the sun has many applications as well, when sufficiently concentrated to reach useful high temperatures. As examples of direct applications, solar energy can heat domestic hot water (DHW) – also called service hot water or SHW in a commercial setting. Solar energy can also heat air to warm a space. Using solar energy for space heating is divided between "passive solar," where windows and insulation are situated to capture incoming sunlight without moving parts, and "active solar," where air or water is actively circulated in a structure using pumps or fans to move solar heat to locations where it is needed. Solar energy can be used to generate steam, either to drive a turbine and generator to make electricity or for mechanical applications such as water pumping. In addition, it can be used to cook food or dry it for storage.

The treatment of this domain focuses on heating water with solar energy because it is one of the most widely used solar thermal applications. A solar hot-water system can supply a substantial part of the DHW in a residence or SHW in a business. At the residential level, an owner may choose to install solar PV for their electricity supply or solar hot water for their DHW supply. They may opt for both. The two technologies compete with each other for the owners' investment dollars and limited roof or ground space. However, once the owner has maxed out the capacity to install one of these technologies, they may have a further opportunity to invest in the other, if they have the funds and available space. Suppose, for example, the owner generates electricity from the

PV system, about equal to their year-round electricity consumption (using an array with net metering available) with a capacity of 3 to 5 kW. Once they have this system in place, they can continue to reduce their environmental footprint by adding a solar hot water system capable of generating 100% of their DHW in peak summer season, rather than continuing to add more PV panels. Alternatively, they could start by installing solar hot water and add solar PV later.

These days, two solar hot-water technologies are competing for market share in the U.S.: the established "flat plate" panel and a more recent "evacuated tube" technology (Fig. 13). Both technologies work by concentrating incoming sunlight in a way that is favorable for heating water or another fluid (e.g., water-glycol mix) that can then be transferred out of the system and into the DHW supply. In a flat plate collector, the water passes through a tube in a sealed chamber that is transparent in front to admit sunlight and insulated in back to increase heating. Fluid passing through tubes in the collector is then heated and transfers that heat to water in a household's hot water tank. Evacuated tubes concentrate heat in a vacuum-sealed chamber that also has fluid transport tubes passing through to take away heat. The difference is a tradeoff between performance and cost: the vacuum tube reduces heat losses by surrounding the absorber tube with an evacuated chamber but also costs more than the flat plate, where the air pressure inside the chamber is the same as that of its surroundings.

Francis M. Vanek

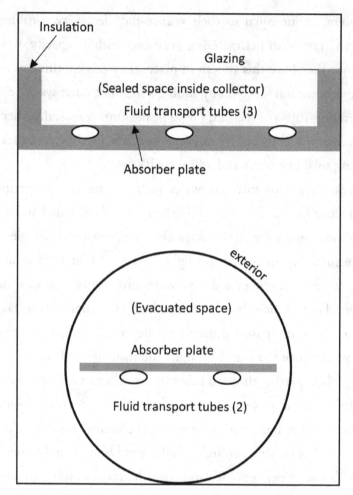

Figure 13 Cross-sectional view of solar hot water heating collectors: flat plate collector (upper) and evacuated glass tube collector (lower).

The two systems do have many common elements: in a temperate climate, they usually have a sealed loop of water mixed with glycol or other antifreeze that is pumped between the panel on the outside and a storage tank on the inside and a means of backup water heating, such as natural gas, for times when the amount of insolation is inadequate. There is no equivalent of net metering for solar hot water: the system

134

can produce extra hot water, beyond what is in immediate need, until its capacity to store extra hot water is filled up; thereafter, there is no "hot water grid" onto which it can release additional output. Therefore, one approach to system sizing in a temperate climate is to design the system so that it produces all the summer demand and falls short in the winter when days are shorter and productivity is lower. This approach leads to some GHG emissions in winter when part of the demand is met by burning natural gas, but it is more economical than sizing to accommodate winter production and having a large amount of extra capacity in the sunny summer months. In a tropical climate, where insolation is more balanced around the year and the user may not care as much about variability in how hot the water is – a lukewarm shower matters less when it is 80°F outside than when it is 8°F! – backup heating may not be necessary.

Whether flat-plate or evacuated-tube systems eventually come to dominate the solar hot-water market, or the two continue to share it, it is clear that there is much room for growth, as solar hot-water systems are still relatively rare. While interest in residential solar energy in the U.S. has gravitated towards PV, a number of our peer countries that possess regions with a good solar resource have focused on solar hot water. Australia, with a population of around 25 million, has more than 1 million households with solar hot water heating. Israel, an early leader in the design and manufacturing of solar hot-water technology, today has solar hot water on more than 90% of residences. And in China, evacuated-tube solar hot water manufacturers have gotten around some of the challenges with installing this technology in a one-of-a-kind, individually designed system, by developing a compact, modular system that is self-contained except for the connection to the DHW piping to the rest of the house. As a result, China in 2019 was estimated to have

70% of the cumulative world solar hot-water systems, in terms of rated capacity.[23]

As an illustration of the potential output from solar hot water systems, monthly values across four years for a household-sized system installed on a rooftop in Ithaca, NY, are shown in Fig. 14. The trend is similar to that of the solar PV array presented in Fig. 4, in the sense that output is low in the winter and climbs through the spring to a peak in the summer, before declining again in the fall. Note that although both the PV array in Fig. 4 and the hot water array in Fig. 14 are in the same geographic location, they respond differently to partial versus full sun, exposure to wind passing over the collector, and other factors, so the shape of the average curve need not be exactly the same. This difference arises because the two processes are fundamentally different. A solar hot-water system is absorbing and retaining heat from the sun to transfer it to the fluid flowing to and from the collector. A solar PV system relies on individual photons of light dislodging electrons in a molecular structure to create a current.

As an indication of the economic value of the investment in this solar hot-water system, the average production per year for the 2011-2014 period is approximately 2000 kWh, or 6.8 million Btu when converted to U.S. conventional units. If a consumer pays $10 per million Btu for natural gas and has a water heating system that is 90% efficient, the same amount of energy in the form of sufficient gas to displace the solar hot water would cost ~$76 per year. This calculation shows one of the important differences between solar electricity and solar hot water. If one divides the $76/year of value among the 2000 kWh generated, the value per kWh is $0.038, compared to values of $0.12-$0.15 for

---

[23] Data sources: for figures on Australia and China, Australian Conservation Center, www.cleanenergycouncil.org.au; for figures on Israel, California Solar Center, www.californiasolarcenter.org. Accessed March 9, 2019.

residential electricity in many parts of the country. It is therefore very important for the installed cost of solar hot water to be kept low, if one wishes to avoid a very long payback period.

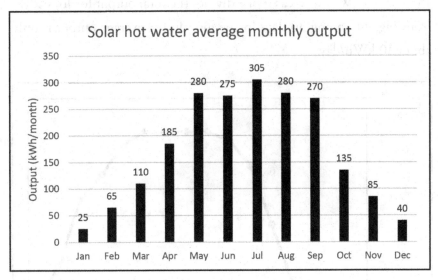

Figure 14 Monthly average output in kWh from a solar hot-water system installed in Ithaca, NY, USA, for years 2011-2014.

Next, Fig. 15 shows representative hourly output for a clear day from the same solar hot water system that is monitored in Fig. 14. The date of the study is June 15, 2011, which is the same date as the solar PV hourly-output study shown in Fig. 8. Since the skies were clear on this date, and the date is close to the summer solstice, the output represents a level at or near the most output it could make, since there are the largest possible number of sunny hours in the day. The system power in kW is measured based on how much the collector is raising the temperature of the glycol/water mix and how fast the solar system's pump is moving the mix between the collector on the roof and the hot-water storage tank inside. Unlike the solar PV where the collector output in kW varies by the hour, the solar hot water peaks at a 2.1-kW rate from 2 to 5 p.m.

This peaking occurs because there is a physical limit on how fast the system can transfer heat from the collector to the tank. Also, because conditions were nearly ideal, the total output for the day shown in Fig. 15 was 19.5 kWh, whereas if one divides the total output for June 2011 from Fig. 14 among 30 days in the month, the average output is only about 10 kWh/day.

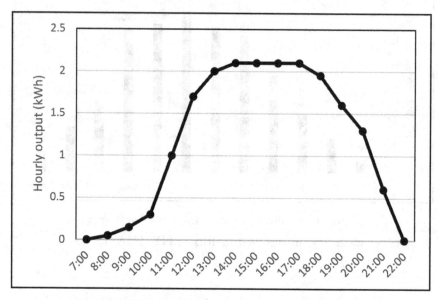

Figure 15 Hourly energy production in kWh for a solar hot water system with 16 evacuated tubes in Ithaca, NY, on June 15, 2011.

In summary, solar hot water heating is a proven technology that in many parts of the world can add to energy derived from the sun. Both residential and commercial buildings use hot water for various applications all year long, so whenever there is sun, they can displace the burning of fossil fuels by taking advantage of a solar water heater. Solar energy users with financial resources can purchase a manufactured system, but where economic resources are limited, users can invest "sweat equity" in building their own solar water heater – many available designs are not complicated.

Solar ovens and solar cookers

Culinary practices in many cultures, including the Cajun cooking native to Louisiana, incorporate an approach to some dishes in which food is slow roasted at a temperature in the range of 160 to 170 degrees Fahrenheit (71 to 77 Celsius), sometimes for four or five hours. When done correctly, the long, slow cooking process at a moderate temperature allows the flavor to penetrate the food gradually, without burning or overcooking, leading to exquisite taste.

This is exactly how a solar oven works when exposed to good sun. Far from being a poor substitute for cooking using fossil fuels, solar cookers are capable of yielding excellent results because they also bring dishes up to cooking temperature slowly and then maintain a moderate temperature for many hours without burning them.

The term "solar cooker" and "solar oven" can be used interchangeably, but the device in question is generally a container made of materials such as wood or sheet metal with a glass opening to allow sunlight to enter (Fig. 16). The bottom and sides of the container are insulated, usually with a material that can withstand high temperature such as shreds of old clothing or sheep's wool. Above the glass opening, reflective panels concentrate the sunlight on the glass. Cooking containers are placed underneath the glass on a dark-colored absorber plate which absorbs incoming sunlight and re-radiates it as heat to the interior of the solar oven. Here the "greenhouse effect" plays a role: the sun's rays can easily pass in and out of the glass opening, but once light energy is converted to heat, the heat cannot readily pass back out through the glass, so the temperature inside the oven rises.

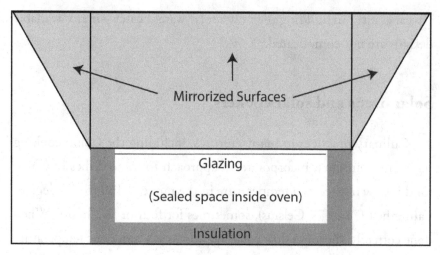

Figure 16 Schematic diagram of representative solar oven, showing sealed space with glazing on top and insulation on sides and bottom, and mirrorized reflective surfaces to capture sunlight.

The reason that the term solar cooker is used (as opposed to solar oven) is that the device can cook as well as bake. Both dishes that bake, such as breads or cakes, and dishes that would generally slow cook on a stovetop, such as grains or soups, can be placed in the device. To adjust for being inside an oven rather than over a flame, a stovetop dish is covered with a black- or dark-covered lid to maximize heat absorption so that it can slow-cook in the oven. Dishes that can be started cold in the solar oven and come up to temperature slowly without losing their consistency, such as dried beans or brown rice, have the advantage of cooking slowly, which often leads to better flavor.[24]

Compared to solar PV or hot water, penetration of solar cooking in the U.S. and other advanced economies is minimal. A PV array or solar hot water system functions automatically with minimal input from the owner, except when it malfunctions. Solar cooking, on the other hand, requires advance planning to set up the cooker early on a sunny day and an opportunity to reposition it once or twice later in the day as the sun moves across the sky. In a fast-paced society where time is scarce, the flexibility to cook with the sun is hard to carve out of the day, especially for those who work nine-to-five jobs. To the extent that there is a region of the world that is the center of attention for solar cooking, it is the developing countries in the global south. Organizations such as California-based Solar Cookers International document projects to disseminate and use solar cookers in many tropical and sub-tropical countries. International service organizations such as Rotary International have supported the dispersal of solar ovens in these regions as well. One of the main obstacles has been the cost of the cookers, but in 2009, a Norwegian inventor based in Kenya, Jon Bohmer, won an international prize sponsored by the Financial Times of London, worth 50,000 British Pounds, for a solar oven design that delivers remarkable cooking and baking performance, for the equivalent of a mere five dollars in materials. There also remains a small but

---

[24] Author's note: In our family, we cook with a solar oven during the warm months of the year, and one of our favorite dishes is "solar rice." The rice is put raw into a dark-colored, covered pot with the appropriate amount of cold water and then slowly cooks in the oven as the day progresses from morning to afternoon. The first pot of solar rice from the solar cooking season is met with great excitement, and on the flip-side, after the oven has been put away for the cold months, the first pot of stove-top rice in the fall is met wistfully.

dedicated group of solar cooker users in the U.S., especially in the sunnier, dryer parts of the country.

As an example of solar oven performance, Fig. 17 shows hourly temperature for a slow-cooking stew on a summer day with abundant sun, using an oven thermometer placed inside the oven within view through the glass cover. The date is June 15, 2011, the same date as the PV and hot water examples appearing earlier. The stew consists of approximately 10 pounds of a mixture of liquid and dry ingredients, placed unheated and uncooked in the oven, in a steel pot weighing approximately 2 pounds and painted black on all sides. At 10 a.m., the temperature is 75°F in the oven, or the same as the ambient temperature. Thereafter, the dish reaches temperatures above the boiling point by noon (240°F) and then slow-cooks between 250°F and 140°F for the afternoon. At 5 p.m., the measured temperature is 140°F, so at this point the dish has finished cooking and is being kept warm by the oven for dinner. After measuring the temperature at 5 p.m., the dish is removed, so the measured temperature of 75°F at 6 p.m. is that of the empty oven only, which has returned to ambient.

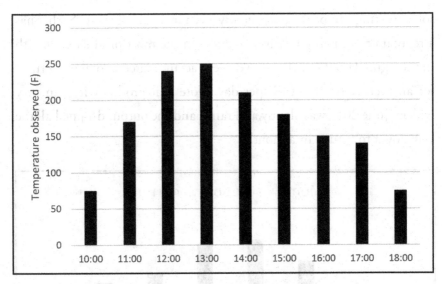

Figure 17 Test-run of a solar cooker on June 15, 2011, in Ithaca, NY, with a 2-pound steel pot containing approximately 10 pounds of liquid and ingredients.

Figure 18 shows the potential productivity of solar cooking in a temperate climate, namely that of Ithaca, NY. The "runs" in the figure are counted as follows: there are two ovens available, and they are both of a size that only cooks one item at a time, unlike that of Fig. 16. Each time an oven is used to cook or bake an item, it counts as a run. Therefore, on a long day in June, if an oven is used to cook one dish in the morning and then another in the afternoon, it can accumulate two runs in a single day toward the monthly total. The measure of productivity is not as scientific as that shown in the PV and solar hot water figures above, since the ovens were not used on every day that sufficient sun was available. Nevertheless, the pattern of productivity is similar, with an off-peak season in April, followed by a peak season from May to August, and returning to an off-peak season in September and October. Due to the cold winter weather, solar cooking is not effective from November to March. However, during the peak summer months, solar cooking can be used frequently, even in a part of the U.S. that has a reputation for being relatively cloudy. In the most productive month in the figure (June 2014), the two ovens accumulated a total of 19 runs, for an average of 0.63 runs per day. Note that productivity can vary widely: June 2013 was cloudy and rainy, and the output dropped all the way down to 7 runs in a month.

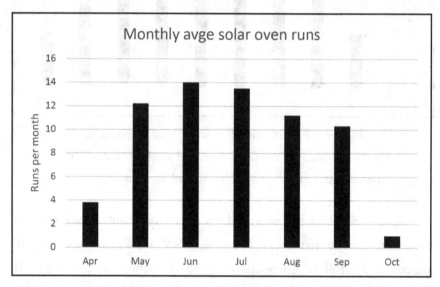

Figure 18 Average number of runs per month for solar cooking operation with two solar ovens in Ithaca, NY, during April-October solar cooking season for years 2012-2014.

Notes: 1 run = one use of the oven to cook or bake a dish from start to finish.

Turning to the global situation with solar cooking, efforts to promote solar cooking focus on developing countries in the tropics because of the potential to displace cooking by gathering and burning firewood. Not only is gathering firewood in many countries very time consuming, but also, the smoke from the fires creates indoor air quality problems. The strong sun is another advantage, not only in arid countries where sunshine is abundant most of the year, but also in wetter countries, many of which have a pronounced dry season for part of the year, when solar cooking can work well. Even the design of solar ovens for tropical locations is different. Solar ovens for use in temperate countries at higher latitudes like the U.S. often have four reflectors all the way around the perimeter of the oven to make the most of the available sun. Ovens in the strong tropical sun, by contrast, often need only one reflector to achieve sufficiently high temperatures, and that single reflector can fold down to cover and protect the transparent opening on top of the oven when it is not in use. Because the one-mirror oven performs well in tropical countries, it does not make sense, especially for solar-oven users who are economically challenged, to spend more on reflective surfaces that are not needed.

More high-tech approaches to using solar energy for cooking are also possible, which typically add some technological pieces to make it possible to cook at other times of day when the sun is not available. A community-scale cooker at the Gaviotas community in eastern Colombia uses the heating of oil with the sun to collect and store solar energy, as well as a small PV-powered pump to move the oil from rooftop collectors to a storage cylinder, and then to the institutional kitchen. A community-scale solar cooking system at the Brahmakumari Ashram in Mount Abu, Rajasthan, India, uses a system of dish-shaped collectors to focus solar energy onto a system of receivers that generate enough steam to cook for 38,000 people per day during peak sunlight periods.[25]

---

[25] For more on the Gaviotas system, see Weisman (1998). For information on the Mount Abu system, see article on "Solar Cookers in India" at http://www.chillibreeze. com/articles/SolarCookersinIndia.asp or description of the system at http://www. digi-help.com/gadgets/worlds-biggest-solar-kitchen.asp.

Opportunities and challenges for solar energy

In this chapter we have discussed several different ways of using solar energy directly, starting with solar PV to make electricity, then heating water or air with solar energy, and even cooking directly with the sun. In the short- to medium-term, we can expect installation of solar energy to accelerate. This is especially true for solar PV, because it is becoming more and more visible all around us, on both a large and small scale. In time, other solar applications may follow.

Some of the growth for solar PV will come just from the competitive prices that are available combined with the pressure on cities, regions, and nations to take action on climate change. In the case of generation on single-family homes, this process can be assisted by increasingly using "bundling" of installation opportunities to streamline the installation of PV across multiple households. Rather than having each owner figure out the system, a group of owners form a "solarize" consortium, negotiate a standard package with the installer and utility, and achieve savings from economies of scale. The installers get the systems up and running faster than doing one-off projects.

Another approach to installation is to have the utility, rather than the homeowner, retain ownership of the system. In this approach, the building owner and the utility enter into an agreement for the utility to install, maintain, and operate the system on the owner's premises. The utility then sells electricity from the system to the building owner at a specified price. In the event that output exceeds consumption in the building, the electricity flows out from the system onto the grid, to be consumed elsewhere. Although this approach is led by the utility rather than the building owner, it creates installation jobs, relieves the owner of having to worry whether or not their system is working, and draws on the utility's long-standing expertise of installing and maintaining electrical transmission equipment.

One challenge with distributed solar systems, both PV and otherwise, is the need to create a system for reliably detecting and repairing malfunctioning units in a larger array. Unlike the repair of a car, where the mechanic can work on the vehicle at their location regardless of the weather, repair of a solar asset is more challenging, as it cannot be moved and can only be tested in the presence of sunlight. At present, many system owners appear to "let slide" the question of prompt troubleshooting. They allow systems to persist with degraded performance for some time, content as long as the majority of panels or evacuated tubes are working – or unaware that there is a problem at all. However, if we are to move to a robust solar future where we truly depend on solar energy as one of the mainstays of our energy supply, this outlook will need to change.

When we take the perspective on solar energy up from the individual household to the "30,000-foot level" of the global industry as a whole, we can see how solar is starting to move toward a robust future and how far there is to go. According to the International Energy Agency, the world reached a total installed capacity of 398 GW of solar PV at the end of 2017 (i.e., the sum of the wattage of all PV panels installed worldwide totaled 398,000,000 kW, or 398 GW).[26] In 2018, the world added 94 GW for a total of 492 GW by the end of the year. If this amount were divided up among 5-kW residential systems, it would be equivalent to the capacity for nearly 100 million homes. At a capacity factor of 13%, the output from 492 GW of solar PV would be about 560

---

[26] International Energy Agency. (2019) Online database of energy statistics. Available at www.iea.org.

Terawatt-hours, or 560 billion kWh.[27] Of the total 492-GW figure, 175 GW, or 36%, was installed in China. The cumulative installed capacity in the U.S. stood at 64 GW, or 13% of the world total.

While impressive, this amount is still only equivalent to about 2% of the total world market for electric power. Other types of solar energy, such as solar hot water, solar thermal-electric generation, and solar cooking, are growing even more slowly. This is not surprising, since solar PV is so versatile – it is available for both small-scale residential systems and large centralized solar power plants and as an electricity source for both stationary applications and electrified transportation. Unfortunately, these trends suggest a long time horizon for solar to fully penetrate the world energy market, even if the pace picks up in coming years.

The monthly productivity figures in Fig. 19 highlight the challenge for solar in temperate climates, i.e., between the Tropics of Cancer and Capricorn and the polar regions. This figure combines monthly average output for solar PV, solar hot water, and solar cooking from Figs. 4, 14, and 18, respectively, into a single representation of average monthly output. For each of the three sources, the month of the year with the highest output is chosen as the maximum, and then the output in the other 11 months is presented as a percentage of the maximum. Each resource has a different maximum month: for PV, cooking, and hot water, the maximum month is May, June, and July, respectively. In all three cases, the equipment is much less productive in the winter months. If the example site were in the southern hemisphere, e.g., Melbourne, Australia, at 38°S latitude, the trough in output would be moved to the period May-August, but the effect would be the same. Much of

---

[27] Interpretation: the capacity factor is the average percentage of the maximum capacity that is actually being used. For example, (492 GW) x (8760 hours/year) x (13%) = 560,000 GWh or 560 Terawatt-hours.

the economic activity of the planet, measured in GDP of output, is concentrated in these regions (North America, Europe, East Asia, etc.). To operate the world economy on renewable energy, each region must have access to a portfolio of renewable options sufficient to meet energy demand in every month of the year. During the "trough" months for solar in higher latitudes, solar energy systems can contribute as much as possible. To make up the balance, either solar energy must be transferred long distances from sunnier regions, or other types of renewables must be developed. These issues are addressed in the next three chapters on wind, other renewable sources, and systems integration.

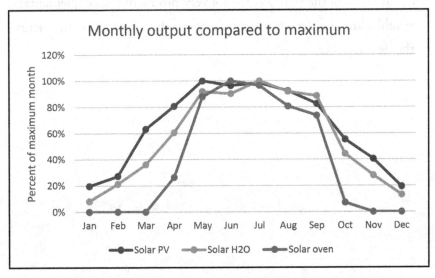

Figure 19 Comparison of observed average monthly productivity for solar systems in Ithaca, NY, 42°N latitude.
Example: for solar PV, the most productive month was May, with an average of 271 kWh of output. The January average was 53 kWh. Therefore, the value shown for January is ~20%.

From this discussion, two goals emerge: 1) develop as much solar energy as possible, and 2) develop complementary technologies that work in tandem with solar. In pursuit of the first goal, many communities around the world will accelerate the rollout of solar energy in coming years. Beyond a point, deeper penetration of solar requires pursuit of the second goal, including new transmission lines to move solar energy over a greater distance and storage systems to save up solar energy when the sun is shining and to release it when it is not. Also, a renewable energy system that relies entirely on solar without using other renewables does not make sense. In many locations, other renewables like wind, hydro, tidal, or wave energy may be quite competitive with solar on a $/kWh basis. Also, many centers of large energy demand are at higher latitudes where at times of the year solar is not very productive. Complementary renewables are in order, starting with one of these sources, wind energy, in the next chapter.

CHAPTER 6

Wind Energy – The Major Complement to Solar

To understand the attraction of wind as an energy source, consider the following design for large-scale solar energy generation. In the early 2000s, developers proposed an enormous solar power station at Mildura, Australia. A sprawling glass-covered canopy several kilometers in diameter would allow air to enter at the edges and then heat it as if it were in a greenhouse, exposed to the strong Australian sun. The heated air would then rush to the center of the canopy where it would enter a one-kilometer-high tower on its way to being released back into the atmosphere through an opening at the top of the tower. As the concentrated hot air rushed up through the tower, it would pass through a collection of turbines, generating electricity.

What a lot of construction and cost to capture solar energy by making air move – a canopy covering many square kilometers, a tower reaching one kilometer into the sky! When we consider wind energy, rather than the sprawling Mildura solar concept, the beauty of wind energy generated at a wind farm is that nature provides two out of three of the components of that solar power station – for free. First, upstream from the wind farm, the sun heats the air that leads to motion in the form of wind. Second, the wind farm is located where winds are channeled together like the air in the power-plant tower, on average, so that they pass over the terrain of the wind farm at elevated average wind speeds. This leaves the wind farm developer with just the cost of designing, constructing, and maintaining the wind turbines. Since nature is doing much of the work of concentrating energy for the wind farm operator, they are able to produce the electricity relatively cheaply. In addition, as technology advances, turbines become cheaper, projects become more cost-effective to build and the cost of production per kWh goes down. For example, prices in the U.S. fell from \$0.07/kWh in 2009 to around \$0.02/kWh in 2017, at the most favorable land-based sites in the middle of the country.

Wind is also complementary to solar. In higher latitudes, for example, solar productivity declines in winter due to the shorter length of the day, whereas wind energy often (though not always) peaks in winter and can compensate for low output from solar.

Wind energy has strong future potential for growth as well. To illustrate this potential, we can compare the situation for wind energy with that of large-scale hydropower (discussed in greater depth in Chap. 7). Whereas large hydro has largely reached its capacity in the United States, we have hardly scratched the surface of wind's potential. For example, a study published by authors at Harvard University suggests that the maximum amount of wind energy that could be captured is around 16 times the annual electricity consumption of the U.S. (Lu et al, 2009).

Our capacity to move toward deeper penetration of wind power has been supported by the U.S. Department of Energy research. The "20 by 30" study published in 2009 to examine the feasibility of producing 20% of our electricity from wind by 2030 was a significant milestone in this direction. The USDOE found that there was potentially 3,000 GW of capacity that could be developed with winds that would provide wind power at a competitive price (U.S. Department of Energy, 2009, p.8). At the beginning of that year, there was 25 GW of installed wind capacity in the U.S.; by the end of 2021, that figure had risen to 135 GW, a more than five-fold increase.

Another advantage is that wind energy development does not appear to claim land in the same way that, for example, impounding water behind a dam does for hydropower. Land inundated for a dam is not available for forestry or agriculture, although it is often available for sport fishing and water recreation. However, with a wind farm, land that was previously used for crops or as rangeland can continue in that use. At a typical wind farm in an agricultural region, there is a circle around the base of each tower with a driveway and grass to allow access to the turbine for maintenance. Outside of that circle, raising crops or livestock continues uninterrupted.

In the rest of this chapter, we will look in more detail at the growth of wind energy around the world and in the U.S., and also some of the challenges this industry faces. To set up this discussion, we first review some basics about how wind energy works.

The Basics of Wind Turbine Technology

The term "wind turbine" denotes a single complete device that converts energy in the wind into electricity (Fig. 1). Large turbines of the type shown in the figure are called "utility-scale" turbine because they are large enough for electric utilities to use them to generate electricity in large quantities for the grid. As shown, blades are attached to a hub that rotates on an axle, turning a generator (mounted inside the box marked "nacelle with generator"). The hub contains a rotation mechanism that allows the angle or "pitch" of the blades to change while the hub rotates, adjusting the amount of wind that the blades catch, like a sailor on a sailboat letting their sail in or out. The axle and generator are housed in a nacelle that can rotate on top of the turbine tower, so that the blades can change direction in response to changes in wind direction thanks to a yaw mechanism that permits rotation. (The term "yaw" means the orientation of any device such as a ship, aircraft, or wind turbine relative to the wind direction.) The nacelle sits on top of a heavy steel tower that in turn sits on a concrete foundation buried under the ground. Note that sometimes the terms "wind turbine" and "windmill" are used interchangeably, but technically a windmill is a different device that engages in mechanical tasks like grinding grain, as opposed to making electricity. Therefore, "wind turbine" is used in this book.

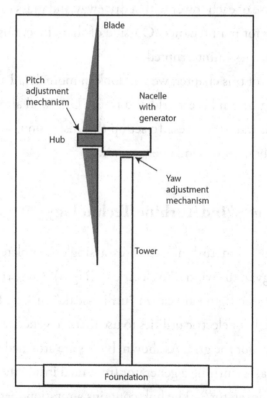

Figure 1 Parts of a utility-scale wind turbine, showing blades, nacelle, and turbine tower. Note that scale has been adjusted to show all components within the figure.

Of the 743 GW of wind turbines installed around the world as of 2020, the vast majority are found in wind farms where multiple turbines feed power to a long-distance transmission line. These wind farms are found both on land and off-shore. A handful of turbines may be deployed by large electricity users such as factories or ski resorts where wind generated power is consumed locally, but these are in the minority.

Turning the focus to large-scale wind farms, offshore farms naturally introduce additional challenges not found when building on land. Until recently, most offshore turbines were installed in shallow water where the foundation could be built into the seabed. Recently, though, some experimental floating turbines have been deployed in deeper water where the floating platform on which they are situated is tethered to the sea floor. Eventually, this effort may lead to the deployment of commercially viable offshore wind farms based on floating turbines.

All large turbines currently being installed are *horizontal-axis wind turbines,* or HAWTs (Fig. 1). As the name implies, the turbine's axis of rotation is parallel to the ground so that the turbine blades rotate in a vertical plane. The alternative is for a *vertical-axis wind turbine,* or VAWT, which have been installed on a pilot project basis in the past. These turbines rotate around a vertical axis (picture a giant egg-beater turned upside-down, with the beater portion sticking straight up in the air). In general, VAWTs remain an area of active research but there do not appear to be any attempts to launch them commercially on the horizon, so the focus of this section is on HAWTs.

In addition to the basic description of turbine components accompanying Fig. 1 above, turbine functions are the following:

- *Turbine blades and hub functions*: The hub at the center of the turbine blades is mounted on the end of the turbine axis and also supports the connection of the end of the blades to the rest of the system. Therefore, there are two distinct types of rotation involved: the hub rotates continuously on the axle of the turbine, and the blades rotate periodically inside the hub to change their angle. The amount of power that the turbine can produce is a function of its *swept area*, or disc within which the turbine blades rotate. For example, a turbine with blades 10 meters long would have a swept area with a radius of 10 meters. Therefore, if we use an approximate value of 3.14 for the value of the mathematical constant pi, the swept area would be about 314 m². A turbine with a larger swept area will produce more power than one with a smaller swept area, all other things equal.

■ *Nacelle functions*: The outer cover of the nacelle first serves to protect mechanical and electrical components from the weather. The nacelle also contains the transmission for adjusting the rotational speed so that it will be correct for generating electricity and the generator that converts the mechanical rotation of the turbine into electrical power. (An electrical generator works like a motor in reverse – a motor inside an electric drill or blender takes electricity and turns it into rotation, but a generator takes rotation and turns it into electricity.) Lastly, the nacelle sits on top of a gearing system that allows the entire turbine to rotate so that it can face the direction of the arriving wind. In a small household-size turbine, this function can be achieved by attaching a tail to the back of the turbine that pushes the device to rotate into the wind. However, because of the massive weight of a utility-scale turbine, the rotation of the nacelle to face the wind is mechanized, with gears and electric motors.

■ *Tower functions*: The tower supports the nacelle at a sufficient height above the ground not only to allow the blade tips clearance when they are at the bottom of their rotation, but also to keep them above slow wind speeds and turbulence that occur close to the ground. (The distance between the ground and the top of the tower is called the "hub height.") Also, much of the weight of the overall turbine system is found in the tower so that it provides stability against the force of the wind acting on the turbine blades. Inside the tower, electric cables pass current from the nacelle to the foundation and away from the turbine, and a ladder or other passageway provides access from the foundation to the nacelle.

■ *Foundation functions*: The foundation provides support for the weight of the tower, nacelle, hub, and blades, and also resistance to the force of the wind pushing against the turbine. In a land-based turbine or off-shore turbine mounted on the sea floor, the foundation is a reinforced concrete pad designed to accomplish both of these goals. The platform of a floating offshore turbine must also accomplish these same functions although materials will be different. For turbines other than floating offshore models, the foundation must be specifically designed to withstand the strong forces of the wind pushing on the turbine and tower, which act like a giant lever. In some instances, turbines with defective foundations have collapsed under the weight of this force.

■ *Distribution system and substation functions*: For a wind farm, the balance of the farm's system consists of a network of access roads and underground electric cables. The network of cables gathers current from the individual turbines and transmits them to a substation. The substation receives the electrical power from the wind turbines and uses large transformers to increase its voltage to levels high enough for long-distance transmission on the grid (typically 115,000 Volts or higher in the U.S.). A substation is critical because favorable wind resources, and hence wind farms, are not typically found next to large consumers of electricity like big industrial plants or populous cities. Therefore, the power transmitted must be stepped up to a higher voltage at the substation for long-distance transmission to load centers far away.

From the dawn of the utility-scale wind energy era around the year 1980, design decisions for a standard large turbine have converged on a number of standards. One is the axis around which the turbine rotates, as mentioned above. Some early wind developers experimented with vertical-axis turbines (VAWTs). Potentially, these have some advantages. For example, the device can receive wind from any direction without needing to be reoriented. However, a downside is that the turbine must be supported at the base, so it is difficult to support with sufficient strength with the thrust of the wind pushing on its entire height above the mount point. By contrast, in the case of the horizontal-axis turbine (HAWT) the thrust is spread concentrically on the blades around the axis of rotation, so that the force is more evenly balanced and easier to support. Because of this, the HAWT eventually emerged as the preferred design solution.

The industry initially experimented with different numbers of blades in large HAWTs and eventually settled on a standard design of three blades. A comparison can be made to propellers in aircraft, where a propeller may have two blades in the smallest two-seat aircraft to six blades in some of the larger twin-engine commercial passenger planes. One difference is that an aircraft is putting kinetic energy into the air to move the craft forward, whereas a wind turbine is extracting energy from the air. The wind-power industry has found that if a three-bladed turbine is the starting point, adding a fourth blade does not pay for itself in terms of the added energy extracted compared to the additional cost. Going in the other direction, most manufacturers have settled on three blades because a two-bladed turbine introduces some instability in the rotational motion of the blades. However, some makers continue to experiment with utility-scale two-bladed turbines, and some household-sized two-bladed turbines are available in the market. (For comparison, a household-sized turbine might be as small as 1 kW, whereas a utility-scale turbine today is between 1,500 and 10,000 kW.)

Growth of the US and world wind markets

Since the publication of the USDOE 20-by-30 report in 2009, U.S. wind energy has grown substantially, and there is every indication that it will continue to grow in the future. In the 20-by-30 scenario, production of electricity from wind would reach 1.2 trillion kWh in 2030 – more than 21 times the estimated production in 2008. Already, it reached 379 billion kWh in 2021, nearly seven times the 2008 value. In each of the last 10 years, national output has increased by at least 9 billion kWh compared to the year before, and in the biggest one-year gain, output increased by 42 billion kWh from 2019 to 2020. (Tax policy sometimes encourages bursts of new installations in some years and not others; see discussion below.)

As wind energy has grown, it has surpassed hydro as the largest source of renewable electricity in the U.S. As shown in Fig. 2, for the period 2001-2021, hydropower averaged 270 billion kWh per year (with low and high values of 217 and 319 billion kWh, respectively), generating about 7% of total production. Hydro production is limited by lack of opportunities to install new capacity, and it has been suffering from the drying effects of climate change in the west where many of the largest dams are located.

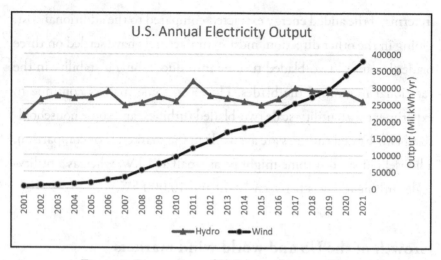

Figure 2 Comparison of U.S. annual output from wind
and hydropower 2001-2021.

Source: U.S. Energy Information Administration.

Wind electric output has grown in the U.S. thanks to an accelerating
rate of installing new wind farms and turbines, especially since 2008
(Fig. 3). As shown in the figure, the annual amount added has been
quite variable as tax policy has sometimes spurred the industry to add
capacity quickly (2012) or slowly (2013). Nevertheless, the "smoothed"
curve in Fig.2 shows a 5-year running average rate of installation, a
consistent 6 GW and 8 GW from 2008 to 2017 before rising to 11 GW
from 2018 to 2020. Accordingly, total installed capacity grew from 25
GW to 135 GW in that time frame.

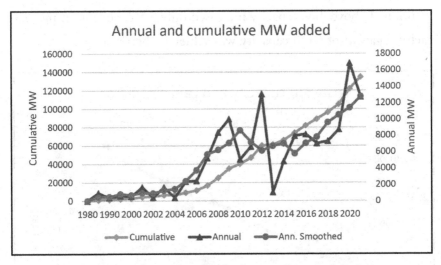

Figure 3 Annual, smoothed annual, and cumulative installed U.S. wind capacity in GW, 1980-2021.

Source: American Wind Energy Association (AWEA).

Note: Annual smoothed curve provides, in each year, the 5-year average annual installed capacity in that year.

Increasing the total number of wind turbines has not been the only reason for growth. Over time, the average capacity factor[28] of the fleet has improved, further boosting annual output (Fig. 4). The capacity factor value improved from 25% in 2004 to 34% in 2017, thanks to a mixture of improvements in technology and advances in operations best practices so that turbines could be available for more hours of the year. Between 2008 and 2017, output increased almost 5 times as

---

[28] Recall from earlier chapters that the capacity factor is the ratio of actual annual output to ideal output if the total wind capacity had operated at full power for all 8,760 hours per year. For example, in 2004 there was 6,719 MW of capacity available, so the ideal output would have been (6,719 MW capacity)*(8760 hrs/year) = (58.9 Million MWh). The actual output was 14.7 Million MWh, so the capacity factor was (14.7)/(58.9) = 25%, as shown.

mentioned above, but capacity increased only 3.5 times, meaning that each Megawatt of wind capacity was achieving better usage.

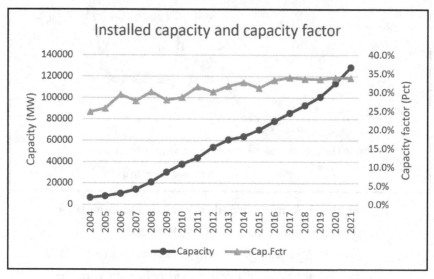

Figure 4 U.S. wind increase in cumulative capacity (MW) and capacity factor (percent), 2004-2017.
Source: American Wind Energy Association (AWEA).

Wind energy has been growing steadily at the global level as well, notably in the continents of Asia, Europe, and North America, which represent at least three-fourths of the world's installed wind turbine capacity (Fig. 5). Wind capacity has increased by at least 50 GW in each year from 2013 to 2020, the equivalent of 10,000 5-MW turbines. Among major users of wind energy in the world, China has led the accelerated growth in wind capacity, rising from 1.3 GW of capacity in 2005 to more than 184 GW in 2018.

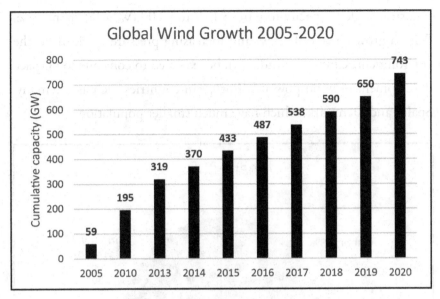

Figure 5 Cumulative global installed wind capacity 2005-2020.
Note: Annual steps 2013-17 included to focus on recent growth. Source: Global Wind Energy Council (GWEC).

It is also important to look at the changing share of installed capacity around the world. Countries such as China and India face a need to address rapidly growing energy demand, deteriorated air quality from burning fossil fuels to generate electricity, and increasing commitments to contribute to global climate protection agreements through expansion of renewable energy. At the same time, they see in wind energy an opportunity to develop a domestic and export industry thanks to their access to cost-competitive manufacturing and increasing research and development capacity. As a result, China moved from not being among the top five nations in terms of wind capacity in 2005 to the number one position by 2020 (Fig. 6). Although India remained in fourth place between 2005 and 2015 and its global share in fact declined from 7% to 5%, the increase in absolute quantity in India was robust: installed capacity rose from 13.7 to 39.0 GW, a 185% increase. With a growing middle class and increasing pressure to clean up the environment, China and India can be expected to continue to outpace development of wind power in European countries such as Germany, Spain, and Denmark, which have much smaller populations.

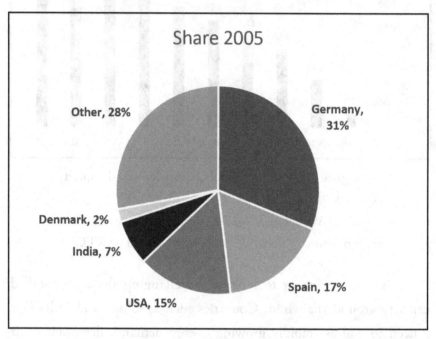

Figure 6a Share of installed wind capacity, 2005 (Total = 195 GW).
Source: Global Wind Energy Council.

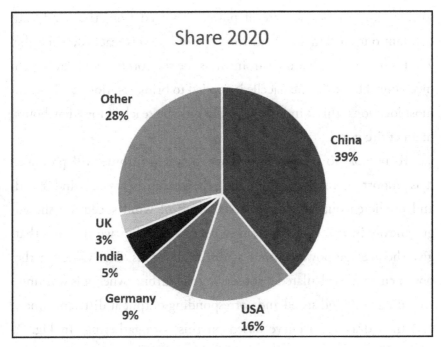

Figure 6 Share of installed wind capacity, 2005 (Total
= 195 GW) and 2020 (Total = 743 GW).
Source: Global Wind Energy Council.

Power curves and turbine efficiency

The intensity of output from a wind turbine depends on how fast
the wind is blowing. Suppose we start with a perfectly calm day. As
wind speed starts to pick up, the turbine will at first remain still if the
wind is too gentle. Then, as the wind speed continues to rise, it passes
the *cut-in wind speed* at which point the turbine begins to turn. At wind
speeds just above the cut-in speed, output from the turbine is small, but
as wind speed continues to increase, it eventually reaches the *rated wind
speed*—in other words, the lowest wind speed at which the turbine can
produce its maximum output. From then on, if wind speed continues
to increase, output holds steady, and the blades feather more and more

to maintain a constant rate of power extracted from the wind and constant output. Finally, if the *cut-out wind speed* is reached, when the wind is so forceful that the turbine must be shut off to avoid damage, a mechanical brake in the nacelle is applied to bring rotation to a halt. In most locations, this wind speed would only be reached for a few hours in an entire year.

To be able to predict how much power a turbine will produce, it is important to understand the relationship between wind speed and predicted output. The various stages of wind speed are shown graphically in Fig. 7 in the form of *power curves* for two turbines that give the average power output at different speeds. The values in the power curve are calculated by observing the turbine when it is working, recording the wind speed and corresponding output at different times, and then drawing a curve based on this data-gathering. In Fig. 7, one turbine has a maximum output of 1.5 MW and the other has a maximum of 1.7 MW. Both turbines have a cut-in speed of 3 meters per second (6.75 mph). After that output from the 1.7-MW turbine rises more rapidly and reaches its maximum output at a lower average wind speed because it has been designed specifically for such sites. To be specific, the 1.7-MW turbine has a rated wind speed of 13 m/s (29.25 mph) because that is the lowest speed at which the 1,700-kW output level is reached. For the 1.5-MW turbine, the rated wind speed is 14 m/s (31.5 mph). For both, the highest wind speed at which they produce power is the cut-out speed of 22 m/s (49.5 mph). The power curves are for "hypothetical but realistic" large wind turbines: although these data are not obtained from actual turbines, if one were to look up power curves for turbines from major manufacturers, they would look similar.

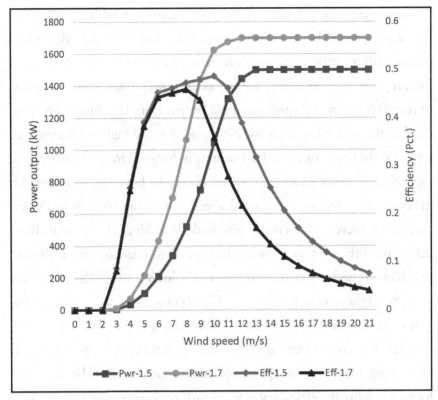

Figure 7 Power and efficiency curves for two representative utility-scale wind turbines for 0 to 25 m/s wind speeds.

Notes: Maximum output for the turbines are 1.5 and 1.7 MW rated capacity, respectively. Wind speed conversion: Range 0-25 m/s equivalent to 0-56.25 mph.

Figure 7 also includes efficiency curves for the two turbines. Based on the density of the air of 1.15 kilograms per cubic meter, as written in the figure, and its speed in meters per second, the wind has a quantifiable amount of power available. Therefore, it is possible to calculate the efficiency of the turbine by comparing the output and available power in the wind. At very low wind speeds, the efficiency is of course zero because the wind is moving but the turbine is not producing anything.

Above the cut-in speed, the efficiency rises rapidly, reaching ~40% at 5 m/s wind speed. The wind speed range from 5 to 10 m/s results in the highest turbine efficiency, which remains between 40% and 50% over this range. Thereafter, efficiency falls as the power in the wind continues to rise with increasing wind speed but output from the turbine remains fixed at the nameplate capacity. Note also that the highest efficiency is lower for the larger turbine. This turbine is designed to reach maximum capacity at a lower rated wind speed. There is, however, a tradeoff in maximizing power at lower wind speed. Once the maximum power output is achieved, efficiency begins to decline. Since the larger turbine maximizes efficiency at a lower wind speed, it does not have a chance to achieve as high a maximum efficiency value as the smaller turbine.

The highest values shown in Fig. 7, of ~49% or ~46% for the two turbines, can be compared to the theoretical *Betz Limit* of 59.3% calculated by Albert Betz in 1919, which is derived from the physics of air moving through the swept area of the turbine blades.[29] The challenge for maximizing the efficiency of wind turbines is that as efficiency rises, more and more energy is removed from the air so that it is moving slower and slower after it passes the turbine. Eventually, if all the energy were removed, the air would come to a complete stop – blocking any upwind air from reaching the turbine blades. Clearly, for the turbine to rotate continuously, 100% efficiency cannot be achieved, and in fact, the Betz Limit works out to 59.3% as the maximum amount of energy that can be withdrawn. Thus, the 46-49% values shown are approaching the limit although they are several percentage points short.

---

[29] An explanation of the Betz Limit is beyond the scope of this book; refer to a more technical work on wind energy such as Manwell et al (2010). As an illustration of the values in Fig.6, at wind speed of 15 m/s, the power available in the wind passing through the 1.5-MW turbine is 7.24 MW, based on the wind speed, the swept area of the turbine (i.e., the circle circumscribed by the blades) and the air density. Output is 1.5 MW, so efficiency is (1.5)/(7.24) = ~20.7%.

Turbine siting and wind-farm design considerations

Whether it's for an individual large turbine or multiple turbines in a wind farm, "siting" wind (finding the best location) depends on the terrain and overall wind resource. For some flat locations, such as the Great Plains or shallow areas of the North Sea in Europe, the wind resource may be essentially the same over many square miles, in which case the output will be more or less constant in any location. On the other hand, in some hilly areas, sufficient output may depend on siting turbines on ridgetops with adequate average wind speed since all other surrounding locations at lower elevations may have wind speeds that are too low. This situation can be problematic from a local impact point of view as a proposed wind farm may be highly visible to those living nearby, leading to opposition to their installation.

The desire to access higher wind speeds far off the ground further confounds the question of visual impact. As mentioned earlier, one of the purposes of the turbine tower is to raise the *swept area* above the ground. For example, the top of the tower, and hence center of the swept area (also known as the *hub height*), might be 80 meters above the ground. If the turbine blades are each 33 meters long, then the turbine would rotate in a disc that is between 47 and 113 meters above the ground. The purpose of raising the turbine in this way is to avoid interference from slow and irregular wind close to the ground caused by wind shear, the frictional force on air as it passes close to the ground. Put another way, air behaves like water or cough syrup when passing over a surface: the fluid (and air, from an engineering point of view, can be treated as a fluid) close to the surface encounters friction and moves slowly, but as you move away from the surface, the effect of that surface decreases, and the fluid moves faster. From heights above about 10 meters above the ground, the increase in wind speed with increasing height is modest because the impact of wind shear near the ground has been fully overcome and the general tendency for speed to increase with height has only a moderate effect. But, as shown in Fig. 8, the effect of raising the turbine height and increasing wind speed is disproportionate: Power continues to increase substantially with increasing height over the range from 10 to 70 meters. For example, since the height of 30 meters is used as the reference value in the figure, increasing height from 30 to 70 meters increases wind speed by only 20% but power available in the wind by almost 70%, as seen in the figure. This trend occurs because the power in the wind is proportional to the cube of the wind speed. For example, if you increase wind speed from 10 to 20 miles per hour, power increases not by a factor of 2 but by a factor of 8.

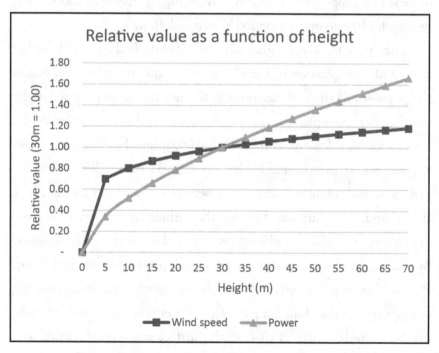

Figure 8 Relative value of wind speed and power available in the wind as a function of height for representative site.

Note: Wind speed and power value set to 1.00 at height = 30m.

When designing a single turbine location and especially a wind farm, designers must also consider prevailing wind direction and strength. Analysts (sometimes called "wind prospectors") can gather historical wind data and compile it into a *wind rose* that shows the percent of time in a year that the wind comes from different compass directions. Figure 9 provides an example from a wind turbine study conducted for a proposed turbine at Ithaca College in Ithaca, NY: there are four main directions and two additional directions between each of north, east, south, and west. The amount of coverage of the rose is proportional to the percentage of time wind arrives from that direction, with concentric circles at 5%, 10%, and 15%. Most of the wind at this location comes from the northwest and south/southeast. For example, starting from due north and moving counterclockwise, due north receives 7% of the wind. Then the next wedge (approximately north/northwest) receives 14.5%; the next wedge receives 14%, and so on.

In a wind farm, upwind turbines tend to interfere with the wind flow arriving at downwind turbines. The designer can lay out the wind farm to minimize interference between turbines when the wind is blowing from the prevailing direction. Conversely, the design can tolerate higher interference from wind directions that seldom occur since the negative impact on productivity will be negligible. For example, for the site represented in Fig. 9, interference when the wind comes from due east would be tolerable because the wind only comes from this direction ~1.5% of the hours of the year. Another factor in laying out a wind farm is the tradeoff between reducing interference and increasing site cost with larger distances between turbines, which increase land acquisition and the cost of royalty payments to landowners such as farmers and ranchers as well as the cost of building underground electrical connections and service roads.

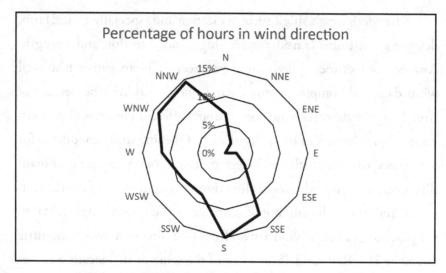

Figure 9 Wind rose for wind turbine site feasibility study for Ithaca College, Ithaca, NY.

Acknowledgment: Thanks to Ithaca College for providing the data for this figure.

Along with understanding the effect of hub height and wind direction on a wind project, another important factor is the distribution of wind speed frequency from completely still air (wind speed = 0 mph) to the strongest winds that occur in a year. To estimate the strength of the wind resource, the wind developer erects an anemometer on a tower at the proposed site and records the wind speed continually, ideally for a period of several years so that year-on-year variability can be observed. If this is not possible, it is also feasible to use data from a single 12-month period, or even from part of a year, and to use statistical techniques to interpret long-term averages. In any case, once the analyst has acquired sufficient data, they calculate the average speed for each hour of the year and then group the hours into wind speed "bins," with each bin having a specific range such as 0 meters/sec (no wind), 0-1 m/s, 1-2 m/s, and so on. Then the number of hours per year, or percent of the year, for each bin can be combined into a wind speed chart.

Figure 10 provides a wind-speed curve for a representative site that would be attractive for erecting a wind turbine. The "Observed" curve in the figure is the actual distribution based on data gathering and analysis. The bins are divided between zero wind hours and 1 m/s bins, each represented by the average wind speed for that bin such as 0.5 m/s for the 0-1 m/s bin, 1.5 m/s for the 1-2 m/s bin, and so on, up to the highest-speed bin at 20-21 m/s. For windy sites, the percent of hours per year at first rises rapidly with increasing wind speed, reaches a peak, and then drops at high wind speeds because the circumstances in nature that generate such high speeds are rare. In this case, 0.9%, or 78 hours per year are completely calm; 1.3%, or 115 hours per year, have winds between 0 and 1 m/s; and so on. Sometimes it is useful to be able to represent the wind-speed distribution in a compact form, and to this end a person with some knowledge of probability and statistics can fit a statistical distribution that represents the wind-speed curve into a "Modeled" form as shown in the graph. The modeled curve requires only the average wind speed for the year (8.1 m/s or 18.2 mph in this case) and the choice of a statistical distribution to present a "smoothed" version of the wind speed bins that approximates the observed shape. The specific distribution used in Fig. 10 is called the Rayleigh distribution. For readers not familiar with the range of different statistical distributions, the idea is similar to the "Bell Curve" or "Normal Curve," but uses a different equation to generate a curve with a single tail that stretches out to infinity on the high end but not on the low one. Both observed and modeled curves predict wind speeds in the range of 6-8 m/s as the most common and higher or lower wind speeds than these as less frequent.

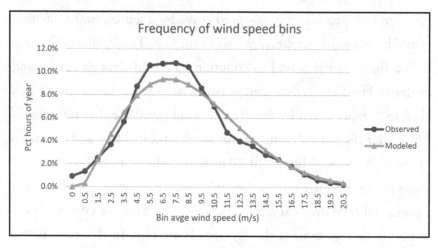

Figure 10 Distribution of percent of hours of the year by wind-speed bin for observed and modeled curves for a representative wind-turbine site.

The value of the wind speed distribution is that it can be combined with the power curve to predict annual energy output from a turbine. Suppose that in the space of a year the observed curve from Fig. 10 encounters the 1.7-MW turbine from Fig. 7. If the average wind speed for each bin is used as the basis for calculating power output, combining hours per year in the bin with power in kW or MW gives energy output in kWh or MWh. For example, the turbine provides 865 kW of output at 7.5 m/s wind speed. This speed is observed over 10.5% of hours of the year (i.e., ~921 hours), so multiplying power by hours gives ~797,000 kWh or 797 MWh of contribution per year. When this process is repeated for all the bins in the figure, the total is 8,080 MWh/y, so the contribution for the 7-8 m/s is 9.9% of the total energy, versus 10.8% of the hours. Figure 11 then compares the percent of hours of the year (same values as Fig. 10) to the percent of contribution to total energy output. Since the higher wind speeds contribute a disproportionate amount of the total energy, they have higher percentage values, and the contribution to annual energy peaks with the 9-10 m/s wind speed bin.

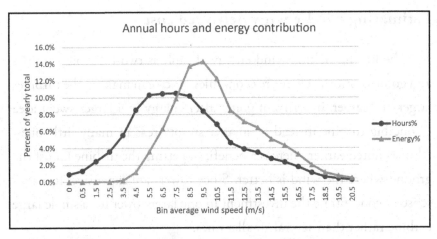

Figure 11 Comparison of percent of hours per year in wind speed bins versus percent of annual energy provided by those bins for representative site and 1.7-MW turbine.

What can be concluded about the 1.7-MW turbine installed in this representative location with average wind speed of 8.2 m/s distributed in the range from 0 to 21 m/s as shown in the figure? Over the course of a year, the turbine would be stationary 8% of the time due to insufficient wind, operating at less than half of its rated 1.7-MW output 24% of the time, operating between half and full output 52% of the time, and operating at full capacity the remaining 8% of the time. (This breakdown does not include down-time for maintenance and a small number of hours where the wind speed is above the cut-out speed.) The predicted 8,080 MWh/year output represents a capacity factor value of 54%. Depending on the cost and complexity of connecting to the broader regional grid and wholesale prices paid for wind-generated electricity, a wind farm with these conditions would be desirable – notice that the capacity factor is significantly higher than the ~33% national average in Fig. 4. This observation brings us to wind cost and revenue, the subject of the next section.

Estimating wind-energy delivered cost

The key to making wind energy cheaply is two-fold: big turbines and good locations. There are economies of scale in making the turbines larger and larger, in terms of going after energy in a larger swept area of one big turbine instead of smaller swept areas in many little ones. Also, as noted earlier, there is a benefit of getting the turbine far off the ground where the wind is better. Since towers are expensive, it makes sense to concentrate the investment in one large tower for a single large turbine rather than several smaller ones.

A turbine with a large diameter also makes slow rotation possible: the turbine can afford the mechanical losses that occur in the gearbox inside the nacelle (see Fig. 1), to go from the slow-moving turbine blades to the fast rotation needed in the generator to generate electricity. This type of slow rotation of blades coupled to a fast-turning generator with a system of gears was not possible in early wind turbines because they were too small, so the losses in gears would have created too great an efficiency penalty. This is good news for birds: modern turbines move so slowly that bird collisions have been greatly reduced, and today, turbines kill relatively few birds compared to deaths caused by vehicles, windowpanes, or outdoor house cats. The Audubon Society, the leading U.S. promoter of bird welfare, has publicly stated that given the overall threat to birds from climate change, they support properly sited wind-energy projects and advocate for research that improves siting procedures and protects birds from being harmed by wind turbines.[30]

Having established that large turbines are the basis for generating electricity from wind on a large scale, we can turn to the broader cost of wind energy projects built around a collection of multiple turbines.

---

[30] U.S. Audubon Society. (2019) "Audubon's position on wind power." On-line resource, available at www.audubon.org. Accessed June 11, 2019.

Most of the cost of wind energy is in the capital cost of building the wind farm, and the majority of the capital cost – 60% to 70% typically – is in the blades, hub, mechanical drivetrain, electrical generator, and yaw mechanism (which allows the turbine to rotate with changing wind direction). The rest of the capital cost is for the tower, foundation, and electrical connection to the grid. This cost breakdown assumes turbines are part of a wind farm, as most are. Individual large turbines can also provide power directly at commercial sites that have a sufficient wind resource and power demand to consume substantial wind-generated output. Examples include the Jiminy Peak ski resort in Western Massachusetts, and Harbec Plastics along the shores of Lake Ontario near Rochester, NY.

In 2017, the American Wind Energy Association (AWEA) estimated the average wind-farm installed cost at around $1,600 per kW, or $4 million per 2.5-MW turbine. This cost includes all the parts of the turbine system and its share of the overhead – the cost of the wind farm's electrical distribution grid, access road for installation and service, and so on. The cost per kW is therefore favorable compared to small-scale wind where a 10-kW turbine on a 100 to 120-foot tower might cost $60,000 installed (i.e., $6,000 per kW).

Cost per rated kW is an important economic measure in wind energy because it is an input into another measure, namely the average cost of electricity production. In addition, the strength of the wind resource at the site also influences the economics, since it dictates the output of the wind farm and therefore the ability to recoup investment. The economic terms of the financial package also influence production cost. Suppose we use the $1600/kW installed cost and the 34% capacity factor figure from Fig. 4 as a basis for economic calculation. Each kW of capacity would then produce 34% of 8,760, or ~2,980 kWh per year. Then, if you were to use simple payback over 20 years to repay the initial cost, you would need to earn $80 per year from the 2,980 kWh, or ~$0.027 per kWh.

Another way to calculate the cost of producing electricity from wind is to apply *discounted cash flow*, which is comparable to the way a homeowner evaluating a mortgage must consider not only the principle value of the home but also the interest that is included with each mortgage payment. Because a major investment like a wind farm is commercial in nature, the developer will need to repay any loan with interest if they receive outside funding from a bank or other institution. Alternatively, if they invest funds they already have in hand, they will typically expect some level of return on investment, beyond simply repaying the principle. Table 1 shows the production cost per kWh for the example of $1600/kW for investment lifetimes from 15 to 25 years and discount rates from 3% to 7%. Under the most favorable circumstances in the table (25 years at 3%), the cost increases to $0.033 per kWh; while for the least favorable (15 years at 7%), the cost rises to $0.059 per kWh. These figures do not include operating cost, which might be ~$0.01/kWh for maintenance, insurance, royalties to landowners, and so on. However, they also do not include any incentives. Where the costs in the table are not competitive in regional power markets with conventional electricity from natural gas or coal, incentives that reflect avoided CO_2 emissions or consumers' willingness to pay a premium for green electricity can make up the difference. Other opportunities to finance wind are programs promoted by a number of states, called *renewable portfolio standards*, in which state law requires electric utilities to derive a certain percentage of the electricity they distribute from renewables. The utilities must in turn procure new sources of renewable electricity to meet these goals.

Life\Rate	3%	5%	7%
15 years	$ 0.0450	$ 0.0518	$ 0.0590
20 years	$ 0.0361	$ 0.0431	$ 0.0507
25 years	$ 0.0330	$ 0.0355	$ 0.0384

Table 1 Production cost per kWh for $1600/kW turbine with 34% capacity factor for 15- to 25-year lifetime and 3%-7% discount rate.

Note: Does not include any non-capital operating cost; see discussion.

We can also use the same figures to model an investment in a representative wind farm with the national-average capacity factor and installed cost per kW. A 100-MW wind farm (40 2.5-MW turbines) of this type would cost $160 million and produce ~298 million kWh per year. As an example, suppose the wind farm can sell the power for an average of 6 cents per kWh but must recover 1 cent per kWh for non-capital operating cost so that the net proceeds are 5 cents per kWh. Revenue for each year would be about $14.9 million. Figure 12 shows the net value of the project calculated out over a 20-year lifetime for simple payback and for discount rates up to 7%. For each scenario, value drops to -$160 million in Year 0 at the beginning of the project when the investment starts but the system has not yet begun to generate power. Then, the annual revenues gradually pay back the investment, with breakeven occurring in Year 11 in the simple payback case (labeled 0% in the figure) or Year 13 in the 3% case. At the other extreme, the investment is still slightly in deficit at -$2.2 million in Year 20.

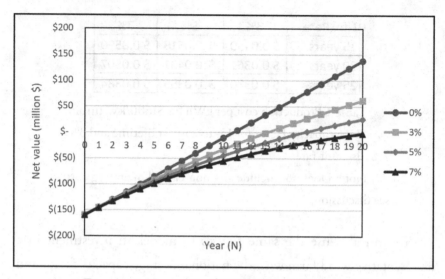

Figure 12 Net value of 100-MW, $160M wind farm investment over 20-year lifetime assuming 34% capacity factor and net $0.05/kWh earnings for simple payback to 7% discount rate case.

As with the cost per kWh values in Table 1, the payback trajectories in Fig. 12 are before any alternative energy incentives. If the payback is not fast enough, incentives such as grants to pay for part of the initial capital cost, or production tax credits that pay the wind farm operator per kWh of electricity produced, can make the economics more favorable.

Wind energy as a complement to solar

Wind energy is attractive not only because it is a large, geographically distributed renewable energy source, but also because it complements solar energy well. One dimension is year-to-year consistency in terms of how much energy is produced each year once the developer has installed a fixed amount of capacity. Chapter 5 discussed how an investment in solar PV over time could have very consistent output levels in terms of kWh produced per year. Wind energy can complement solar by providing output at night or during the winter when solar output falls off, provided it is consistent by season. This consistency is beneficial even if wind is intermittent because systems for storing and distributing intermittent production can fill in the gaps in the short run, as long as wind is consistent over longer periods. Fortunately, wind energy is driven by arriving energy from the sun and the rotation of the earth, both of which are consistent over time, so even if productivity of a wind farm varies from one day to the next due to changing weather, output tends to level out over time. Figure 13 shows an example for annual output at a wind farm in Benton Lake, MN, in the Minnesota "wind belt." Over an 11-year period, the capacity factor is never lower than two percentage points below the mean of 33%, except for one year (in 2004 it is 27%). In general, this means that once the investment in wind is made the operator can count on the long-term productivity of the wind farm within a tolerance. Even in the one low-performing year the farm still makes 80% of the average value. This type of data is difficult to obtain because it is commercially sensitive – wind farm operators do share the number of turbines or total capacity in MW, but they are reluctant to share annual output because it reveals how well the turbines are performing. Therefore, it is not possible to show values for multiple wind farms. However, it makes sense that this trend would be representative of wind energy generally because the underlying drivers are the arriving sunlight and the turning planet.

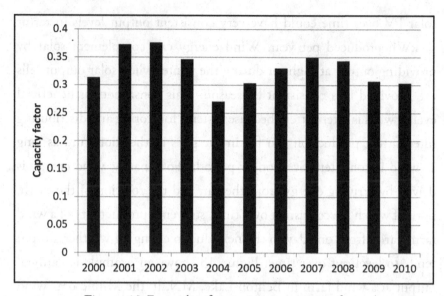

Figure 13 Example of variation in capacity factor by year for wind farm at Lake Benton, MN, 2000-2010.
Note: For 11-year data set, mean value and standard deviation of capacity factor are 33.0% and 3.26%, respectively. Source: Wan (2012).

Solar and wind also complement each other because their month-by-month productivity values are often counter-cyclical: when solar panels are losing productivity in late fall and going into winter, wind farms in many locations are reaching peak output. This trend suggests that across the year ongoing basic energy demand could be met using an appropriate mixture of solar and wind, combined with some amount of storage and demand-side management to cover the inevitable variability. Figure 14 compares monthly solar and wind farm output for a range of locations around the U.S., including actual wind farms in Wyoming, Colorado, and Oregon, as well as predicted wind farm output for a proposed wind farm site in New York State. For the New York site, average capacity factor was calculated by taking the average wind speed for the 12 months of the year and applying a representative turbine-power curve to predict wind farm output, and from that, finding the capacity factor. The trends for CO, NY, and WY are representative of many wind sites around the world, both in the U.S. and in other countries, and also of off-shore as well as on-shore locations. Harsher winter weather also leads to higher average wind speeds and greater productivity of turbines. The sites in CO and WY have a higher average capacity factor because they are close to the wind belt of the U.S. Great Plains, which is known to have one of the best wind resources in the world. The NY site may have lower capacity-factor values, but it also follows the same general trend of better performance in winter than in summer.

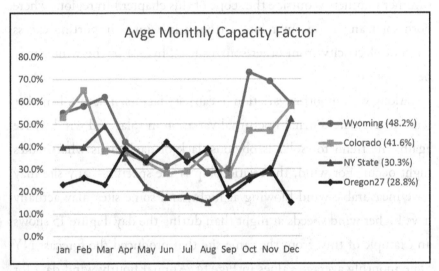

Figure 14 Observed and/or predicted capacity factor values for wind farms in representative U.S. states.
Sources: Energy Information Administration for CO, WY; Oregon Dept. of Environmental Quality for OR; author's calculations for NY. See text for explanation.

The Oregon data in Fig. 14 shows how there are also examples where the rule of greater productivity in winter does not hold. The State of Oregon Department of Environmental Quality has compiled an average CF value by month for 27 wind farms in Oregon, which together have an average value of ~28.8%. This collection of wind farms has higher values in the period April-August and drops off in the other months of the year. In this way, wind is different from solar: Increased incoming solar energy in the temperate regions of the planet is precisely the reason that summer occurs, so inevitably available energy from solar panels will be increased. For wind, however, the month-on-month trend is influenced by local factors, so that some sites have increased productivity in the summer, not the winter. (A detailed explanation of local factors that lead to wind peaking in winter in some locations and summer in others is outside the scope of this chapter.) In regions where both solar and wind enter into a trough in winter, importing excess wind or electricity from other sources (e.g., hydro) in the winter may be an option.

Along with monthly variation in capacity factors, it naturally makes sense to evaluate diurnal-nocturnal variation in solar and wind. Once again, the trend for solar is obvious: lack of daylight is what makes night occur. For wind, the relationship is site specific – any site may have measurable wind blowing at night, and some sites may actually have higher wind speeds at night than during the day. Figure 15 shows an example of this, from the same site that produced the forecast NY State monthly average values in Fig. 14. Annual hourly wind data for this site was compiled to find the average power available in the wind over 24 hours, and the average was found to be highest between 9 p.m. and 5 a.m. Since the site is at 42°N latitude, the average insolation on the summer solstice is shown at that latitude between 6 a.m. and 6 p.m. At either 6 a.m. or 6 p.m., the insolation is only about 65% of the maximum, but then it rises above the average between 9 a.m. and 3 p.m. Note that the summer solstice is used only as an illustration in this case; the pattern would look different at either the equinoxes or the winter solstice. Nevertheless, the comparison shows how the higher output of wind at night might compensate for the lack of sunlight so the two might be mixed in some appropriate way to provide a balanced mix of power.

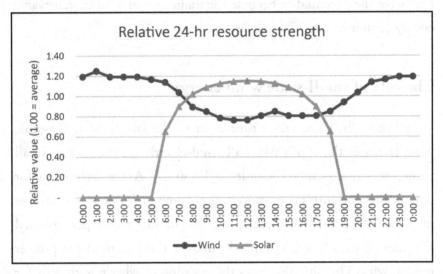

Figure 15 Diurnal-nocturnal variation in wind and solar output for a representative location in Ithaca, NY. Wind data shown is for a proposed wind farm site in Enfield, NY. Average values for wind and solar are 132 W/m² and 759 132 W/m², respectively. See text for explanation.

Sources: ASHRAE Handbook of Fundamentals, as quoted in Vanek et al (2016, Table 9-3, p.297) for solar; author's calculations for wind.

To sum up, wind energy presented in this chapter is a desirable "dance partner" for solar energy as presented in Chap. 5. Often (though not always) wind is more productive in winter when solar is less productive. Over the long term, wind turbines are productive at night as well as during the day, and sometimes they produce more at night than during the day. Lastly, both wind and solar are consistent in terms of annual average output. Although for either source it is not possible to predict with certainty the output on a date in the distant future, for both sources the high- and low-productivity days balance out over time, so that the average becomes predictable. In combination, they have the potential to become the mainstays of a future renewable energy economy.

The role of small-scale wind energy

Historically, there was a time prior to the launch of utility-scale wind farms in the 1980s when all wind-electric generators had small nameplate capacities, on the order of 10-50 kW. As the technology for large-scale wind turbines advanced, they came to dominate the market for electricity from wind, partly due to the lower cost per installed kW mentioned above, and partly due to the potential for greater productivity. This situation begs the question of what role there is for small-scale wind turbines.

The response to the question is two-fold. On one level, big wind turbines are here to stay: they tap an inexhaustible renewable energy resource in a world that is carbon-emissions constrained, and they are cost-effective. In the middle of the twentieth century, we did not build large wind turbines because we simply did not have the technology to build them strong enough to stand up to the power of the wind over time. An interesting case in point is the experimental 1-MW wind turbine erected in Castleton, Vermont, in the 1940s. After only about 700 hours of use, it collapsed and needed to be removed. For decades, no new attempt was made to build such a large turbine. However, this technological challenge has been overcome. Large turbines now have an insurmountable cost advantage over small ones. As long as we continue to use wind energy to make electricity, most of it will come from big turbines.

However, there will still be a niche role for small-scale wind, for at least two reasons. First, there will always be remote, windy locations where the grid cannot reach, where customers want electricity, and where an off-the-grid wind system provides the most cost-effective way to meet the need. Having enough wind is site-specific, but in some locations with a good wind resource, a small wind turbine may be more cost-effective than a PV system for off-grid remote power, especially in cloudier locations. This is especially true at higher latitudes where a solar array may have very low productivity around the winter solstice and wind generation may be essential to make sure there is sufficient electricity overall to meet demand.

As a second and perhaps more philosophical motivation, small wind systems installed in suitable locations exploit a renewable energy resource that otherwise would not be available. Large wind farms can be delayed for all sorts of reasons: turbine-production backlogs, grid-connection problems, or local opposition. In the meantime, every increment of renewable energy large or small helps. If there is a good site for a small wind turbine on your property, chances are that no one but you will develop it.

Other wind site and system sizing considerations

Regardless of whether a proposed project is for a single small turbine or a large utility-scale facility, local topography greatly influences how fast the wind blows on average, from one potential site to the next; features such as mountains, hills, valleys, and water bodies channel, divert, or diffuse the wind, affecting its power. In this sense, wind is different from solar: if you get a certain amount of sun in one part of the locality in which you live (such as your county or greater metropolitan area), then you will probably get about the same amount in any other part, assuming the site is not shaded. For wind energy, the developmental approach is to find the windiest possible sites that are accessible both to the transmission grid and, from there, to markets where there is demand for electricity. If the project is a single turbine that makes electricity for a local use, such as a factory (e.g., Harbec Plastics in Ontario, NY) or a ski resort (e.g., Jiminy Peak in Massachusetts), then the grid connection concern goes away.

The industry standard is to first use a *wind map* of a region, which could include a single U.S. state or several states. Wind maps give a rough estimate of average wind speed in locations on the map based on regional prevailing winds and local terrain. The map indicates relative wind strength using color-coding. A wind professional or homeowner scouting for a new location or evaluating a specific location can get an initial sense of the relative wind strength from the map color. In the east, good locations for wind are typically on the tops of ridges that catch prevailing winds from the west, for example on hilltops to the south and east of Lake Ontario in New York State, or on ridge tops in the Allegheny or Blue Ridge Mountains further south. In the Great Plains, vast areas have sufficient wind for wind farms so that developers can predict output based on nearby existing wind farms. Similar options arise in other major wind markets such as China and the European Union.

The need for height above the ground and access to mountain ridges creates a dilemma for wind. Opinions about the aesthetics of big wind turbines are mixed. Some people do not mind them, or even think they look "cool," but others dislike or even detest them. For persons living in a rural location that is at first surrounded only by forests and fields, it may feel as if the arrival of a wind farm in their neighborhood is leading to the industrial development of the countryside and greatly affecting the bucolic feeling of a location.

Big picture view: The role of wind in the renewable portfolio

As we have seen, wind energy production has been growing around the world, spurred on by strong wind resources available in many locations and an ever more cost-effective technology. In the case of the U.S., back in the 2000s the "20 by 30" report envisioned a robust role for wind energy, and the industry has made great strides toward that vision, with wind emerging as the most productive renewable electricity source in the country.

Even as U.S. wind capacity has grown, however, the rate of wind energy installations in the U.S. has slipped compared to the pathway needed to reach 20% market share of electricity by 2030, as envisioned in USDOE's report. The shortfall may be partly due to local opposition to specific projects and perhaps due to lack of sufficient policy support. As shown in Fig. 16, installations actually outpaced the 20x30 pathway up through 2012. From 2013 onward, however, the national industry slipped into a pattern of installing 5 GW to 13 GW per year whereas the report proposed a goal of installing 16 GW per year starting in 2018 and keeping this pace approximately to 2030. The only exception was the year 2020, when the industry actually exceeded the 16 GW target, installing 17 GW in that year. Historic installation rates vary widely because of tax policy; for example, 2012 was an outstanding year, with 13 GW installed because a tax incentive was on the verge of expiring. Nevertheless, examining the historical 2006-2021 trend as represented by the dashed line in Fig. 16, shows the long-term average reaching only 11 GW in 2021. Put another way, the 2021 value from Fig. 2 is

~380 billion kWh/y, and if the linear trend were to continue, output would grow by another 378 billion kWh/y in the ensuing nine years. The resulting 758 billion kWh/y in 2030 is approximately double the 2021 output, but well short of the 1.2 trillion kWh that the 20-by-30 report envisions.

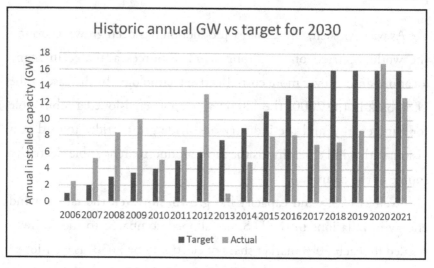

Figure 16 Actual annual installed capacity trajectory of U.S. wind 2006-2021 versus 20-by-30 pathway, with linear trend line fitted to actual installed capacity.
Sources: for actual installations, American Wind Energy Association; for 20-by-30 pathway, U.S. Department of Energy.

One possible way out of the not-in-my-back-yard dilemma is to concentrate wind development in the Great Plains and grow long-distance transmission. Another strategy is to build wind turbines offshore instead of on land. On both the coasts and in the Great Lakes, average winds are typically even stronger than those on the ridgetops of the northeast, and if the turbines are built far enough from land, they are over the horizon and not visible. This strategy has worked well in

Europe where the North Sea has large areas of shallow water far from land where the turbine foundations rest on the sea floor. Unfortunately, as the developers of the now-defunct Cape Wind Project in Nantucket Sound in Massachusetts can attest, the shallow water along the eastern seaboard is often too close to land to put turbines out of visual range from the beach, leading to local opposition.

Nevertheless, even though Cape Wind did not come to fruition, efforts in the region around Rhode Island, Massachusetts, and Long Island have continued. The first offshore wind project in the U.S. to successfully reach completion and come online, the five-turbine, 30-MW Block Island Wind Farm, started producing power in 2016. As of 2019, its developer, Deepwater Wind, is designing a much larger 1000-MW project between the eastern end of Long Island and Martha's Vineyard. The development of floating turbines is emerging as another possible solution. Wind developers can position these devices in deeper water but anchor them to the sea floor to keep them in place. Not only might floating turbines solve the aesthetic problem, but they could go after even stronger wind resources that are found further out from shore. Also, floating turbines would greatly increase the total resource that is available along the U.S. eastern seaboard since locations with sufficient wind, shallow water, and sufficient distance from the shore to avoid aesthetic objections are limited. As of 2022, floating turbines are in the testing stage; there are not yet any large-scale commercial wind farms based on this technology.

Lastly, with continued installation of on-shore wind farms and the expansion into offshore wind, the wind energy sector can evolve into a vast and robust complement to the solar sector, and together they can complement each other to provide power day and night in summer and winter. However, these are not the only renewable energy sources. Renewable options can be highly location-specific, and a specific community or region may be endowed with other types of renewable sources. These others may not be as large as wind or solar, but they still have a role to play. The next chapter considers other renewables, such as water-based sources, biomass, and geothermal energy.

CHAPTER 7

A Supporting Role for Other Renewable Sources

The previous two chapters covered solar and wind energy, which together can provide a foundation for an energy system based on renewables. The energy sources covered in this chapter represent a collection of resources that can play a supporting role in the renewable energy economy. Their total availability in terms of maximum amount of energy is less than that of solar and wind, and they may not be as widely distributed. However, the technologies in this chapter usually also have some unique advantage that creates their niche within the overall energy mix. For hydro, tidal, and wave power, it is the concentration of energy in the form of moving water, which is more energy dense than wind or sunlight since water is a relatively heavy medium. For geothermal and biomass energy, it is dispatchability: we can control when the energy system does or does not produce, which is handy for an energy market where the timing of energy consumption is not known in advance. Some of the resources discussed also do double duty, as they extract energy from waste, thereby reducing the waste stream and at the same time generating energy. The reasons for these advantages are explained in greater detail later in the chapter.

From these various niche sources, a blueprint for a diverse renewables-based energy future emerges that is more cost-effective than one based purely on solar and wind. It is also a blueprint that can address both the short- and long-term variability problems that confront dependence on intermittent solar and wind energy.

Large-scale Hydropower

In terms of large amounts of renewable energy being made available in a concentrated form, there is perhaps no better example than large-scale hydropower. Large-scale hydropower is also the oldest form of electrical generation from a renewable energy source. Developers began generating electricity from hydropower at Niagara Falls as early as 1882.

Hydropower draws on the hydrologic cycle of evaporation and precipitation– circulation between the earth's surface and the atmosphere – by tapping into the downward movement of water from high points on the land to low points, with sea level usually as the lowest point. Fully one-fifth of the incoming energy from the sun flows into evaporating water at the earth's surface and lifting it into the atmosphere.[31] From there, it eventually falls back down to the surface of earth, where much of it falls in the oceans, is absorbed by plant life, or sinks into the water table below the ground. However, some fraction runs off into streams and eventually into larger rivers, which provide the basis for hydropower.

Hydropower is similar to wind power from Chap. 5 in that a "fluid" (water instead of air) flows past a device that converts natural motion into mechanical, human-made motion. There are differences as well. Hydropower and wind power both produce energy in proportion to the speed of the fluid, so the more water or air mass that is moving through the device, the higher the output, up to the rated maximum output of

---

[31] Sorensen, Bent, 2002, *Renewable Energy: Physics, Engineering, Environmental Impacts, Economics, and Planning.* Elsevier, London.

the device. However, for hydropower, the height from which the water is descending (also known as "head") also impacts the output since higher head increases output. To understand this point, consider that a person would do more work to carry a bucket of water up to the top of a mountain than to the top of a small hall. This logic works in the other direction: Water at a higher elevation can do more work when it arrives at the bottom of an elevation than water that starts at a lower elevation. Therefore, the operator of a large hydropower dam desires to keep their reservoir at a higher level so that the turbines in the reservoir can be more productive.

As an illustration of the impact of flow and head, consider a large hydropower dam with 100-MW turbines, where the efficiency from water arriving at the turbine to electricity output is 80%. Suppose in the base case the flow is 100 m³ per second, and the height of the water is 100 meters vertical above the turbine (Table 1). The output would then be 78.4 MW, or ~78% of the maximum.[32] In Scenario 2, output is increased to 94.1 MW by increasing the water level behind the dam to 120 meters. Scenario 3 achieves the same outcome by keeping height constant at 100 meters and increasing flow to 120 m³/second. Note that in both cases the capacity factor has increased to 94% but output is less than the maximum possible from the turbine. In summary, the table shows how a dam operator might increase output either by holding back more water so that the water height behind the dam increases, or by allowing more water volume to flow through the dam. In practice, both options are available to the operator in a real-world setting.

---

[32] This calculation uses the density of water of ~1,000 kg/m³ and the gravitational constant of 9.8 m/s²: Power = (1,000 kg/m³)x(9.8 m/s²)x(100 m height)x(100 m³/s flow)x(80%) = 7.84×10^7 Watts = 78.4 MW.

Scenario	Flow rate (m3/sec)	Height (m)	Output (MW)
S1.Base case	100	100	78.4
S2. Increase height	100	120	94.1
S3. Increase flow	120	100	94.1

Table 1 Illustration of flow and water height scenarios for a 100-MW, 80% efficient hydropower dam.

In comparison to wind energy, hydropower also benefits from the high density of water. A cubic meter of air passing through a wind turbine weighs about 1 kilogram, in rough numbers. A cubic meter of water weighs about 1,000 kilograms. Combine many, many cubic meters per second with a long drop before the water enters the turbine at a dam site, and you are talking about a serious amount of energy. The Hoover Dam, which spans the Colorado River between Nevada and Arizona and was finished in 1939, has a turbine capacity rated at a total of 1,500 megawatts and produces about 4 billion kWh of electricity in a typical year. For comparison, the Fenner wind farm near Syracuse, NY, consists of 20 turbines with a total capacity of 30 MW, typically producing 85 million kWh per year. Output from the Hoover Dam is nearly 50 times higher.

Hydropower is also cost-effective. Although any one large dam is a major investment, the price per kWh is low because dams are so productive. The Hoover dam cost $50 million to build in 1939, or $940 million in today's dollars. That amount is equivalent to just three or four years of electricity revenues, at typical wholesale market rates.[33]

Dam operators manage the amount of water built up behind the dam, the rate of power production, and the amount of flow downstream

---

[33] Cost taken from Bureau of Reclamation website, U.S. Department of the Interior. Cost conversion made using Consumer Price Index (CPI) value of 0.053 for conversion from 1939 to 2018 values. Revenue estimated based on $0.06/kWh paid wholesale.

against multiple and sometimes competing goals. They generate electricity to earn revenue, but they also sell water for irrigation. Sometimes the power production from the dams acts as a complement to production from other sources or variability in demand, rather than to make as much power as possible. Boating or fishing above the dam may depend on a certain minimum level, and swimming and whitewater rafting below the dam may require flow in a certain range, high enough to be viable but not so high as to be dangerous. Like power and agriculture, recreational activities contribute to the regional economy. In addition, waters above the dam may provide habitats and wildlife refuges for fish, animals, or birds. In times of drought, the dam operator may curb output so that some minimum amount of water is available for contingencies. When rains are heavy and extreme rainfall is predicted, the operator may accelerate the release of water through the dam to create space in the reservoir to be able to buffer an expected influx and prevent downstream flooding.

Opportunities for large-scale hydropower have largely been used up around the world (Table 2). In earlier years, the largest dams were in the United States, such as the current largest U.S. dam, the Grand Coulee in Washington State. Over time, dams in other countries have surpassed Grand Coulee: The James Bay complex in Canada, the Itaipu Dam on the Parana River between Brazil and Paraguay, and most recently the world's largest dam, the Three Gorges Dam on the Yangtze River in China.

Name	Country	Capacity (MW)
Three Gorges Dam	China	22400
Itaipu	Paraguay/Brazil	12600
St James Bay complex	Canada	10000
Grand Coulee	USA	6480
High Aswan	Egypt	2100
Hoover Dam	USA	1500

Table 2 Examples of major world hydropower dams

The pace of building large new hydropower dams has dwindled in large part because public opinion that was originally favorable has now turned against them. "In the view of conservationists," writes John McPhee about the life and work of environmentalist David Brower, "dams represent...the absolute epicenter of Hell on Earth (McPhee, 1971, p.158)." Even if hydropower reduces air pollution and greenhouse gases (GHGs) emitted from burning fossil fuels, the effect on local ecosystems and local communities can be profound, not to mention the inundation of unique natural landscapes and GHGs from any inundated plants and trees as they decay. Historically, hydropower started with the least intrusive sites and gradually developed more and more contentious ones. Take one of the earliest large hydropower resources at Niagara Falls: the impoundment area for this hydropower facility was the entirety of Lake Erie, and all that was needed was the channel to go around the waterfall. The Hoover Dam was met with enthusiasm and support in the 1930s, both because it brought much-needed jobs and investment during the Great Depression, and also because it put an end to devastating flooding along the lower Colorado River. Starting in the 1950s and 1960s, however, opposition grew. The Glen Canyon Dam, with the flooding of Lake Powell, was built over public opposition based on concern over inundating picturesque canyons and loss of access to land. Other dams proposed for the southwest were planned but not built at all, thanks to the opposition of Brower, the Sierra Club, and other groups.

On the international stage, other more recent dams have been completed at the expense of profound local effects, often because the terrain is flatter than that of mountainous regions such as the Rockies in the western U.S. The flooded area needed to be much larger to create a high enough dam to deliver the desired amount of energy. In a number of cases, it seemed that authorities might finish one dam project but leave such a bad taste in everyone's mouth that there was no stomach for further projects. For example, the Hydro-Quebec project in the northern reaches of the province of Quebec in Canada generates power for much of eastern Canada and the northeastern U.S., but it has also inundated the ancestral lands of the Cree nation. Protests both by the Cree and their supporters in the region confronted much of the building of the project during its construction phase from 1970 to 1984; latter phases of the project have been shelved and may never be built. The Itaipu Dam on the Parana River in Brazil and Paraguay generates up to 90 billion kWh of electricity per year, but it has also flooded a vast expanse of forests. Perhaps the most controversial is also the largest of all, namely the Three Gorges Dam in China, whose first turbine began operating in 2003. At a total output of more than 22,000 megawatts, it dwarfs the Hoover Dam, but it also has a 400-plus mile long catchment area and has displaced more than a million residents and covered up numerous historical sites. In terms of life-cycle analysis of carbon emissions, any dam has a certain amount of embodied energy in its construction materials that must be accounted for, but the Three Gorges will also lead to the release of vast amounts of captured carbon from trees and other plants whose carbon content will be released to the atmosphere as they decay. The dam will therefore require years of electricity output to "pay back" these emissions before it can begin having an impact on reducing China's net CO_2 emissions. The World Bank originally supported this project but before long withdrew support due to concerns about negative side effects.

Along with opposing the construction of additional large dams, the U.S. has moved in the direction of deconstructing smaller, antiquated U.S. dams. The largest deconstruction project in recent years has been that of the 15-MW Elwha River Dam in Washington State, which was removed in 2012. In this case, the negative impact of the dam on the local environment including the salmon habitat outweighed any carbon-free electricity benefit, and the decision was taken to remove the dam.

Outside the U.S., there are still some places in the world where large dams in the hundreds or thousands of megawatts are under construction or planned. A leading example is the Rogun Dam along the Vakhsh River in Tajikistan, which has been under construction in this landlocked central Asian country by fits and starts for the past 30 years. The site is located in a remote, deep mountain valley, and if finished as planned would be the world's highest at 335 meters from the base to the top of the dam, with a capacity of 3,600 MW. In 2018 the Tajik government opened the first phase of this dam with the completion of the first 75 meters of the dam. Another example is the proposed 2,000-MW Kambarata-1 Dam in nearby Kyrgyzstan, which is planned, but on which ground has not yet been broken. The Rogun and Kambarata Dams are found in locations that are favorable to large hydropower: they have low population density, are found in mountainous regions so that the amount of inundated land is less, and are not competing with other land uses such as agriculture or forestry. Slow progress comes not from local opposition but from challenging economic conditions in Kyrgyzstan and Tajikistan, as well as the challenging, remote construction sites.

Small-scale Hydropower

A single large dam may be able to generate thousands of megawatts of power, but significant amounts of hydropower can also be developed through many small-scale hydropower systems that are distributed over a wide area. Of the approximately 70 GW capacity currently in use in small-scale hydro worldwide, some 38 GW are installed in China and allocated among thousands of village and rural systems, constituting more than the rated capacity of the Three Gorges Dam. According to the U.S. Office of Energy Efficiency and Renewable Energy, there is potential in the U.S. for an additional 30 GW of capacity in 49 out of 50 states (excluding Delaware), spread across more than 5,000 sites (USDOE, 2010).[34]

There is not a precise dividing line between large- and small-scale hydropower, but small-scale hydro can be considered as systems up to 10 or 20 MW. Many of these systems fall under the heading of *run-of-the-river* hydropower, which divert a portion of a river's flow to turn a hydroelectric turbine, generating electricity. These projects are attractive because they do not require impounding large amounts of water behind a dam, inundating land, or relocating human settlements. On the other hand, they do generally require some type of structure upstream from the plant at the point of siphoning off a part of the stream, such as a *weir*, a type of dam that allows water to pass over the top but also has an intake point for the plant. Also, they are susceptible to seasonal changes in water flow and cannot regulate output by storing up water to be released through the turbine during periods of peak demand. Finally, at the low-capacity end of small hydro, there is a separate category of *micro-hydropower* devices that can be used for a single household and have ratings as small as 500 Watts. For example, a home might be located next to a stream that runs continuously through the year with

---

[34] Source: U.S. Department of Energy (2010).

a measurable elevation drop so that a micro-hydro turbine could be installed in the stream, and then the power could be transmitted to the house via electric cable.

The history of small hydro for electricity begins at the same time as the development of large hydro sites such as that of Niagara Falls. It predates the small-scale generation of electricity from both wind and solar PV. Already in the late 1800s, small hydro turbines were being used to power early local electricity grids. The passage of the Public Utilities Regulatory Policy Act (PURPA) in 1978 opened a new chapter for small run-of-the-river plants as some plants that had fallen out of use in the 1960s and 1970s found a new opportunity to provide green energy under a regulatory framework that favored small producers.

The following presentation on small hydro uses two examples local to the area of Ithaca, NY. The first example is Cornell University's 1.2-MW hydropower plant, an operating small hydro system built on Fall Creek within the Ithaca city limits that contributes to the electricity supply of the campus. The published maximum capacity of the turbines in this plant is 1.9 MW, but the capacity of the *penstock*, or upstream pipe that delivers the water from the creek to the plant, limits output to no more than 1.2 MW. Geographically, the region around Ithaca features many lakes and valleys with waterways dropping hundreds of vertical feet over distances of a few miles, so it lends itself to hydropower development. One of the first local lighting systems in the U.S. was built on Fall Creek in Ithaca and used a small turbine to power electric lights starting in 1883. The Cornell plant operates today in the same location as this initial turbine. First put in service in 1904, the plant fell out of use in 1970, but it was renovated and reopened in 1981. Water is diverted at an upstream location and drops via the penstock over a vertical distance known as *head height* of 42 meters, or 138 feet, into the turbine to provide power.

The following calculation illustrates the output from this facility. First, there are losses in the water traveling from the intake to the turbine due to friction and turbulence in the water flow, so the practice is to use a "net head" value that is lower than the physical drop. In this case the net head is 35 meters or approximately 115 feet, a reduction of 7 meters (23 feet) compared to the unadjusted head height. The efficiency of the system in terms of electricity output as a function of power available in the water flow is approximately 80%. The maximum flow that the turbine can accommodate is 4.4 m³/second (~155 ft³/sec); any flow above this amount simply remains in the stream and flows past the plant. The product of head, flow, the density of water, and the gravitational constant then give the output of 1.2 MW (Table 3). At the low end of water flow, the operator must always leave the first 10 ft³/sec in the stream, and additionally the plant requires a minimum of 7 ft³/sec of net flow to begin turning. Therefore, at times when total flow in the creek drops below 17 ft³/sec, the plant output drops to zero.

Factor	Units	Value
Vertical	Meters	35.00
Flow	m3/second	4.40
Density	kg/m3	1000
Efficiency	--	80%
Gravity	m/s2	9.8
Output (Approx)	Watts	1200000
	MW	1.2

Table 3 Example calculation of conditions at maximum output for Cornell University Hydropower plant.

As with solar output in Chapter 4 and wind output in Chapter 5, seasonality of small hydro is an important factor. Figure 1 shows monthly output for this plant for the years 2011, 2012, 2015, and 2016. During 2013 and 2014, the plant was taken off-line for many months during each year for renovation and upgrade, so these years are not included in the figure. This region experiences a typical northeastern U.S. climate where monthly rainfall declines into a trough in the summer months; consequently, plant output also drops so that capacity factors are in the 1%-15% range.[35] In July of 2016, output fell to zero for the month. Overall, annual output ranged from a low of 4.1 million kWh (2012) to a high of 5.5 million kWh (2011) for the years shown. Assuming that this seasonal pattern would be representative of small hydro in the region generally, it can play a complementary role to solar PV, which peaks in the summer months (see Chapter 4).

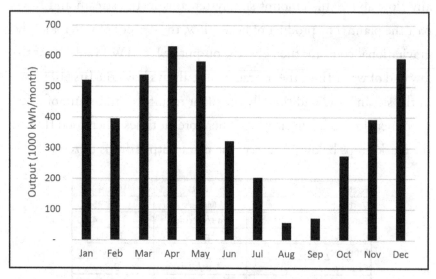

Figure 1 Cornell 1.2-MW hydropower plant average monthly production 2011-2016 in kWh.

Data source: Cornell University Utilities & Energy Management.

---

[35] Recall from earlier chapters that the capacity factor is the ratio of actual production to production that would have occurred if the plant had operated at its maximum capacity for a given period of time. For example, a month with 30 days has 720 hours, so the maximum possible production is (1.2 MW) x (720 hr.) = 864 MWh. If the plant were to produce 8.64 MWh in a given September, its capacity factor would be 1%.

The data from this plant also show how small hydro can achieve very high capacity factor values when flow is high. During the highest producing month in the figure, May 2011, the plant produced 800,000 kWh over 31 days. If it had operated continuously at 1.2 MW, it would have produced ~893,000 kWh, so the capacity factor is roughly 90%. That means that if the maximum possible flow is 4.4 m³/s, as in Table 3, the average flow would be 90% of this amount, or about 3.9 m³/s. The overall annual capacity factor is lower in large part due to the drop-off in production in the summer months. Averaged across the four years in the figure, the average annual output is 4.6 million kWh, which works out to a capacity factor of 44%.

The second example of hydropower is based on a feasibility study for a small hydro system in Ithaca, NY, in Six Mile Creek, a parallel creek to the above example.[36] The location is called First Dam, which is a small dam with a 59-foot vertical drop to a turbine location where power could be generated. The site was in fact used to power a drinking water treatment plant up until 1911, when the plant switched to a gravity-fed water supply system and power from the plant was no longer needed. Analysis is based on a turbine with a rated mechanical capacity of 277 kW and electrical capacity of 256 kW, based on the characteristics of the flow that was available.

For a small hydro system of large enough size to produce electricity for public use (as opposed to a household-sized system), the analysis begins with data on the historical distribution of flow levels. For the U.S., the U.S. Geologic Survey gathers flow data at their network of "stream gages" around the country. These devices track the flow in cubic feet per second over time, and the USGS then uploads the

---

[36] Results are found in Jeyapandian et al (2017). Acknowledgment: Thanks to Cornell Engineering students Lesslie Jeyapandian, Arriman Makmoen, Garret Quist, and Defeng Tao for their work on this study.

historical record of the data to a government website. The analyst can then calculate average annual flow and the distribution of flow values around the average.

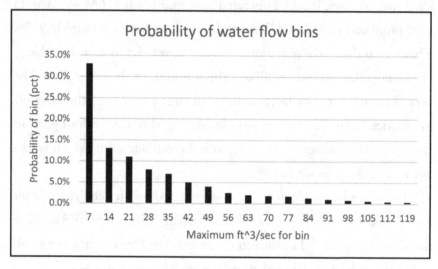

Figure 2 Estimated flow distribution at First Dam, proposed hydropower site on Six Mile Creek in Ithaca, NY, based on historical 2003-2015 USGS stream gage flow data.

For the proposed hydropower site, the analyst team used data from two nearby stream gages to interpolate the approximate distribution of flow at the site (Fig. 2). The flow value in cubic feet per second (cfs) is shown along the horizontal axis; for example, the first bin on the left represents all the times in an average year when flow is between 0 and 7 cfs. Then the vertical axis gives the probability that flow is in the range shown in the bin. When compared with the pattern for a representative windspeed distribution for a wind energy site given in Chap. 6, there are both similarities and differences. Both curves have several bins at the upper end where the probability of being in the bin is low, but when the values do occur, output is high. (To keep the figure compact, a small number of high flow and low probability bins are not shown.) Unlike the wind speed distribution, however, the lowest flow bin (0-7 cfs) has the highest probability, and from there, the probability declines continuously as flow speed increases. Overall, the mean flow is ~23.2 cfs.

Estimated average output from the plant uses the predicted hours per year of flow at different values, as in Fig. 2, combined with a proposed turbine and generator technology to predict electricity output. The chosen turbine technology achieves maximum output at 70 cfs; any quantity of flow available in the stream above this amount simply remains in the streambed and bypasses the plant. The system has approximately constant efficiency at 77.5% for either partial (<70 cfs) or full flow, from the motion of the water to electrical output from the generator. Due to losses, the effective head is reduced from 58.9 to 55.8 feet (from 18.0 to 17.0 meters).[37]

When estimating output, flow values from Fig. 2 are modified to reflect limitations on the function of the turbine plant. First, the plant is required to allow the first 4 cfs of flow (assuming there is some measurable amount) to pass the plant at all times of year to maintain the health of the waterway between the intake and outlet of the hydro plant. Second, the plant must receive a minimum of 7 cfs before the turbine begins to turn. Therefore, whenever the output is between 0 and 11 cfs, the plant will not operate. Based on the data in Fig.2, this amounts to a substantial fraction of the year since the first two bins (0-14 cfs) account for 46% of the hours of the year.

Annual output is estimated from the number of hours per year in each bin, the average power in the bin based on the average flow for the

---

[37] The turbine used in the analysis is an Ossberger model A-4098 with 277-kW turbine and transmission to a 256-kW generator. The maximum output calculation can be verified using 1000 kg/m³ density water, 77% efficiency, 17-meter head, 9.8 m/s² gravitational constant, and 1.98 m³/sec flow to arrive at 256 kW of output.

bin, and the system efficiency. For example, for the 14-21 cfs bin, the average flow is 17.5 cfs. Therefore, the flow available to the turbine is 6.5 cfs, and the number of hours per year is 11% or 964 hours per year. The output at 6.5 cfs is 23.8 kW, so the total contribution to output is ~22,900 kWh/yr. This process repeats for all bins in the distribution, including the top bin, which is simply the combination of all bins where flow is >70 cfs and full output is possible. The complete calculation for each individual bin is not shown here, but Table 4 summarizes the contribution from partial and full output conditions, also showing 2,891 hours per year where usable flow and hence output is zero. The process estimates total output at 575,000 kWh/year, for a 26% capacity factor. The system operates at full 256-kW output for 963 hours or just 11% of the year, but this period contributes a disproportionately high amount to the total because the system is so productive. Note that as a simplification, the need for repair and outage downtime when sufficient flow is available does not appear in Table 4. This need would slightly lower the output value.

Output	Flow range	Avge flow	Power	Time	Output
	(cfs)	(cfs)	(kW)	(hrs/yr)	(1000 kWh)
Zero	0 to 11	0	0	2891	0
Partial	11 to 81	31.2	67.0	4906	328.7
Full	81 and up	70	256	963	246.5
TOTAL	All	23.2	65.7	8760	575.2

Table 4 Summary of contribution to estimated annual output for proposed 256-kW hydropower plant from stages of turbine operation at First Dam, Ithaca, NY.

Table 4 concludes the example of analyzing a small proposed hydro system. The benefit comes from ~575 MWh/year of carbon-free energy and the compact nature of the hydropower system. In the region in question, producing the same amount of electricity annually using solar PV requires three acres of panels, so there is some benefit to using small hydro instead of solar in terms of saving space. Otherwise, lack of information about project costs and the open-ended nature of the project complicated efforts to fully estimate the cost per kWh. In terms of estimating the cost per kWh to produce electricity, the capital cost of the generating equipment is known accurately. Other costs are not as clear. For example, the dam was already built, but it requires some upgrading and refurbishment, the cost of which is uncertain. The cost of connecting the plant to a load is also uncertain. Lastly, the cost of completing the environmental impact statement and evaluation of impact on the stream is difficult to estimate, because in recent years there are few examples of small hydro systems coming online in the U.S. where the developer paid for this process. Instead, growth in the small hydro market has been driven by opportunities to take currently permitted and operating hydro plants and to upgrade the technology to increase output. To conclude, it would be premature to try to estimate the cost of dam repairs, grid interconnection, and environmental impact assessment. However, one first step toward a cost estimate is possible: the quoted cost for just the turbine and generator system is $250,000, so if one were to recoup this cost in 10 years using simple payback using the estimated ~575,000 kWh/year output, each kWh sold would need to recover $0.0434 to pay back this investment. Including all other elements would significantly increase the cost per kWh.

Other Energy Sources Based on Water Movement

The remaining water motion-based energy sources are those available at or near the ocean shore using tides, waves, or currents. Energy systems based on thermal energy in water are covered later in this chapter.

209

With tides, different designs are competing to exploit this resource. Locations for any of these designs are chosen so that the underwater terrain, combined with large tides, provides a sufficient flow of water with each ebb and flow tide to produce significant amounts of energy. The energy is of course available only with the movement of the tides, but it is very predictable compared to other intermittent resources such as wind or sun since tidal patterns are known with great accuracy. A 20-MW tidal power station at Annapolis Royal, Nova Scotia, Canada has operated since 1984 by allowing high tides into an area through a sluice that then closes at ebb tide, forcing the water out through the turbine. A 240-MW station at Rance on the Normandy coast of France opened in 1966 and operates in a similar way. More recently, the Korea Water Resources Corporation opened the 254-MW Sihwa Lake Tidal Power Plant in 2011.

Other tidal power designs are also under development that resemble water-power turbines from hydroelectric stations immersed in coastal water without creating a structure to capture and channel the high tide. As an example of this type of tidal energy development, Marine Current Turbines Ltd. of the United Kingdom first began operating an experimental 300 kW turbine off the southwest coast of England in 2003. From 2009 to 2017 MCT operated a commercial-scale 1.2-MW turbine in Strangford Lough in Northern Ireland. This resource could also be developed on the U.S. side along the Maine coast. In general, though, the U.S. has fewer good locations for tidal energy than countries at more northern latitudes such as Canada or the European Union because higher latitudes generally have larger tides, and larger tides provide greater opportunity for power generation. The Golden Gate Narrows adjacent to San Francisco and the East River around New York City are some exceptions because of the characteristics of tides that flow in and out of these bodies of water.

Another form of energy available along coastlines is the energy in waves. One design for a wave energy station consists of a structure that channels the incoming wave into a chamber with an entry on one end for the waves and an orifice for air to pass on the other end. As the air pressure in the chamber changes due to the entry and exit of the waves, air flows in and out of the chamber through the orifice, driving a turbine mounted on the other end of the orifice, thereby generating electricity. An experimental, grid-connected 250-kW station based on this principle operated on the island of Islay in Scotland between 2000 and 2012. As an example of a different type of wave energy, developers in Sweden began operation in 2015 of a prototype 3-MW wave energy conversion system with devices that rise and fall in the waves to drive a turbine and generate power.

The U.S. may also have a large ocean-energy resource available in the form of currents, specifically in the Gulf Stream, if a successful technology can be developed. One concept for developing this resource is to suspend below the surface an underwater turbine, tethered to the ocean floor, which rotates as the current passes through it. Although there are no prototypes currently in trial use anywhere in the world, the potential development of this energy source has appeal in that the current is close to shore (15 or 20 miles away) and provides energy in a concentrated fashion (the speed at its core is four miles per hour or more), and unlike tidal energy, flows continuously. Challenges include keeping a tethered object under water at the right depth to capture the current (and also well below levels where they might interfere with shipping) and creating a very durable device that can remain submerged for long periods of time or possibly for its entire useful lifetime. In general, coastal energy systems that depend on waves, tides, or currents operate in a harsh, salty environment where durability is a challenge, but they may eventually provide significant amounts of power that are frequently located close to coastal population centers.

Francis M. Vanek

Biological Energy Sources

Biological energy in its essence accesses solar energy that has been stored in the physical structure of plants or trees and converts it into heat, electricity, or both. This section focuses on bioenergy from crops or forest products. Bioenergy from the waste stream is covered in the next section, and bioenergy for passenger and freight transportation is covered in Chap. 8.

In its simplest form, humans have used bioenergy for cooking and warmth since prehistoric times. Dispatchability is one of its key features. With proper storage, supplies of dried wood, wood products, or plant products can be accumulated and retained until the energy is needed, at which point they are combusted for the chosen application.

One of the challenges with bioenergy is that it is very heterogeneous. Both plant materials and wood products have a wide range of characteristics based on the different species of plant or trees. Sources can vary in terms of the regions in which they can be grown, the productivity per acre or hectare of land, the energy density of the eventual energy product (in terms of Btu per pound for example), and other factors. Growing conditions are also variable and uncertain, and crops will respond in different ways to variation in amount of sunshine, temperature level, or amount of rainfall. Some representative values for crops and forest products used for heat and for biofuels are shown in Table 5.

Energy type	Source	Million Btu/acre/yr
Wood	Hardwood forest	12.5
	Softwood forest	7.5
Ethanol	Corn crop	27.1
	Sugar cane crop	42.4
Biodiesel	Soybean crop	6.9

Table 5 Representative values of energy productivity per acre for bio-energy sources and biofuels from agriculture and forest products.

Note: Table assumes one harvest per year. Values shown are subject to variability and are influenced by specific species of tree or hybrid of plant grown, positive or negative growing conditions in a given year, and other factors.

A starting point for evaluating crop bioenergy is assessing the amount of energy that can continuously be harvested per unit of area of land. Although variability for the above reasons affects productivity, a typical rate for harvesting wood as a heat source that can be sustained long-term without depleting the forest is half a cord of wood, or 64 cubic feet, per acre per year. There is substantial variability in wood energy content, with hard woods having higher energy content and greater weight per cord. As an average, 64 cubic feet of wood translates to 10 million Btu of energy content (the average of hardwood and softwood values shown in Table 5). Therefore, since one acre produces 64 cubic feet or 10 million Btu, a forested area 10 miles on a side (i.e., 100 square miles or 64,000 acres) could produce 640 billion Btu per year for heating purposes. One strategy to increase the productivity of woody material production for heating per acre per year is "short-rotation coppicing." In this approach, the manager grows a species, such as willow, continuously on a parcel of land, and woody branches are frequently harvested for energy purposes.

Once a supply chain for gathering wood- or plant-based crops exists, there are several possible applications for energy conversion. The simplest is to heat a single structure with a wood-burning stove of some type. In past centuries, society could allow fireplaces and stoves to be inefficient and buildings poorly insulated because the overall human population was much smaller, and the amount of heated space was lower. At the present time, however, wood combustion in single homes (or small businesses of a similar size) must be energy-efficient if wood is to make a measurable contribution to overall winter heat energy demand in the U.S. and other countries. Furthermore, society has become much more demanding of local air quality levels than in past centuries, meaning that household-size wood stoves must have effective and robust emissions control systems to have a consequential impact on the overall heating load.

A high-efficiency wood-burning stove in regions with a moderate winter such as the northeastern U.S. might heat a well-insulated, medium-sized home (1500 to 2000 square feet) with one cord of wood per winter. This amount is equivalent to the harvest from two acres of forest on a continual basis. This standard sets an ambitious target for heating with wood. Many factors, including a less-efficient stove, less insulation, larger number of square feet of heated space, or a harsher winter could contribute to greater wood consumption.

In a more complex option, a single larger burner can combust wood in a central location and then distribute the heat to multiple buildings in a heating district. Large-scale, centralized burning has the potential for lower cost per building and higher burn temperature, leading to fewer particulate emissions generated. The Cobb Hill community in central Vermont uses a system like this to provide heat to 23 homes with a single heating center. During the heating season, a central hot water tank is kept continuously hot by periodically burning loads of wood. As heat is needed in the heating district, pumps circulate hot water from the heating center to the houses. Water is then returned to the heating center to be heated again.

The most complex option is to burn wood for generating electricity, either on its own or in combination with coal or natural gas. Byproduct heat may also be circulated for heating purposes to create a combined heat and power (CHP) system. In 2014, 43 billion kWh or about 1% of the U.S. electricity supply came from wood.

As an example of what it might cost to generate electricity from wood, an economic analysis is provided here using representative values for a 50-MW wood-burning plant. This is the same size as the 50-MW Joseph McNeil generating station outside of Burlington, Vermont, which generates electricity from wood biomass. The calculations use representative capital, operating, and fuel cost values from the literature. The example plant generates steam that turns a turbine and generator, with an overall efficiency from fuel to electricity output of 35%. The energy content of the wood is 18.6 million Btu per ton, and the cost to the plant operator is $32 per ton including delivery. The plant consumes 138,000 tons of wood per year; so based on the wood energy content and efficiency, the output is 899 billion Btu per year, which converts to ~264 million kWh per year.

Turning to the investment required, the unit capital cost of a wood plant is $4300 per kW, which is higher than that of a large natural gas fired plant. Therefore, the total cost for a 50-MW plant is $215 million, or $17.25 million per year when annualized.[38] Operating cost not including

---

[38] Capital cost calculated using a 20-year lifetime and 5% discount rate. For comparison, if the cost of electricity were based on 20-year simple payback instead, the reader can verify that the annualized capital cost would be $10.75 million, and the production cost would be ~$0.082/kWh.

fuel is estimated at $0.0245/kWh, or $6.45 million per year for the proposed 50-MW plant. The fuel cost is $4.42 million per year.

The results are summarized in Table 6. The plant has an overall higher levelized cost of $0.107/kWh. This price is higher than the production cost for electricity from natural gas although the CO_2 emissions are 100% from biological energy at the combustion stage since no fossil fuels are combusted. The relatively small plant size keeps the total forested area required to fuel the plant small and therefore regional in nature, compared to fossil-fired plants that draw from a national delivery grid for coal or gas, where fuels can come from hundreds or thousands of miles away. As shown, the plant is built with a 50-MW nameplate capacity, but produces at an average of about 30 MW, for a 60% capacity factor.

Component	Value	Units
Technical components		
Wood fuel input	138000	tons/yr
Equiv. energy input	2,569	bil.btu/year
Overall efficiency	35%	
Electricity output	899	bil.btu/year
	263.6	Mil.kwh/yr
Average output	30.1	MW
Capacity factor	60%	
Economic components		
Capital cost	$17.25	million/year
Operating cost	$ 6.45	million/year
Fuel cost	$ 4.42	million/year
Total cost	$28.12	million/year
Unit production cost	$ 0.107	per kWh

Table 6 Summary of technical and economic analysis for example 50-MW wood-fired power plant.

There are several challenges with electricity from biomass energy. Often, wood-fired plants require a backup fossil fuel source since wood supplies can be seasonal and in certain months the full supply needed to meet a given demand level may not be available. In this case, the plant maintains steady output but of course is no longer delivering 100% fossil-free electricity. Another concern is local air pollution since some U.S. plants have been cited for excessive emissions and encountered local opposition on this point before. Woody materials are also more susceptible to deterioration as a feedstock than fossil fuels and require greater care, for example, to protect them from water and moisture.

There are some general limitations that apply to all types of biomass used as an energy source. Compared to solar and wind, they are not as productive per unit of land area, so they are not as able to cover a large fraction of overall energy demand. For example, a community seeking a carbon-free heat source during the winter months might choose to purchase wind-generated electricity that is produced on windy but agriculturally poor land, perhaps at some distance from their location. The community could then use ground- or air-source heat pumps (described in a later section in this chapter) to efficiently heat their built infrastructure. This solution avoids problems associated with on-site fuel combustion, emissions, and air quality problems. Even if biomass and biofuels are not an ideal national energy solution, they may be an excellent local one. In smaller communities, in sparsely populated rural America with land available for growing crops or maintaining forests where sun or wind are not as plentiful but soil and rainfall conditions are good for growing, this energy source may work very well. Also, this solution does not rely on long-distance transmission of wind energy, so the community may prefer it if they prioritize a locally independent energy supply.

Energy Recovery from the Waste Stream

Extracting energy from the waste stream comes in several forms. This energy source does double duty not only to meet energy needs but also to reduce the volume and burden of waste disposal. It has an economic advantage as well. Often, the disposer provides the feedstock free of charge or even pays to dispose of it rather than the energy generator needing to pay for it. The size of the waste stream limits the amount of energy that can be generated: Even a robust national system to capture and convert waste can only cover several percent of the overall energy budget, not more. The limiting factor is the amount of embodied energy in the solid waste that society discards as well as the total amount of biological material and heat ending up in our wastewater stream. Still, to the extent that waste energy is feasible, the combined ecological and economic advantages are attractive.

Waste energy recovery resembles biomass energy covered in the previous section because much of the energy content comes from biological sources. However, some of the content does not. Raw materials and products manufactured from plastics and other fossil fuel derived inputs make their way into the solid waste stream and wastewater. When combusted, carbon-based materials release CO_2 and other GHGs into the atmosphere that otherwise would not end up there. Nevertheless, other benefits of energy recovery, such as the prevention of waste plastic making its way into the natural world and oceans, may outweigh the negative consequences of contributing to atmospheric carbon, so some locations may choose to pursue this energy source.

The waste stream can come from many sources, including lumber yards, poultry plants, agroforestry operations, or dairy farms. For example, in the case of dairy farming, agricultural wastes like manure are used as field fertilizer, but farmers can only use the fertilizer at certain times of year. With waste-to-energy conversion, the farmer can dispose of waste to the energy company frequently and on a regular basis year-round, eliminating the hazard associated with accumulating residues for long periods of time.

The remainder of this section covers two examples: wastewater energy recovery at a wastewater treatment plant (WWTP) and energy recovery from municipal solid waste (MSW).

Energy Recovery at Wastewater Treatment Plants

Wastewater energy recovery consists of separating biological materials from treated water, digesting them in an anaerobic digester to make methane, and then combusting the methane to make electricity and heat either for industrial processes or space heating (also called combined heat and power, or CHP). After leaving the biodigester, the gas must be processed to remove CO_2 and trace contaminants (e.g., hydrogen sulfide) so that it can be combusted in a reciprocating engine or turbine without damaging the equipment.

If it does not process the sludge coming from wastewater treatment in some way, a typical WWTP must pay a large fee on an ongoing basis to ship it to a landfill. Therefore, WWTPs have a strong incentive to reduce the volume of flow and possibly capture energy contained in the by-products of water treatment since they can both reduce both landfilling and gas/electricity costs. Table 7 shows a sample of U.S. WWTPs that generate part of their electricity requirement from sludge with microturbines, reciprocating engines, or fuel cells. For many WWTPs, the total energy available in sewage and contents of septic tanks delivered by trucks ("septage") does not generate enough electricity to make the plant self-sufficient for electricity. Therefore, the plant can adapt its biodigestion system to receive other outside waste (e.g., food waste from food processing facilities, waste streams from institutions that may be high in waste food content, etc.) to increase the total potential for electricity production so that the plant can become self-sufficient and even a net generator for neighboring residential and commercial electricity customers. Some WWTPs are seeking to rebrand themselves as "energy centers" at the heart of an energy district, for which the wastewater stream is just one among several energy sources.

Location	Plant Average Flow	Energy Capacity
	(Million gal./day)	(kW-e)
Albert Lea, MN	5	120
Chippewa Falls, WI	2	60
Fairfield, CT	9	200
Flagstaff, AZ	3.5	290
Ithaca, NY	5.5	260
Lewiston, NY	2	60
Santa Maria, CA	7.8	300

Table 7 Average water treated per day and electrical generation capacity for selected U.S. wastewater treatment plants.

Source: U.S. Environmental Protection Agency.

The remainder of this WTTP case study focuses on one of the facilities in Table 7, namely the Ithaca Area Wastewater Treatment Facility, or IAWWTF. It serves approximately 100,000 people with an average flow of approximately 5.5 MGD (million gallons per day) although it has a maximum capacity in peak periods of 30 MGD. The IAWWTF started energy recovery from wastewater treatment when it was opened in the 1980s, and it has recently been expanding its capacity to receive "truck waste" (waste food and other waste biological materials) to reduce the regional waste flow to landfills and reduce its internal electricity purchases from the grid. In 2006, the plant replaced the original Cummins reciprocating engine generators with four 65-kW Capstone microturbines, for a capacity of 260 kW.

The goal of this case study is to estimate the cost of the ancillary equipment needed to generate electricity from waste at the IAWWTF and to calculate the cost of electricity production in $/kWh. Figure 3 shows the flow of waste into and energy products out of the system where each bubble in the schematic includes, if possible, the physical flow volume, energy flow, and revenue or cost (if any). In the configuration shown, the energy that is eventually converted in the microturbines arrives 50% from sewage and 50% from "truck waste" (including septage, food processing waste, portable toilet waste, and animal processing waste). Although the energy contribution is equal, the physical volume of the truck waste is much smaller as the wastewater flow is mostly water (20,000 gallons per day of truck waste, or 20 KGD, versus 5.5 MGD). Energy content passes through the biodigester, enters the CHP system as part of the biogas supply, and is allocated to electricity, heat supply, or thermal losses. Some energy content is of course lost with the sludge that comes out of the biodigester and goes to the landfill ("solids to landfill" in the diagram), but these are not quantified here. Also, the byproduct heat from the CHP does not make a monetary contribution in this case because it is used to heat the biodigester, but in another context, it might be used to reduce grid gas purchases and create another revenue stream.

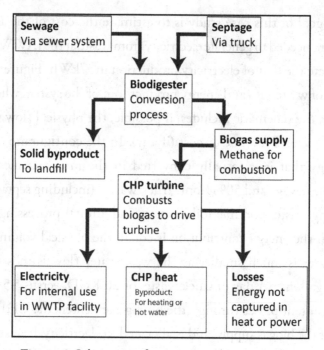

Figure 3 Schematic of wastewater, biogas, and energy flows in wastewater energy recovery system from sewage and truck waste.

In terms of cost or revenue, the WTTP charges a fee to truck waste haulers, which varies according to the desirability of the waste (high energy content versus high contamination) but on average generates $750/day in revenue for 20,000 gallons per day of flow. This amount is slightly more than the daily cost of landfill solids disposal, which amounts to $687 per day at a typical rate of $68.70 per ton. The electricity output of 5800 kWh per day amounts to approximately 2.1 million kWh per year, which is equivalent to a 92% capacity factor for the 260-kW turbine system. At an avoided cost of $0.105/kWh (currently paid by the IAWWTF in this case), the output is worth ~$605/day. The net revenue per day is $668 per day, or ~$244,000 per year. Also, with an additional investment in capital equipment to dry the 10 tons of sludge per day sent to the landfill, this cost can be reduced or even turned into a revenue stream if the quality of the output material can achieve standards set by the U.S. Department of Agriculture, known as "Class A Biosolids." This investment would increase the net revenue over the long term.

The savings, from capturing waste energy in the treated water, comes from a calculated investment in a system to capture and convert organic material (Table 8). The biodigesters are assumed to be in place already since they are required to meet environmental quality requirements for the plant. The capital cost of the remaining required system is estimated at $2,883 per kW, or $749,000 for the 260-kW system, and includes additional equipment beyond the microturbines to purify the gas stream leaving the biodigester. With discounting, this investment converts to ~$60,100 per year.[39] An additional maintenance cost is estimated at an average of $0.02 per kWh generated leading to a total of $42,000/year. Fuel cost actually appears as a credit in the table: If we consider only the net revenue of charging for truck waste but paying for landfill solids, the net positive flow is $23,000 per year. The result is a levelized cost of $0.038/kWh, substantially lower than the avoided cost.

---

[39] $749,000 discounted at 5% over 20 years.

Francis M. Vanek

Component	Value	Units
Technical components		
Energy input	33.73	Bil. Btu/year
	9.5	Mil. kWh/year
Overall efficiency	22%	
Electricity output	7.42	Bil. Btu/year
	2.1	Mil.kwh/yr
Average output	240	kW
Nameplate capacity	260	kW
Capacity factor	92%	
Economic components		
Capital cost	$60,100	per year
Operating cost	$42,000	per year
Fuel cost	($23,000)	million/year
Total cost	$79,100	million/year
Unit production cost	$0.0377	per kWh

Table 8 Summary of technical and economic results for electricity generation at WWTP plant.

Extensions of the system in Fig. 3 are possible. Wastewater flow grows only at the rate that the size of the community grows, but truck waste could be increased to make the plant a net generator of electricity. If so, surplus electricity could be sent to the grid. Another concept is to make the WWTP the core of a district heating and electricity generation system where a district heating loop from the plant would extend to surrounding homes or businesses. These customers could also receive some of the electricity generated as part of the energy district.

Waste-to-Energy Conversion

The second example of waste energy recovery is waste-to-energy, or WTE, applied to municipal solid waste. WTE entails separating combustible materials from non-combustibles (e.g., metals, glass), combusting them in a specialized power generation plant, recovering any residual metals for recycling, and then safely disposing of ash. As an energy source, WTE has the advantage of reducing the volume of space required for landfilling and generating electricity at a relatively low cost because fuel is a credit rather than a cost. WTE requires careful combustion and specialized pollution controls because the burning of certain waste materials such as plastics has the potential to generate toxic byproducts. As mentioned above, WTE is not strictly a zero-CO_2 source, but it may reduce GHG emissions because decomposing waste made of hydrocarbons in a landfill generates methane, a potent GHG, which might be avoided if the hydrocarbon is converted to CO_2 instead.

WTE generated 21.3 billion kWh in the United States in 2014, or about 0.5% of the total electricity supply generated, according to the U.S. Energy Information Administration. WTE facilities are distributed around the country, such as the 39-MW Jamesville plant outside of Syracuse, NY. No new WTE facilities have been opened in the United States in approximately the last 20 years due to disappointing performance on pollution controls and resulting public controversy from an earlier generation of WTE technology. Peer countries in Europe and Asia, notably Japan and Denmark, have in the meantime forged ahead to reduce overall emissions from WTE combustion, and today the general opinion of WTE in those countries, especially as an alternative to landfilling solid waste, is more favorable than in the United States. In Denmark, *fully 97% of the solid waste stream is either recycled or combusted using WTE*, with only 3% going to landfills. WTE facilities in Denmark often operate within or near the urban built environment, reducing haulage distances.

The rest of this section uses the feasibility of a 50-MW WTE plant to explain how this technology works and explore its cost. One possible opportunity for WTE at present is the closing of coal-fired power plants due to unfavorable economics of generating electricity from coal. For example, in the 2012-2015 period, the Cayuga generating station on

Cayuga Lake near Lansing, NY, became uneconomical to operate as a baseload, coal-fired plant and began a conversion process. Often the owners of these plants convert to natural gas combustion to reduce cost as well as emissions. However, some plants might be converted to WTE instead to reduce the need for landfill capacity as well as to generate energy. All figures used in the example come from the U.S. Energy Information Administration, and other government sources, or from similar facilities currently in operation.

The study assumes a 60% capacity factor, which is typical of a coal-fired plant that WTE might replace, to put the two options on equal footing. The capital cost of the proposed WTE plant is $2,060 per kW, or $103 million initial cost, which converts to an annualized capital cost of $8.26 million.[40] The plant would have an overall efficiency of 28.4% from energy content in the waste to electricity going out. This relatively low value reflects the presence of moisture and non-combustibles in the fuel. The favorable economics of the incoming waste stream compensate for this low value, however. The waste has a projected energy content of ~12 million Btu per ton. This energy density value is lower than that of coal (typically on the order of 25 million Btu per ton), so the plant must be prepared to handle a higher volume and mass of incoming waste to generate the same amount of energy. The plant would charge $55 for each ton of waste delivered, and each ton processed would result in revenue of $8 on average, from metals that are recovered after combustion and sold.

The results are shown in Table 9. The process starts with 263,600 tons per year of MSW delivered to the plant, which has an equivalent energy content of ~3.16 trillion Btu. Based on the efficiency of the plant and converting Btu to kWh, the output is 262.8 million kWh per year.

---

[40] The annualized capital cost is the equivalent of $103 million discounted at 5% for 20 years.

The combined annual capital and operating cost for this operation is approximately $28 million per year, but this amount declines to $11.4 million/year after including revenue from MSW tipping fees and earnings from recovering metals. Based on the electricity generated and net cost annually, the production cost is 4.3 cents per kWh.

Component	Value	Units
Technical components		
Energy input	33.73	Bil. Btu/year
	9.5	Mil. kWh/year
Overall efficiency	22%	
Electricity output	7.42	Bil. Btu/year
	2.1	Mil.kwh/yr
Average output	240	kW
Nameplate capacity	260	kW
Capacity factor	92%	
Economic components		
Capital cost	$60,100.00	per year
Operating cost	$ 42,000.00	per year
Fuel cost	$ (23,000.00)	million/year
Total cost	$79,100.00	million/year
Unit production cost	$ 0.038	per kWh

Table 9 Summary of technical and economic results for WTE electricity generation at 50-MW plant.

Compared to other electricity sources, WTE has some unique features. The plant has a relatively high capital cost, and especially high operating cost, compared to a natural-gas-fired plant, due to the complexity of combusting solid waste and the relatively small capacity of the plant, compared to natural-gas-fired plants that may be 1000 MW in size or more. However, it appears that in countries such as Japan or Denmark a network of small, decentralized WTE plants is favored so that the hinterland for obtaining waste for any one plant is not too large, and it is likely that WTE plants will remain relatively small (40–50 MW typical maximum capacity). WTE has the benefits of relatively low cost per kWh, low price volatility thanks to a steady supply of municipal waste, partially avoided CO_2 emissions from combusting waste not derived from fossil fuels, and avoided use of space for landfilling. However, the maximum scope for WTE is limited. Based on typical per capita rates of waste generation and maximal recovery of waste possible, the most electricity that could be generated from WTE would be on the order of 3% of national demand.

Heat Pumps and Energy from Ground, Air, and Water

This section covers a range of technologies and systems that function by moving heat itself, as opposed to technologies presented earlier that either access kinetic energy available in water (i.e., hydropower) or energy available from burning combustible materials (biomass and waste combustion). Here, either technologies move heat into a location that is desired to be warm, or out of a location that is desired to be cool. Sometimes the name "geothermal" energy is applied to this type of energy, but strictly speaking geothermal energy comes from energy found under the ground in reserves of steam or in the temperature of the earth itself. Geothermal energy in the earth can either be shallow (just below the surface, typically at ~50° F) or deep (far below the surface, and much hotter than atmospheric temperature). However, in addition to geothermal energy from under the ground, the atmospheric air surrounding our built environment (air-source heat) and flowing water and bodies of water (water-source heat) can provide heat in a similar way. Systems can extract this energy on different scales, ranging from small household systems to major industrial systems. Along with using these systems to heat spaces during cold weather, these same principles can be applied to cooling spaces during hot weather by using ground, air, or water as a destination into which to move heat, thus cooling a climate-controlled space. A mantra in the industry is the saying "don't make heat – move heat."

Some of these systems use a device called a *heat pump*. Heat normally wants to flow from hot to cold, so systems that exploit this tendency can be relatively simple. For example, suppose you wish to cool a space and have access to a large reservoir of cold water in some form. If you continually circulate cold water from the reservoir through the space, heat will tend to transfer to the cold water, and all that is needed is a device that encourages heat transfer called a *heat exchanger*. However, if you wish to transfer heat against the direction it normally wants to flow, in other words from a colder to a hotter location, then a heat pump is required.

Geothermal Electricity Generation

Geothermal electricity generation is an example of geothermal energy. In these systems, steam from underground is piped into a power plant and run through a turbine to generate electricity, in the same way that a coal-fired power plant expands steam in a turbine. Residual heat downstream from the turbine can be used for process heat or circulated in a district heating system. The steam comes from geologic faults or other underground locations where sources of heat come into contact with subsurface water close to the earth's surface. This resource is attractive because of its low cost, dispatchability, and lack of emissions other than excess steam. The first geothermal power plant opened in Italy in 1904, and today the U.S. is one of the leading producers of geothermal electricity in the world, with 17 billion kWh produced in 2018 (Fig.4), representing about 0.4% of total electricity production. The largest U.S. production is at The Geysers in the Mayacamas Mountains in Northern California, which has a nameplate capacity of 1.5 GW and an average capacity factor of 63%, thus producing 8.3 billion kWh/year, or nearly half of the national total.

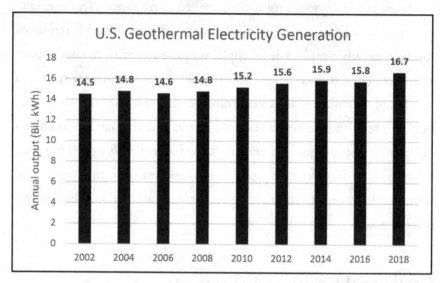

Figure 4 U.S. annual production of geothermal electricity 2002-2018. Source: U.S. Energy Information Administration.

One concern with geothermal power plants is that to be truly renewable, they can only extract steam at the rate that the underground heat source can replenish the available steam. For some geothermal plants, demand for electricity leads to production levels that outstrip this replenishing capacity, and eventually, the plant goes into decline. Also, the development of near-surface steam power generation requires access to sites that have the resource available, and unexploited sites are in limited supply in the U.S. As shown in Fig.4, output increased only slightly from 2002 to 2018, and in any case the figure of 15-17 billion kWh/year is small compared to the overall demand of ~4 trillion kWh. Other countries are better positioned to derive a substantial fraction of their electricity supply from geothermal: Iceland already makes widespread use of geothermal resources for electricity and heating, and Indonesia has large untapped potential.

Another concern is that geothermal plants may contribute to local environmental impact in some cases. A recently opened geothermal plant at Hellisheidi near Rejkyavik in Iceland has suffered from noticeable amounts of hydrogen sulfide mixed in with the released steam, leading to premature deterioration of synthetic components in vehicles, need for more regular cleaning of area houses, and other deterioration.

Enhanced Geothermal Systems

Given the geographic limits of geothermal electricity generation, interest is growing in an alternative that has more widespread potential, called Enhanced Geothermal Systems, or EGS. This technology injects water deep underground to make steam instead of depending on steam resources near the surface. In one approach to the design of an EGS site, geologists identify a stratum of rock underground where high temperatures are available at relatively accessible depths, or through top layers that are relatively easily penetrated. A power plant is then situated on the earth's surface above the underground high-temperature resource, and the two are connected by an injection well and a production well, which go down in the range of 5000 to 20,000 feet below the surface to reach the resource. Water is injected into the injection well and then permeates the region of hot rock at the bottom of the well. As the water boils, the pressure forces the steam up the production well to the top where it is expanded in a steam turbine.

Unlike the surface steam resource, hot rock strata that are suitable for EGS are widely distributed beneath the U.S. land mass. EGS plants are also dispatchable (i.e., able to vary the rate of water injection as demand rises and falls), and as long as the thermal resource is not extracted too quickly, heat from the surrounding rock replenishes heat removed by the working fluid, and the process can continue. One large challenge with EGS is the cost of drilling, which must often take place in rock strata that are harder and deeper than those previously encountered by other industries, such as the oil and gas industry. EGS is still a concept at this stage, but if it can be developed cost-effectively and without major adverse side effects, it could become a large renewable energy supply in the future. As an example of an early project using drilling to access deep geothermal resources, the city of Erding near Munich in the region of Bavaria in southern Germany has drilled several wells 3-4 km in depth to generate steam for district heating and electricity generation. Separately, they drilled a 2.3-km deep well to provide hot water for a recreational water park. There are several other deep geothermal projects working and under development in Bavaria.

Low-temperature Applications

Next there are several low-temperature thermal applications. By "low temperature" we mean that the temperatures are in a narrower range close to room temperature, compared to high-pressure, high-temperature steam being tapped at a geothermal electricity generating station. For example, in winter a house in North America may seek to maintain indoor temperatures of 65-75°F compared to outdoor temperatures of 10-20°F. In summer, the same house may seek 65-70°F compared to outdoor temperatures in the 85-105°F range.

Many of these applications use heat pumps. Figure 5 shows the function of a heat pump in a simple form. The working fluid (sometimes called a "refrigerant" in this case) circulates between cold-side and hot-side heat exchangers, passing through a compressor in one direction and an expansion valve in the other. A pumping system keeps the fluid moving from station to station. The arrows on the left and right side of the figure represent the movement of heat from a source to a destination. Initially, the fluid enters the cold-side heat exchanger at a temperature that is lower than the ambient low temperature so that the ambient temperature will naturally tend to heat the fluid. For example, in the case of a ground-source heat pump, the fluid pipes may pass through the ground at 50°F, so if the fluid is at 38°F heat will transfer from the ground to the fluid. Next, the compressor raises the pressure and with it the temperature of the working fluid so that it arrives at the entry of the high temperature heat exchanger at a temperature higher than the surrounding temperature of the destination. Suppose the air in the destination is kept at 75°F: If the fluid enters the heat exchanger at 95°F, heat will naturally flow from the fluid to the surrounding room. Finally, the fluid passes through the expansion valve so that its pressure and temperature can fall, and the cycle repeats.

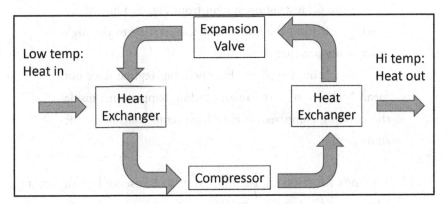

Figure 5 Basic components of a heat pump system, showing winter configuration for moving heat from the low outdoor temperature to the high indoor temperature.

The heat movement shown in Fig. 5 is in fact the winter configuration where heat moves from the cold outdoors to the warm indoor space. In summer, the movement of heat reverses so that heat moves from the inside of the house, which is now cooler than the hot outdoor summer air (Fig. 6). The physical components of the heat pump stay in place (heat exchangers, compressor, and expansion valve); changes in the valves in the system (not shown in the diagram, for simplicity) achieve the routing change so that the fluid flows from the indoor heat exchanger to the compressor, and not to the expansion valve.

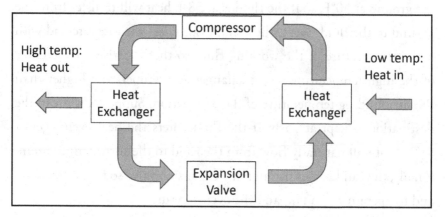

Figure 6 Heat pump system from Fig. 5, adjusted for moving heat from the low indoor temperature to the high outdoor temperature in summer.

Note: "Low temp" in this operating regime does not mean "cold" – it is the relatively low temperature inside the building compared to the "high temp" outside in the summer air.

Heat pumps function in a similar way to household refrigerators, but on a larger scale. A refrigerator keeps food cold by expelling heat from its insulated interior to the warm kitchen air outside using a fluid compression-expansion cycle. The refrigerant (i.e., fluid inside the refrigerator) passes through the cold interior space at low pressure, after which it is compressed and pumped to the exterior condenser coils so that it can shed heat to the outside air at room temperature. Thereafter it passes through an expansion valve to return to low pressure, and the cycle repeats. In the analogy to the heat pump in winter, the roles are reversed, with the inside of the refrigerator equivalent to the outdoor air and the room temperature in the kitchen equivalent to the heated air inside the house or other heated space. Thus, heat is being moved from a cold space to a warm one in both the refrigerator and the heat pump, but in the former, the objective is to cool the cold space while in the latter it is to heat the warm one.

Specific applications of heat pumps for space heating and cooling can be divided between ground/water source and air-source heat pumps. In the first type of system, heating of a building is accomplished by pumping fluid through a horizontal trench or vertical well and then transferring it via a compressor inside the building. Once the high-pressure fluid carrying heat is inside, it can heat either water or air to be circulated to the various rooms, similar to a conventional boiler heating water or furnace heating forced air. These systems can also be designed to run in reverse during the hot season, in which case heat from inside the building is expelled into the trenches or wells. These systems revolve around the stability of temperature below a certain depth: starting at depths at or deeper than around 8 feet below ground, the temperature in the ground remains at around 50 °F year-round in the middle latitudes. If the heat source is water instead of air, the function is like that of a ground-source heat pump, with the system tapping into a mass of water that has high thermal mass and low variation in temperature year-round.

In place of a ground or water source, homeowners may instead install air-source heat pumps that tap the thermal energy available in the air surrounding the structure. The energy available in the air is less dense than in the earth or water, so for a given desired amount of heat, the air-source system must work harder and therefore consume more energy. Also, an air-source heat pump can extract heat from air even in the winter when air temperature is at or below freezing, but it will need to work harder to transfer the heat into the building, increasing electricity consumption. In a worst-case situation where the outside air temperature is extremely low, it may no longer function efficiently enough to operate in a cost-effective way whereas a ground or water source pump is not subject to the same low temperature limit because the heat source has more or less constant temperature. However, the air-source pump also avoids the high upfront investment cost associated with trenches, wells, or piping through water. The choice therefore depends on the owner's tradeoff between upfront and ongoing cost.

There are some other practical considerations for ground-source and air-source heat pumps. They combine well with large-scale wind energy development in the U.S.: since wind farm output peaks in the winter months in many locations, this energy supply could be coupled with heat pumps to carry much of the nation's heating energy load. One other consideration is that ground-source heat pumps require a space adjacent to the building for drilling or excavating trenches or wells, and air-source pumps are suitable for low-density residential developments or rural areas, which may not be possible in all locations.

Table 10 presents a case study of a ground-source heating system to show how much energy it can deliver and how much it costs to operate. This study uses a house like the one introduced above for heating with wood in a high-efficiency wood heater and requires a total of 7 Mmbtu of energy during a cold winter month (1 Mmbtu = 1 million Btu). The heat pump system has a "coefficient of performance," or COP, of 4.38; for each unit of energy input from the compressor, the system provides

4.38 units of heat to the destination.[41] The energy input required from the compressor is 1.6 Mmbtu/month (~468 kWh/month), and the amount of heat extracted from the ground source in this case is the difference between heat delivered and compressor input, or 5.4 Mmbtu/month.[42] The additional system electricity consumption is given as a nominal quantity of 40 kWh/month; this quantity is not calculated precisely, but it is known to be small compared to the compressor energy requirement. The total electricity budget at 508 kWh/month at $0.14/kWh leads to a monthly bill of ~$71 to heat the space.

Component	Quantity	Units
Heat required	7	Million Btu/mo
Coef. Performance (COP)	4.38	
Compressor input	1.60	Million Btu/mo
Heat from ground	5.40	Million Btu/mo
Compressor electricity	468.4	kWh/mo
Other electricity (approx.)	40	kWh/mo
Total	508.40	kWh/mo
Unit cost	$ 0.14	Per kWh
Cost per month	$ 71.18	per month

Table 10 Ground-source heat pump example for high-efficiency home requiring 7 million Btu of heating energy during a cold winter month.

Note: *COP = Coefficient of Performance.

[41] This calculation uses a simple interpretation of COP, using only the ratio energy output to electricity input to the compressor. A complete calculation of COP considers all aspects of energy input including not only the compressor but also energy consumed to pump the fluid around the system and other energy inputs. COP also uses net energy delivered to the heating load after considering losses due to heat escaping and friction. For both of these reasons, actual COP would be lower than calculated in this simplified example. A complete understanding of the relationship between the energy input and amount of temperature change and heat delivered requires an explanation of thermodynamics that is outside the scope of this book. Most modern textbooks on engineering thermodynamics cover the refrigeration cycle and heat pumps.

[42] Conversion: 1 kWh = 3,412 Btu.

Several comments about the heat pump example are pertinent. First, one could expect that any option to heat a home in the depth of winter will have significant cost, and heat pumps are no different: Electricity consumption increases in a non-trivial way. For a house that consumes 6,000 kWh per year or 500 kWh per month before introducing a heat pump system, the increase of about 500 kWh/month effectively doubles monthly consumption during the winter months.

The cost of heating with the heat pump can be compared with conventional fuel in the form of natural gas. Suppose the homeowner pays $12 per Mmbtu for gas including supply and delivery. With an 85% efficient heating system, the 7 Mmbtu per month of heat delivered translates to 8.2 Mmbtu/month of natural gas purchased for $99/month. Comparing the gas-fired heating option to the heat pump, the savings amount to $28/month, so the question then becomes one of how long it takes for the savings from the heat pump to pay for the incremental cost of upgrading from a gas-fired boiler to a heat pump. The cost of ground-source trenches or wells varies widely based on site-specific conditions, so this example does not include an estimated capital cost or payback timeline.

The decision about whether or not to invest in a heat pump system may include avoided emissions as well as economic payback. The 8.2 Mmbtu per month of natural gas purchased in the conventional heating alternative represents 4.8 tons of CO_2 per month emitted to the atmosphere. The heat pump uses 1.73 Mmbtu/month (including the 40 kWh/month of additional electricity consumption beyond the compressor) to move 5.4 Mmbtu/month of carbon-free energy from the ground into the heated space. If the 508 kWh/month of electricity can be derived from 100% carbon-free sources, the emissions savings can be significant for a single dwelling.

Turning to other examples that use heat pumps for heating and cooling, applications can be centralized as well as decentralized. A single source, such as a river or lake, can be accessed by multiple heat pumps each serving a separate building.

Effluent Thermal Energy Recovery

Wastewater gathered by urban sanitation networks provides another potential source for thermal recovery under the heading of Effluent Thermal Energy Recovery, or ETER. Wastewater retains heat from various sources (e.g., domestic hot water) and remains at temperatures typically between 50° F in the winter and 75° F in the summer. Also, the wastewater flowing in sewer mains and through a wastewater treatment plant (WWTP) provides a ready supply of heat without needing to invest in infrastructure such as trenches or wells through which to circulate a refrigerant to transfer heat from source to destination, reducing capital cost. Along with accessing ETER at the WWTP, it is also possible to directly tap into sewer mains as they pass underneath buildings to use ETER for heating and cooling. This approach has the benefit of proximity compared to ETER in a WWTP that must be distributed to surrounding buildings.

As an example, the 5.5 million gallons per day flowing through the Ithaca Area Wastewater Treatment Facility (IAWWTF), discussed above as an example application of biogas extraction from the waste stream, also can potentially provide significant thermal energy (Table 11). Energy extracted from the flow is based on the amount of temperature reduction in the effluent as it passes through the initial ETER heat exchanger system. The temperature change may appear modest, but 5°F of temperature reduction results in 229 Mmbtu/day

extracted because the flow volume is so large.[43] The working fluid of
the ETER system leaves the heat exchanger at 50°F and can be boosted
to 115°F with a heat pump. A heat pump system can achieve COP = 4
over this range of temperature lift, so 22,379 kWh/day, or 76.4 Mmbtu/
day added to the heat results in 305.4 Mmbtu/day of heat available.
This amount is equivalent to the daily heating requirement of 1,300
of the high-efficiency living units introduced above regarding heating
with wood or ground-source heat pumps. Of course, it would be a huge
capital investment to extract all of the heat and to distribute it to so
many living units. Also, the electricity consumption figure is large: it is
equivalent to four times the total output from the CHP system in Fig.
3. Nevertheless, this example gives an order-of-magnitude sense of the
potential scale of ETER.

Component	Quantity	Units
Water flow	5.5	Mil.Gal/Day (MGD)
Temperature change	5	Degrees F
Heat extracted	229	Million Btu/Day
Coef. Performance (COP)	4	
Compressor energy	76.36	Million Btu/Day
Heat delivered	305.43	Million Btu/Day
Entering hot temperature	115	Degrees F
Electricity consumed	22,379	kWh/Day
Equivalent living units	1300	High-efficiency homes

Table 11 Summary of energy potential and input
compressor electricity required for Effluent Thermal Energy
Recovery (ETER) system based on Ithaca Area Wastewater
Treatment Facility flow

ETER is not yet in wide use in WWTPs in North America, but there
are some early examples. The 34 MGD James Kirie plant in Chicago
extracts heat from effluent and uses it internally for applications such as

[43] Based on the constant of 8.33 Btu per degree of temperature change per gallon
of water.

space and service hot water heating. The Southeast False Creek Energy Utility in Vancouver, Canada, extracts heat at a WWTP and exports it off site to buildings for heat and hot water.

Other Types of Energy Extraction from Lakes and Oceans

Another way of exploiting the energy in water is through *lake-source cooling* or *ocean-source cooling* (LSC or OSC). When a large summer-time cooling load (for example, air conditioning of buildings in a city or town) is located next to a body of water deep enough to have a layer that remains at cool temperature through the warm months, it is possible to pump the water out, transfer interior heat from buildings to it, and return it to the body of water. This process raises the temperature of the circulating water a few degrees, but provided the cooling load is small relative to the mass of water available at the source, the effect on source water temperature is negligible. The system consumes some energy for pumping, but it can save 80% or more compared to the energy required for conventional cooling using air-conditioning chillers. These systems are in use in Scandinavia and The Netherlands, as well as in Toronto and at Cornell University in Ithaca, NY. A large urban OSC system has been proposed for Honolulu.

Since there is a 500-foot change in elevation between the lake and the cooling load, Cornell's LSC system uses a heat exchange building at the level of the lake and a separate, sealed water loop that circulates between the lake level and the campus. This solution reduces the pumping energy required because the cooling water is not lifted to the campus due to the force of the returning water on the rising water, in the same way that an elevator in an elevator shaft reduces the amount of energy required by being suspended from a counterweight. Overall, the LSC system saves between 20 and 25 million kWh of electricity per year, compared to providing the same amount of cooling with conventional air conditioning chillers. For example, in a typical year, August might be the month with the heaviest air conditioning load. Where in the past the campus would have required up to 6 million kWh in a month to operate air conditioning, LSC consumes only 600,000 kWh in a month for pumping and controls for the same amount of cooling.

One other water-based energy concept known as *Ocean Thermal Energy Conversion*, or OTEC, also captures energy for human use from temperature differences instead of water motion. The principle behind OTEC is that where a large temperature difference exists between surface ocean water temperatures and temperatures at depths of 1000 meters or more, in theory, a heat engine can operate on the temperature difference by extracting thermal energy from water pumped between the two layers and then expelling the water in the colder layer. In many parts of the subtropical and tropical Atlantic, Pacific, and Indian Oceans, conditions exist where the surface temperature is 70°F or more, but the temperature at depth is 40°F or less, which is suitable for OTEC.

Although the potential energy that could be extracted from this resource is very large, no prototype system for OTEC has been tried up to the present, due to both technical and economic challenges. The low maximum efficiency and challenges surrounding the construction and maintenance of the hardware needed are both barriers to its development. First, maximum efficiency of heat engines is a function of temperature difference, and 30-40°F is not much compared to the hundreds of degrees of temperature difference achieved in fossil-fuel powered electricity generating plants. Furthermore, there is a big energy loss associated with pumping large amounts of water between such large depths. Also, the equipment for generation and for transmitting power to the mainland would need to be able to withstand storm conditions at the ocean surface, adding to the cost. However, certain island electricity markets like Hawaii or Puerto Rico may eventually provide niche markets for OTEC because they are adjacent to deep waters and pay high prices for conventional electricity.

The Renewable Energy Portfolio: Broader is More Resilient

In this chapter we have seen a wide range of sources, including hydropower, wave, tidal, biomass, geothermal, waste-recovery, and heat-pump energy. Taken together, these resources can play a substantial supporting role in the U.S. economy, and in other countries, they might be a dominant energy source (e.g., geothermal energy in Iceland, hydropower in Switzerland). These resources can support the intermittency of solar and wind energy. They will also be used in location-specific situations, such as a small hydro project in a favorable location or rural communities that are best served by exploiting locally available biomass and biofuel options.

The use of biomass, small hydro, or coastal energy sources may not appear to be major national sustainable energy sources, but that does not matter. A risk in looking just at national numbers is not seeing the important role of local solutions for sustaining local communities. For the local community, what matters most is that reliable energy is available locally, and if that energy comes from local sources, there may be advantages, such as keeping economic activity local.

The portfolio of many energy options creates a stronger, more robust, and more flexible renewable energy solution than relying on a single energy source. It is not a coincidence that we have other forms of energy, many of them derived from solar such as hydro or biomass, and that we are developing them. They each bring niche advantages that make the overall portfolio more attractive. Some complement the seasonality of solar energy: for example, small hydro is often stronger in seasons other than summer. Others allow us to store and dispatch renewable energy in a controlled way.

Extracting energy from the waste stream, including wastewater, municipal solid waste, and biological byproducts such as those from food processing is a distinctive resource. This source has the dual benefit of providing alternative energy and reducing the size and disposal cost of the waste stream. Often, the economics are favorable because the fuel source appears as a credit rather than an operating cost in the business plan. One limitation is that a properly functioning market economy discourages production systems from generating waste, so there are limits on the total amount of energy that can be recovered, relative to the size of the national energy budget.

The other distinctive resource in this chapter is the heat pump. Strictly speaking, heat pumps are not a primary energy source because they always rely on another primary source for the electricity needed for operation. In the short run, they can reduce fossil fuel use and GHG emissions because they act as a "multiplier" of energy input into heat energy delivered, reflected in a metric called the "coefficient of performance." Longer term, heat pumps can be coupled with renewable sources to provide carbon-free heating and cooling.

Lastly, the vision of combining renewable electricity from wind or hydro with heat pumps to heat homes and businesses without burning fossil fuels points to the next direction that we need to go: systems integration. We have seen a wide range of energy sources beyond solar and wind in this chapter, but they also need to be organized into a complete system that works together effectively. Some of the energy applications that this system will serve are stationary, like heat pumps, but others are mobile applications like all the vehicles that we use, from cars and trains to ships and aircraft. Systems integration is the focus of the next chapter.

CHAPTER 8

Systems Integration and Transportation Energy

For several years, the NYSEG (New York State Electric & Gas) energy utility in the region around Cornell University and Ithaca, NY, ran an advertising campaign in print media and also on billboards on ski lift pylons at the local ski resort. The billboards on the ski lifts depicted a child's pinwheel toy (emblematic of a wind turbine), with the caption "choosing renewable energy: easy as child's play" next to it.

On one level, they had indeed made renewable energy easy. Although it is not spelled out anywhere on the billboard, many skiers (or local news-media readers who encountered the ad elsewhere) would know from context and previous exposure that the ad is for selling "renewable energy blocks" to utility customers. For a certain fee each month, you can buy a "block" of electricity from renewable energy sources (100 kWh, 200 kWh, etc.) that will offset your conventional energy use. The fee is on top of your normal electricity bill, the assumption being that environmentally conscious customers will pay extra for this, the way they pay extra for organic fruits and vegetables. For a modest price, electricity becomes carbon-free. In terms of bookkeeping, each kWh of carbon-free electricity from wind or solar has a "credit" associated with it, and as long as that credit cannot be double-counted, then the NYSEG customer is guaranteed that the environment is getting the green benefit they have purchased even though the kWh of energy has not directly flowed to their home meter.

On another level, however, when we think more broadly about the issue, choosing renewable energy is ever so much more difficult than child's play. The largest problem is that when utilities sell and consumers buy carbon-free electricity in this way, they are benefitting from the modest share of the overall energy market. What if every residential, commercial, industrial, and government customer signed up all at once? NYSEG and other utilities like it would quickly run out of "shovel-ready" locations to install renewable energy generating assets or ways to manage its intermittent flows. The market would feel the shortfall not just in generating assets such as wind and solar farms but also in storage and transmission/distribution capacity to deliver renewable energy. What if these customers want not just electricity for existing loads but also for charging millions of cars and trucks that previously ran on gasoline and diesel? The shortfall would be even more acute.

The Role of Systems Integration

For some aspects of this problem, the solution is more manufacturing capacity to build devices such as wind turbines and solar panels. For other aspects, however, the solution lies in improving *systems integration*, meaning that the existing technological components work together better or in a new way to give us the quantity and quality of energy that we want. This is especially true of a renewable energy future where we will need to generate energy when it is available, move energy around, store it if required, and match demand to available supply. Systems integration brings its own unique set of design problems, separate from the individual technologies that make up the components of the system.

These problems include the need to understand synergies between components, design interfaces correctly, and sometimes modify or design new components that fill a gap.

One challenge for finding systems integration solutions is that the economic marketplace tends to reward discrete end-use products, and especially consumer products, more readily than a systems integration solution that improves the way existing components interface with each other. Take the example of electronics. The marketplace has rewarded discrete products such as information technology, computer hardware and software, and wireless communications equipment with rapid growth in the economic size of the market and great wealth for the most successful entrepreneurs. Where systems solutions have been the most economically successfully, they have tended to be new systems of networks that have a small physical footprint and can be implemented by private companies (e.g., cellular telephone networks, the internet). In a relatively short time, global wireless communication companies have advanced through many generations of network technologies, from First Generation to Fifth Generation (commonly abbreviated 1G to 5G in the media), and so on.

By comparison, electricity grid or transportation networks in the U.S. have not modernized as quickly; they have, in fact, suffered from deteriorating conditions due to inadequate investment. Wind and solar technology have improved, and costs have declined faster than was predicted 20 years ago. However, large-scale deployment of renewables to the point that they become the major energy source in the U.S. or globally is a massive infrastructure project more akin to rebuilding highway or transmission grid networks than a new wireless network generation. The fitful pace of building wind and solar infrastructure (as discussed in Chapters 5 and 6) has slowed their penetration into the market, especially relative to our aspirations for shifting from fossil fuels.

On the transportation side, electric vehicles, public transportation, or intercity passenger rail all require infrastructure in good working order. Unfortunately, the funds to both repair existing infrastructure and create new linkages have fallen short.

Current Function of the Grid and the Role of Renewables

A major piece of infrastructure to consider is the nation's electricity grid. As an indication of the condition of the grid in recent years, consider the Northeast blackout of 2003. In this event, transmission-line failures in northeast Ohio cascaded into a massive power failure affecting 55 million people because systems meant to contain failures functioned poorly or not at all (see U.S.-Canada Power System Outage Task Force, 2004). Fully recovering the grid and restoring normal function throughout the region took days.

At the other extreme, a modernized grid, at the heart of a system linking renewable-generating assets with modern, efficient electrical devices, could go a long way toward meeting the twin goals of stopping the buildup of CO_2 in the atmosphere and reliably delivering energy for the long term.

At the outset, it is important to understand the function of the current grid where conventional energy from natural gas and coal dominate, and how it might function if renewables were dominant. Figure 1 shows how demand in a typical regional electricity market varies, with demand falling in the middle of the night and early hours of the morning, rising during the day, and falling again at night. Note that the peak demand is lower on the weekend, as many workplace locations are closed or less active. Also, the values are for a particular time of year that is not disclosed, but the peak value in a week (about 42,000 MW in this case) varies depending on the location on the globe. For example, a location that experiences hot summers would see the highest peak levels in summer weeks on weekdays when air conditioning load is at its maximum.

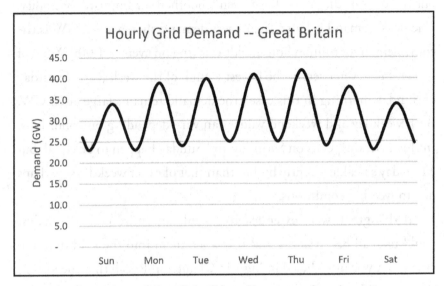

Figure 1 Typical load profile curve for electricity demand in GW for a representative week in the United Kingdom.

Source: National Grid Great Britain. Note: Curve in the figure has been smoothed from the original hourly data to improve visibility.

Figure 1 shows hourly demand for a representative 168-hour week from Sunday to Saturday for the National Grid in Great Britain, including England, Scotland, and Wales, but not Northern Ireland. The shape of the hourly demand over a week tells a story about how electricity demand for an entire country with a population of about 60 million functions. The daily demand follows a similar demand each day: at midnight at the beginning of the day, demand is falling and continues to fall until it bottoms at 3 a.m. or 4 a.m., and after that it increases through the morning. In the middle of the day, it reaches a peak, where it stays until evening when it falls again toward midnight, and the pattern repeats the next day. The daytime peak is actually more of an undulating plateau than the smooth curve shown in Fig. 1, but the data in the figure have been smoothed for improved visibility. The peak demand is large: the largest demand shown at 42 GW is the equivalent of 42 million households drawing on average 1,000 Watts of power. However, even in the lowest trough of the week (early Saturday or Sunday morning in this case), the demand remains large at 23 GW. Both weekday and weekend values can vary depending on conditions. In this case, the peaks on Saturday and Sunday happen to be equal, but Thursday's peak is slightly higher than that of other weekdays, perhaps due to weather conditions.

If this graph were extended to include an entire year, an analyst could take all 8,760 hours and rearrange them into the load duration curve that was introduced in Fig.1 in Chapter 4. Recall that the load in that curve had a maximum value of 18 GW of capacity on the highest demand hour of the year. The government agency that regulates the grid will require that the grid has some extra capacity so that if some generating units fail in the hours when demand is at its yearly peak, the grid will still be able to meet demand. For an anticipated peak of 18 GW, this buffer might amount to 15%, or 2.7 GW, extra. The region then plans to meet future demand with a mix of baseline plants that run most of the time and variable-output plants that adjust to changing demand as was shown in Chapter 4, Table 4.

The load duration curve and the knowledge of how demand varies hour by hour on weekdays and weekend days is a useful starting point for planning how to operate the grid in a region. Total power requirement in a market (including both individual residential users and larger commercial and industrial accounts) fits an approximate profile over a 24-hour period, based on day of the week, time of year, weather conditions, and other factors. Although the exact future amount of electricity that will be demanded from one moment to the next is unknown, based on weather and other factors, it is possible to make a reasonable prediction a day or two in advance. With this prediction, producers can schedule close to the amount of electricity needed. In real time, the final excess or shortfall can be compensated for by certain producers that are especially flexible in their ability to change output. Some of these producers participate in a "spot market" where they agree to sell power into the market with very little advance notice to make up for any shortfall in the moment. Large-scale hydropower is useful here: Dam operators can vary output to complement differences between changing demand and output from other generators. Another option is to transfer extra power into large-scale storage, such as a pumped storage system, or to take power out of storage to make up for a shortfall. See discussion of energy storage later in this chapter.

The Independent System Operator, or ISO, oversees changing demand patterns and makes sure that, after considering any use of energy storage, generators are matching demand to keep the regional grid stable. Each state or multistate region in the U.S. has its own ISO, which uses information technology to track demand and then every few minutes to electronically signal how much power to put out to plants within its district. This does not exactly match production to the amount of electricity being pulled out of the grid by all the loads down to the exact number of electrons. However, some slack is allowed; the imbalance in input and output shows up in the form of slight variation in voltage. Electronic devices large and small can accommodate this variability up to a point. However, if the grid voltage varies too far from what is expected, electricity-consuming devices are put at risk of damage, at which point the grid delivery of electricity must be interrupted to restore correct function, and a blackout ensues.

Blackouts are costly, but not as costly as destroying all of the electricity-consuming equipment in an entire region.

Intermittent renewable energy sources fit into the current systems because their percent contribution is small, with wind and solar together at around 7%. Distributed household and small commercial solar PV systems produce an additional increment of electricity "behind the meter," but this amount does not count toward the percentage. Since the grid is adapted to handling uncertainty in the match between load and production anyway, renewable energy input shows up in the form of an amount subtracted off the load, and the ISO covers the shortfall with dispatchable resources, such as peaking plants and hydroelectric stations. The ISO generally maintains a rule that because wind and solar do not pay for fuel and have very low variable cost, and furthermore because they avoid GHG emissions, their sale into the market is prioritized. On the other hand, grid capacity can become congested, and in some cases a wind farm may be shut down, even though wind is available, because the transmission lines do not have room to move the power to markets at the other end.[44]

Grid Function in a Future Renewables-Dominated System

The current grid can integrate intermittent renewables into the mix of power sources – up to a point (!) – because it is able to adjust to variability in their output, in the same way it adjusts to variability in demand. Issues come up if there is too much intermittent renewable production. If there are wide swings in renewable output due to large buildup of generating capacity, the economics become unviable for

---

[44] See article in the *New York Times* (Wald, 2008).

conventional power producers because they would be expected to have large amounts of capacity on call, much of which would not actually be used. Alternatively, if renewable assets were to replace much of the conventional ones, and conventional plants were decommissioned and no longer in service, the grid would become unreliable whenever there was a shortfall of solar or wind production.

The economics of investing in renewable generation becomes complicated as well. The conventional grid benefits from the mixture of capital-intensive, low-variable-cost generation for base level demand that is continually present and low-capital-cost generation for peaking plants (see Chapter 4). With the move from conventional to renewable power, the low-capital-cost option disappears because renewables are essentially all high-fixed-cost, low-variable-cost systems. Along with high initial cost, intermittent renewables do not have their full rated capacity guaranteed on call at any given hour in the future, and with seasonality and day/night variability, there are certain months of the year or hours of the day when the likelihood of availability is depressed.

To counteract these challenges with renewables, we can implement three strategies overall. First, we can invest in energy storage to smooth out peaks and valleys in renewable energy production. Second, we can expand grid transmission capacity and especially high-voltage, long-distance capacity. Instead of putting extra energy into storage, it could be moved from a region where excess production is available to another that is falling short. Lastly, we can deploy the "smart grid" that exerts control over energy loads large and small in a region so that they rise and fall in response to changing energy availability. This solution would transform the grid from today's approach in which customers decide their behavior independently and the ISO and producers are expected to follow suit.

There is in fact a fourth strategy, but it does not get as much attention as the other three because it is not as appetizing. As the system moves closer and closer to 100% reliance on renewables, it may turn out that storage, transmission, and a smart grid may not be able to entirely guarantee reliability on a year-round basis. Therefore, it may be necessary to build additional renewable generating capacity to be used during periods of peak demand and then idled outside of it. At present, seasonal electricity consumption is uneven across the year, especially at a regional level. It may not be possible to entirely balance this out. An operator of a peaking plant in the present day does not expect their plant to operate for 7,000 or 8,000 hours per year. There may in the future be some renewables that also only operate some of the time. Fortunately, there is plenty of room to deploy the first three strategies and get close to a balanced grid operation of generation, storage, transmission, and demand, even if they do not achieve 100% coverage of all the demand in the grid.

Energy Storage

Energy storage provides a means of handling the variability between demand and generation in the grid system. If plants are producing too much electricity in the moment, some electricity can be diverted to storage to be released into the grid later. Storage is also used to generate and store energy when real-time market prices are low at night and then to provide electricity from the storage system when market prices are high during the day. The discussion in this section includes pumped storage and stationary batteries as well as less-developed options such as flywheels and compressed air storage.

Pumped Storage

Historically, the most common method of energy storage has been pumped-hydro storage where water is pumped uphill to store energy and then released later to transmit the energy to market, so it makes sense to look at this resource first. Table 1 shows location and capacity for a sample of six pumped-hydro storage facilities around the U.S., which together account for 10.9 GW or about 49% of 22 GW of pumped-hydro storage capacity in the country. By power capacity, Dominion Bath County in Virginia is currently not only the largest domestically but also the largest in the world. Most facilities in Table 1 are located in mountainous regions, but the Ludington plant in Michigan uses high dunes along the shores of Lake Michigan as a basis for pumping water up to higher elevation.

Name	State	Capacity (MW)
Dominion Bath County	VA	3003
Ludington	MI	2712
Raccoon Mountain	TN	1652
Castaic	CA	1247
Northfield Mountain	MA	1168
Blenheim-Gilboa	NY	1100

Table 1 List of representative pumped storage facilities in the U.S., including location and maximum power output. Source: U.S. Energy Information Administration.

Pumped storage capacity in the U.S. is small relative to the overall size of the electricity market. Figure 2 shows the total amount of electricity production transferred into pumped storage from 2004 to 2018, which ranged from 4.5 to 8.5 billion kWh per year. The largest figure in the graph of 8.5 billion kWh in 2004 represents just 0.2% of total demand in that year. Note that the values in the figure represent the net amount of energy stored, i.e., the total amount stored minus the total amount eventually extracted, with the difference constituting round-trip losses from the beginning of the storage process to the eventual end of the extraction process. Taking the 2004 figure as an example, if round-trip losses amounted to 22%, then the 8.5 BkWh shown actually represents the 38.6 BkWH originally stored, of which 8.5 BkWh is eventually lost. The remaining 30.1 BkWh is returned to the grid as usable energy. However, even if we use the 30.1 BkWh figure, it amounts to just 0.8% of total demand, reinforcing the observation that storage capacity is small compared to demand.

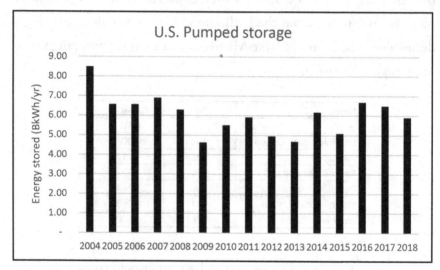

Figure 2 U.S. annual pumped storage volume in billion kWh per year, 2004 to 2018.
Source: U.S. Energy Information Administration.

To illustrate the size, function, and capacity of large-scale pumped storage, consider the hypothetical system in Table 2. The location has available an average vertical drop of 300 meters from the uphill reservoir to the turbines, ignoring head losses due to friction in the pipes and other factors. The system is capable of a maximum flow of 425 m³/sec of water through four 250-MW$_e$ turbines. The system efficiency is 80% from kinetic energy flow in the water arriving at the turbines to electric power output. Based on these inputs, the system is capable of an output of 1,000 MW, as shown.[45] If the reservoir has a maximum capacity of 20 million cubic meters of water available for the pumped storage system, then the turbines could run at full flow and full power for approximately 13 hours, providing 13.1 GWh of output. This hypothetical system is like the Blenheim-Gilboa plant in Table 1, which has a nameplate capacity of 1,100 MW, average head height of approximately 300 meters, and capacity of 19 million cubic meters.

Component	Quantity	Units
Maximum flow	425	m3/sec
Head height (vertical)	300	meters
Density of water	1000	kg/m3
Gravitational constant	9.8	m/s2
System efficiency	80%	
Power output	1.00E+09	Watt
	1000	MW
Storage capacity	2.00E+07	m3 water
Time at full power	47,059	seconds
	13.1	hours
Maximum energy given	13,072	MWh

Table 2 Parameters and capacity for a representative 1,000-MW storage system in a mountainous region with available 300-meter head.

With the push toward more renewables and intermittent energy sources, there is growing interest in expanding pumped storage. According to USEIA, there are proposals for an additional 34 GW of pumped storage capacity in early stages of the Federal Energy Regulatory Commission's permitting process, along with the 22 GW currently operational.

---

[45] Calculation: Power = (425 m³/s)*(300 m)*(1000 kg/m³)*(9.8 m/s²)*(0.8) = ~1.0 x 10⁹ Watt.

Utility-Scale Stationary Battery Storage

The next storage means to consider is the use of utility-scale batteries to store and then discharge electricity. A utility-scale battery is an industrial product that typically fits in a 20-foot or 40-foot shipping container for ease of shipment and can deliver more than 1 MW of power and store more than 1 MWh of energy. Improvements in lithium-ion battery technology have dropped the storage cost in utility-scale batteries from more than $1,000/kWh ten years ago to prices on the order of $200/kWh at present. Cumulative installations in the U.S. have grown from less than 100 MW in 2013 to more than 1,000 MW in 2018 (Fig. 3). Along with pumped hydro, battery storage stands to become one of the main forms of energy storage as renewables continue to grow.

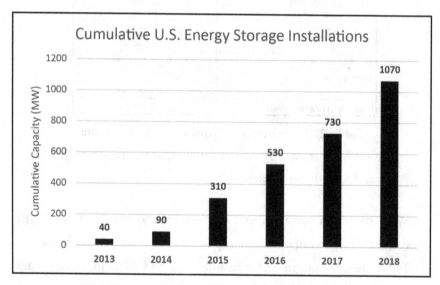

Figure 3 Cumulative growth in U.S. deployed battery storage capacity 2013-2018.

Source: Wood Mackenzie Power & Renewables. Note: 2018 cumulative figure is preliminary.

To understand how stationary battery systems work, consider a representative utility-scale battery that is contained in a 20-foot container with a maximum power output of 3 MW and maximum energy storage capacity of 1.2 MWh (Table 3). The production cost of the battery is $200/kWh, so the entire battery costs $240,000. If the fully charged battery were to discharge at the maximum 3 MW, the battery would be completely discharged in 24 minutes. However, the draw on the battery may be shorter, or may be for less than the full 3 MW, in which case the battery will not be fully depleted during the discharging phase.

Component	Quantity	Units
Storage capacity, energy	1.2	MWh
Maximum power output	3	MW
Unit cost of storage	$ 200	per kWh
Total system cost	$ 240,000	
Lifetime cycles	10000	MWh
Expected cycles/year	1000	
Expected lifetime	10	Years
Expected cycles/day	2.74	
Wholesale power cost	$ 0.06	per kWh
Efficiency, r/t	90%	
Purchase per kWh out	1.11	kWh
Cost	$ 0.067	per kWh
Cost per cycle	$ 0.024	per kWh
Total cost	$ 0.09	per kWh

Table 3 Summary of technical and economic characteristics of 1.2-MWh utility-scale stationary battery.

*Note: i.e., this quantity is the amount of electricity in kWh that must be charged into the system to eventually discharge 1 kWh due to round-trip losses in storing and then discharging energy; see text.

To calculate the economics of the stationary battery investment, suppose that one "cycle" of the battery is counted as 1 MWh stored and discharged, and that it has an expected lifetime of 10,000 cycles. (In reality, periods of charging and discharging would occur in different sizes and lengths, but for simplicity assume they are uniform.) If the useful lifetime of the battery system were 10 years, then the expected rate would be 1,000 cycles per year, or 2.74 cycles per day. This rate implies that the average discharge from the battery would be 2.74 MWh/day. Since the maximum power is 3 MW, the battery would in theory be capable of 72 MWh/day if it were physically possible for it to sustain this rate for 24 hours, so the average rate is only 4% of the maximum. This percentage value implies that the battery is available to charge and discharge at a much higher rate if required, so it has a deep capability to support grid reliability.

Beyond the cost of generation itself, the cost of electricity stored and discharged from the battery must cover two elements: the impact of energy lost as electricity is stored and discharged (sometimes called "roundtrip" losses) and the capital cost of the battery. If the roundtrip efficiency is 90% and the generated electricity costs $0.06/kWh, then for each kWh sold from the battery, 1.11 kWh must be purchased, at a cost of $0.067/kWh. The cycle lifetime is equivalent to 10 million kWh charged and discharged, so the capital cost per kWh is $0.024/kWh. Therefore, the total cost is $0.091/kWh, and if transmission to a final customer at $0.06/kWh is included, the price rises to $0.151/kWh. The same electricity costs $0.12/kWh without storage. Thus, the cost is somewhat higher with storage included. However, much of the customers' electricity consumption would come directly from generation and distribution without passing through storage, so the storage price would be blended into the overall mix, reducing the economic impact.

Various applications of stationary batteries are possible. A network of batteries can be combined into a single storage bank on-site at a solar or wind farm, smoothing output for transmission on the grid. One battery maker, Saft, proposes a connected system of batteries in 20-foot containers installed in a "storage farm" capable of providing up to 50 MW of instantaneous output in support of renewable farms. Battery power centers may also work in locations separate from solar and wind farms, closer to electricity consumption in major population centers.

Battery storage centers can also replace natural gas fired "peaker" plants that traditionally meet the few hours of the year with the highest demand on the load duration curve. For reasons discussed in Chapter 4, these peaker plants are the most inefficient in the fleet of generation plants. They also emit a disproportionate quantity of harmful emissions such as NOx, often on days that are the hottest of the year and therefore the most subject to poor air quality. States such as California and New York have recently enacted laws to force a transition from peaker plants to battery storage centers designed to meet peak demand.

In lieu of locating storage capacity in centralized plants, battery storage may also be distributed to the household level in the form of small family-sized battery storage. An example is the Tesla "Powerwall," which has 13.5 kWh of storage capacity, 5 kW of continuous maximum output, and 7 kW of short-term peak maximum output per unit. Depending on the application, the user can chain up to 10 of the units together to meet their needs. One application is a home with a solar PV array that might charge the storage units during the day with solar power and then discharge them at night rather than purchasing grid electricity. In an extended power outage, the same home would continue to receive uninterrupted power from the combination of solar panels and battery storage.

Flywheels and Compressed Air Storage

Besides pumped hydro and stationary batteries, storage systems that play a niche role at present include flywheels and compressed air. A flywheel stores kinetic energy in the spinning motion of a large, heavy wheel. When energy demand arises, it is transferred out of the flywheel by having it drive an electric generator, thereby transferring power back to the grid and simultaneously slowing the flywheel. Now, flywheels are currently mainly used in "regulation" of the alternating current oscillations of the current in the electricity grid, which can be made more regular at times by either putting power into or taking power out of a flywheel.

The leading concept for using compressed air as a means of energy storage is in conjunction with natural gas fired power production. Much of the energy required for generating electricity from natural gas involves compressing air to be mixed with the gas during the combustion process. In a typical gas-fired plant, 25% to 35% of the gross energy generated by the turbines in the plant must be diverted to compressing the air that is mixed with the gas. If solar or wind is used to compress air and store it in a reservoir such as an underground cavern, the compressed air can then be withdrawn and used in the power plant. Since less of the energy derived from natural gas is used to compress air, overall GHG emissions per unit of electricity produced decrease. With additional research, it is possible that in the future flywheel or compressed air storage technology might expand into some of the more general storage applications alongside pumped hydro and batteries.

Improving Long-Distance Transmission

Some renewables provide attractive opportunities for distributed generation, such as household-size solar PV arrays. These sources can reduce the need for long-distance power transmission since power can be generated and consumed within a local area. In other contexts, however, long distance transmission would continue to play a role, and it might also expand. Renewable sources such as wind farms, large-scale hydro, and large solar farms all depend on long-distance transmission. For example, the 250-MW Mount Signal Solar Farm mentioned in Chapter 4 is about 200 miles from the large energy market in Los Angeles. Building large solar farms in unpopulated and unobstructed lands can provide capacity for large-scale production beyond what is available in rooftop solar in Los Angeles alone. In some situations, it may be imperative to increase long-distance transmission from major renewable production centers to grow the overall fraction of energy from renewables. This is especially true because, in major population centers like Los Angeles, New York City, and the like, there may be large commercial or industrial energy loads whose demand far exceeds what could be generated using solar installed on the footprint of the facility itself.

In the U.S., transmission grid upgrades will take place on a network of regional transmission grids that primarily focus on flow within their respective regions but also allow some amount of energy movement between regions. Transmission line size is measured in kilovolts or kV (1 kV = 1,000 Volts). High voltage reduces the fraction of energy lost in transmission, so long-distance transmission is rated at 100 kV or above. Common transmission voltages for major lines are 115, 230, 345, 500, and 765 kV, although other voltages are possible. Higher transmission voltage requires a larger initial investment, but also reduces energy losses, and therefore cuts operating cost.

Most high-voltage transmission in the U.S. network is alternating current (AC) as opposed to direct current (DC). (The difference between AC and DC is that AC periodically switches direction, on the order of 50 to 60 times per second in most countries, whereas DC only flows in one direction.) Alternating current is used in the grid because it is easier to change voltage using industrial-size transformers at junctions where lines of different voltages meet. However, direct current (DC) has lower losses per unit of distance, and the most efficient line is a 1,000 kV DC line, that operators claim loses just 3% of transmitted energy per 1,000 km of distance. The downside of DC transmission is the complexity of organizing the endpoints where AC power enters from the surrounding grid at one end and is dispersed back into the AC grid at the other end. Therefore, high-voltage DC lines are found not in a web-like network but in certain key linear corridors where the high capital cost is justified by large transmission volumes.

Examples of DC transmission include the Pacific DC Intertie on the U.S. west coast and the Hydro-Quebec Trans-Energie DC line in eastern Canada. To focus on the first example, in the 1960s the Los Angeles Department of Water and Power (LADWP) and partners including the Bonneville Power Authority in the Pacific Northwest conceived of a high-efficiency transmission system that would bring inexpensive power from hydroelectric stations in Washington State and Oregon to the southern California market for the summer peak air conditioning season. The result was the 1000-kV Pacific DC Intertie that opened in 1970 between Rice, OR, and Sylmar, CA. This line helps to balance demand for electricity production in the northwest as northwestern states use hydroelectric power for heating in the winter, and electricity demand actually declines in the summer, which is the reverse of the California market.

In the future, the U.S. might improve transmission to accommodate major solar generation in the southwest or wind generation in the Great Plains or along the Atlantic and Pacific Coasts. Currently, the national grid is divided into an Eastern and Western "Interconnect" and a third region covering the state of Texas and some adjacent regions run by ERCOT (Energy Reliability Council of Texas). This division creates three separate regions where the various ISOs in each region are relatively well coordinated and can easily trade power with each other.

Transmission between the three regions exists but is limited. Stronger connections, perhaps using DC connections as a link between the AC networks on either side, would facilitate wind power transmission westbound or solar power eastbound. Alternatively, dedicated long-distance 1000-kV transmission could be used for line-haul transmission of large amounts of power, which could then be broken up into AC transmission at lower voltages. For example, a 3000-km DC line from future solar farms in eastern Arizona to the middle of Ohio would deliver about 91% of its transmitted energy, using the statistic of 3% loss per 1000 km.

Implementing Smart Grid Systems

The smart grid is an evolution of the electricity grid in which the electricity generation system begins to control the behavior of some of the electricity demands in the network, rather than the demands always dictating how the generation side must respond. To understand its potential impact, we can start by thinking about the ways in which the current ("non-smart") grid makes it difficult to integrate large amounts of electricity from an intermittent source.

Take a typical workday as shown in Fig. 1 above. As individual users wake and begin their morning routines, businesses open for the day, and so on, demand on the grid increases. The ISO tracks this demand and makes sure generation keeps up with rising demand by calling on dispatchable generators to increase. The ISO also benefits from forecasting capabilities based on factors such as knowledge of the impact of weather and temperature on energy demand, which allows them to predict the likely path of real-time demand during the day.

The electrons entering and leaving the transmission and distribution system sort themselves out based on *Kirchhoff's Law*, which dictates that current flows in a network from high to low concentrations of electrons. For example, if a household has a solar PV array, and in the middle of a sunny summer day it is producing more current than the house is consuming, the "extra" current will find its way onto the grid and to some place that is in a net deficit. No active control is required: Kirchhoff's Law takes care of it. Kirchhoff's Law can be compared to a swimming pool with a water slide on one side. Suppose a person takes a whiskey barrel full of water to the top of the slide and pours the water down it. The water falling into the pool will not stay under the slide; the water redistributes itself all around the pool so that eventually it comes to rest and is level once again.

In terms of renewable energy, a single household PV array is small enough that the grid can adjust to its oscillations over time. The challenge for a multi-megawatt solar or wind farm is larger. These types of generation can throttle downward easily and precisely: if either type of generation is producing at a high rate and demand on the grid begins to fall, or if generation output is increasing faster than grid demand, wind turbines or solar panels can have their output dampened in real time to keep pace. However, if demand grows faster than output, or if output begins to fall due to intermittency, some other intervention is required, or else the grid voltage will be in danger of moving outside of its safe range.

In the smart grid, we change the assumption so that now the ISO's algorithm and wireless communications can talk to the loads in real time. Loads become variable based on the amount of power available to the grid. In Chapter 4, we discussed a new generation of electrical appliances and devices that would help to reduce energy consumption and CO_2 emissions by using energy much more efficiently. This same new generation of appliances and devices can also be designed to communicate with the grid and respond to requests to reduce or cut off power consumption temporarily to reduce maximum power requirements during a peak load period. For example, suppose the collection of renewable energy farms and ISO in a region are networked with a collection of refrigerators in a city. Refrigerators may be able to safely stay off for 10 or 15 minutes without putting any of the food content at risk. In an event where the grid needs to reduce peak demand, the ISO might rotate through the bank of refrigerators, turning off each group for a time before moving on to the next. Other appliances and electric vehicles that are parked and stationary (see next section) could be programmed the same way. Data centers might function in a similar way: certain energy-intensive procedures might wait for a peaking of intermittent energy supply, and then taper off when the supply drops again.

Arrangements where grid operators have authority to cut off or curtail power to certain customers actually predate the coining of the term "smart grid." For several decades, some utilities have arranged with certain large customers such as manufacturing plants for reduced cost per kWh in return for the right to restrict power provided during a period of high demand on the grid. During that period, the manufacturer might need to slow production to accommodate a lack of full power. However, they were happy to agree because even with potential delays now and then, they could reduce overall operating cost over time because at all other times they could purchase electricity at a discount. Utilities like this arrangement because they can potentially pass through a high-stress period without needing to resort to "rolling brownouts" in which portions of their service area take turns having their power cut off involuntarily. The smart grid pursues this same aim, but it involves a much broader range of customers and manages power distribution more precisely using algorithms, information technology, and wireless communication. The capacity to forecast day-ahead wind- and solar-farm output within a tolerance is advancing as well, so the smart grid will in the future be able to plan how to balance production with loads and storage.

Even without a major influx of renewable generating assets, the interaction between the smart grid and smart appliances can help reduce the stress on the grid due to peak demand periods. The grid is vulnerable to blackouts at these times because most or all generating units will be online. If any units fail, there is a risk that supply will be unable to meet demand, and a load must be shed.

Electrical appliances could be further adapted to be used with the combination of renewable resources and the smart grid by designing them to harness periods of high energy output so that they might store energy internally for down periods. For example, a household refrigerator, freezer, or air conditioning system might take the extra energy and store away ice in a reservoir, which these devices could then draw on later. Similarly, during cold weather, a storage heating unit might take the extra output and store it as heat in thermal bricks or some other heat storage reservoir for later use.

One way to bring this system into being is to offer a two-tiered rate structure. Ratepayers who want to be 100% guaranteed that power will be available (except of course during system-wide unscheduled blackouts) would pay the full rate. However, other ratepayers could get a reduced rate if they were willing to allow appliances to turn off in this way or to allow the grid operator to interrupt their entire central air-conditioning system one time per year.

Lastly, all of these trends related to the evolution of the grid are taking place in the context of growing concerns about cyber-security in society in general and in energy systems in particular. Even without adding smart grid capabilities, ISOs and other stakeholders increasingly rely on digital communication to monitor and control the grid. These activities are vulnerable to cyber-attacks. Unfortunately for the future of the smart grid, as of 2019 national governments such as those of the United States, Russia, Iran, China, and North Korea are ramping up their capability to launch cyber-attacks on one another, including on electricity grids. There is a perception (perhaps incorrect) that these attacks can be carried out to cause economic hardship on rival countries without catastrophic loss of life, making the target a tempting one. In the short- to medium term, cyber risks will likely slow the growth of the smart grid, both because of actual attacks that may occur and the headache and financial cost of needing to harden newly added grid elements against cyber-attacks.

Electricity Microgrids

An electricity microgrid is a network of energy sources and control systems that can serve a local collection of energy loads, for example in a neighborhood or corporate/academic campus. Microgrids include three key features:

1. They are physically connected to the larger regional grid – they are not remote stand-alone electricity systems
2. During normal operations, they produce electricity in parallel with the regional grid so that the owner can recoup the investment in generating capacity by producing and selling electricity.
3. During a regional grid blackout, they can "island" (i.e., cut off the connection to the regional grid) and safely generate power for the loads included within its boundaries.

To qualify as a microgrid, a system must be connected to two or more electricity accounts. This means that the electricity generated crosses property boundaries. Crossing boundaries requires a specific agreement with the utility responsible for electricity distribution since the utility generally has the exclusive right to perform this function. A *nanogrid* is a system that can generate and consume electricity in island mode during a blackout but that is contained within the boundaries of a single utility account.[46]

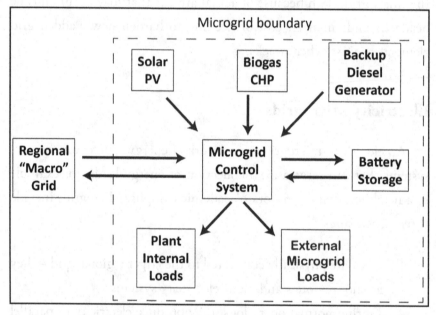

Figure 4 Elements and energy flow relationships in a representative microgrid.

---

[46] Note that there is not universal agreement on this nomenclature. Some locations use the term "microgrid" to describe a single utility account connected to the regional grid that can island and run in stand-alone mode and use the term "mini-grid" to describe the cluster of multiple accounts that can island together and run as a stand-alone during a regional grid failure.

Figure 4 shows a representative electricity microgrid that incorporates several possible elements and energy flow relationships. This microgrid would be retrofitted into an existing plant or facility that already has some backup power, represented by the backup unit ("Backup Diesel Generator") in the figure.

Energy sources in the microgrid include an intermittent source ("Solar PV") with nameplate capacity in the range of 100-1,000 kW, a renewable dispatchable source ("Biogas CHP", i.e., combined heat and power) that combusts biogas to rotate a turbine and a generator, and a diesel-powered and hence fossil fuel consuming backup generator.

During normal operating conditions, the microgrid generates electricity from the CHP unit based on available biogas and from the solar PV when there is sun. The diesel generator is expensive to run because diesel is a high-price fuel for electricity generation, so it remains off. The microgrid controller distributes power from the local generation to the loads (bottom of the diagram), and as needed draws power from the regional macro-grid and pushes it onward to the loads. The backup "Battery Storage" is optional in the microgrid. Depending on the arrangement with the regional utility, the microgrid owner may have authorization to sell extra CHP and PV production to the macro-grid for credits against purchases, or they may store the power in the battery system for later use.

Loads are divided between internal and external, for the case where the microgrid is retrofitted into an existing facility that typically has some type of backup generation. The internal load is the electricity consumed within the plant and on the same utility account where the microgrid control system is located; thus, between local generation and consumption no electricity crosses a property boundary. For example, a large facility such as a hospital or wastewater treatment plant may already consume millions of kWh per year and possess mandatory backup generation prior to the implementation of the microgrid, due to the critical nature of the load. Solar and biogas generation, system control, and internal load would then all appear inside the facility boundaries. Alternatively, it is possible to build up a microgrid entirely separate from any one customer so that effectively all loads are "External Microgrid Loads."

The use of islanding and backup power systems predates the influx of microgrids. For decades, regulations have required critical facilities such as water treatment plants or hospitals to incorporate sufficient backup generation to run in stand-alone mode for all their load, or perhaps a subset that is judged especially critical. Large industrial generators on the order of 500 kW of capacity are typically used since they can start quickly in an emergency, and the diesel fuel can be stored on site in tanks for long periods without degrading. The regulator might require both a certain power capacity, such as three or four 500-kW units, and sufficient diesel fuel storage to be able to operate in standalone mode for three or four days to be able to ride out an extended regional blackout. The microgrid is much more than a backup generating system: It also allows distributed generation to work in tandem with the macro grid so that the microgrid operator can avoid purchasing long-distance delivered power and pay for the investment.

One option that the microgrid operator may consider is an uninterruptible power supply system to allow the microgrid to shift seamlessly from connected to island mode during a regional grid blackout. With this system in place, the microgrid generation and optional storage takes the place of long-distance transmission and distribution as the regional power shuts off, and loads continue to receive power, so that, e.g., a customer does not lose power to a computer system where otherwise data might be lost. Uninterruptible power is convenient for the customer but also adds to microgrid cost. Without it, in a power failure the microgrid at first shuts down along with all surrounding loads. It then "islands" (i.e., physical pathways for electricity to flow to and from the macro grid are uncoupled) and performs a "black start" whereby a generating unit begins to generate AC power so that the other generation and storage can sync their output with the oscillations of the startup unit. Typically, where it exists, the diesel backup generator performs this function since it is already built into the emergency power system of the facility, and devices are already in place for these generators to power a black start.

Microgrids aim to achieve several potential benefits. One benefit is to improve reliability, especially for critical loads. For example, a microgrid district might include several commercial and residential accounts, and these account holders would continue to receive power in the event of a macro grid failure. Some customers that are viewed as "critical loads," such as fire and police, housing for the elderly, or schools, might especially benefit from the presence of a microgrid. For example, a feasibility study in Ithaca, NY, showed that a microgrid based at the local wastewater treatment plant might also link to the nearby city high school. In the event of an extended emergency, the high school would continue to receive power, and it might even serve as a temporary emergency shelter for residents who had lost power in their homes.

Microgrids may also encourage development of renewable distributed generation where it might not otherwise be feasible. For example, a neighborhood might have a number of properties where solar PV is not feasible due to shading. However, if the microgrid can be constructed so that a single large PV array in a sunny location in the neighborhood supplies power to the microgrid control, it may be possible for the affected homeowners to collectively invest in the large array and then achieve the economic benefit of avoided grid electricity purchases.

Integrating the Grid with Transportation Electrification

At first glance, the subject of transportation energy might appear to be so distant from that of electricity grids that it should appear in a separate chapter. Increasingly, though, transportation and electricity are moving toward each other through the process of "electrification", so transportation energy is included as part of the discussion of systems integration in this chapter. For certain transportation energy applications, electrification does not appear to be a suitable solution at present, so other alternative fuels like biofuels and hydrogen are discussed later in this chapter.

As with better appliances and more efficient power plants, improving technology to reduce total demand for transportation will get us to a certain point, but after that we need to think about substitutes for fossil fuels. Improved efficiency alone will not meet sustainability goals, in the short run because CO_2 emissions will continue to be excessive even in the most ambitious efficiency scenarios, and in the long run because of the decline of oil supplies—first conventional, then non-conventional. Eventually, we need to be able to draw on non-fossil resources to solve both problems.

At present, transportation energy derived from petroleum is intimately linked with the vast infrastructure that extracts, ships, and refines crude oil, and distributes and dispenses the finished product to all manner of vehicles. To varying degrees, any replacement for oil-based transportation implies replacing some or all of the infrastructure – which is expensive and time-consuming and may leave us with the problem of "stranded assets" if parts of the old infrastructure are abandoned before the end of their useful life.

Lastly, and uniquely to transportation among all energy uses, most mechanized vehicles that we use on land, sea, and air are "free-roaming":

they need to carry their energy source on board, in a compact, cost-effective form. Certain vehicles that connect directly to the grid through overhead wires called *catenary*, such as electrified railroad lines, operate from electricity that is delivered from off-board sources, but these represent only a small fraction of our total transportation energy use and greenhouse gas emissions. By contrast, cars, trucks, and aircraft (which account for more than 90% of all transportation greenhouse gas emissions[47]) depend on compact and cost-effective storage of fuel so that each has sufficient range between refueling stops, but the space and weight taken up by energy storage (i.e., the fuel tank) does not dominate or distort the design, shape, or function of the vehicle. Aircraft are particularly sensitive to this factor: private car owners do not generally think about keeping their cars at no more than half a tank full to have a lighter car that consumes less gas, but in commercial aviation, matching the amount of fuel in the tank to the length of the flight is an integral part of holding down operating costs by minimizing airborne weight.

The number of possible energy carriers for free-roaming vehicles is limited to basically three types at this time: hydrocarbons (like gasoline, ethanol, etc.), electricity, and hydrogen. These three are connected in a progression. If you start with electricity and add protons, you have hydrogen atoms, and if you start with hydrogen and add carbon, you have the various hydrocarbons, such as gasoline or diesel. Outside of

---

[47] According to Davies et al (2007), the total U.S. emissions for passenger cars, light duty trucks, heavy highway vehicles, and aviation constituted 1.7 billion tonnes of GHG equivalent (mostly CO_2 but also including the CO_2 equivalent for methane, etc.) out of 1.9 billion tonnes across all types of transportation. The breakdown of heavy highway vehicles was not given in this source, but it is well known that the vast majority are large trucks, as opposed to intercity passenger buses. The source also does not give a global transportation emissions breakdown or one for peer industrial countries, but because the mix of vehicles and aircraft is similar, the breakdown of emissions is by necessity similar as well.

these, there are no others on the horizon. Ammonia has been proposed as a means of using nitrogen to carry hydrogen in a vehicle or ship. Proposals for flywheels or compressed air onboard the vehicle for energy storage have not led to a commercially viable product, nor are they expected to for the foreseeable future.

If only we could provide some other feedstock to existing petroleum refineries that would result in liquid transportation fuels that did not increase atmospheric CO_2, the transition would be simplified. We would just need to replace oil drilling rigs with whatever apparatus was needed to obtain this other feedstock, and the rest of the infrastructure we could keep, from refinery downstream to filling station and motor vehicles. Unfortunately, no such feedstock exists: the closest thing is biofuels (discussed later), and these require a fundamentally different type of refining process for which a petroleum refinery is not suitable.

Electrification of the transportation sector aims to eliminate CO_2 emissions by switching from fossil fuels in internal combustion engines to electricity in motors. At first, some fraction of the electricity will still emit CO_2 because it is derived from fossil fuels. However, as the electricity supply shifts to more and more renewables, those emissions will gradually be phased out.

Electrification of Passenger Cars and Small Trucks

The focus of this section is on private passenger cars, either traditional sedans, station-wagons, etc., or the "small trucks" that have become more popular in recent years, including vans, minivans, pickup trucks, and sport utility vehicles. Hereafter, these are referred to as "light-duty vehicles." Light-duty vehicles are the single largest user of transportation energy worldwide. Other types of transportation energy users are covered later in the chapter. These include all manner

276

of electric vehicles such as electric streetcars, subway trains, light-rail vehicles, trolleybuses, and short- and long-distance electric trains. They also include urban and long-distance trucking, ships of all sizes, and aviation.

Light-duty vehicles are also the dominant user of transportation energy in the U.S., and this is why electrification of light-duty vehicles is such an important initiative (Fig. 5). Over the period 1970-2018, the largest change in transportation energy consumption has occurred with vans, pickups, and sport-utility vehicles or SUVs ("LT" in the figure) as both the number of drivers owning this type of vehicle and the average distance traveled per year has grown. When combined with passenger cars ("PC" in the figure, which include sedans, station wagons, hatchbacks, coupes, and so on), the combined energy use is by far the lion's share of the total energy covered in the figure. For example, in 2018 the combination of passenger cars and light trucks consumed about 14.4 Quads (14,400 trillion Btu, to use the units in the figure), or about 84% of the total of all four curves. Aviation energy use has grown as well, although not as much as light trucks. All other transportation energy use, including the combination of motorcycles, buses, subways, and other types of public transportation, fall within the "Other" curve in the figure and constitute only a small fraction of the total.

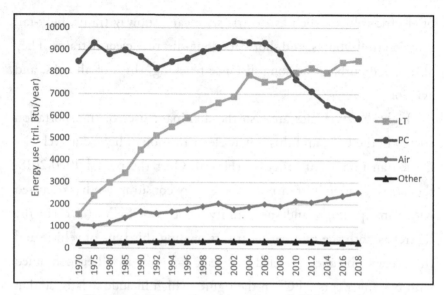

Figure 5 Energy consumption of U.S. passenger transportation modes in trillion Btu, 1970-2018.

Abbreviations in legend: "PC" = passenger car, "LT" = light truck; see text. Source: U.S. Department of Energy, Oak Ridge National Laboratories.

Light-duty vehicles are a good fit for electrification not only because they are the biggest energy opportunity but also because their usage pattern lends itself to electric charging. A typical car drives around 80% of its miles in short-range daily driving, with the remaining 20% on long trips. For around-town driving, the electric vehicle range is sufficient to allow the vehicle to start the day with a full charge, complete all daily driving, and return to its home base at night to recharge for the next day. In the U.S., some vehicles are parked overnight in public locations that lack charging access, such as a car belonging to an apartment resident that is parked on the street. However, a great number of vehicles park at single-family homes where charging infrastructure can be installed.

Vehicles can charge using 110 Volt (U.S.) wall current (called level I charging), but with an investment in a 240V charger (level II charging), home charging can become much more efficient and reliable. Many of the major automakers (Nissan, General Motors, etc.) have converged on a standard charging nozzle so that the equipment is interchangeable and public chargers can accommodate the various makes. Some fully electric vehicles (EVs) can accommodate fast charging at 480V DC (direct current) charging stations (level III). These stations cannot be installed residentially for reasons of both safety and cost, but where they can be installed in a public location, they add economic value by charging many vehicles per unit of time to recoup the investment cost. Direct current is useful because it can be transferred directly into the battery without being first converted from AC to DC so that the charging goes faster.

In other countries such as China where motorists typically reside in high-rise apartments and not spread-out suburbs, or in dense urban areas in the U.S., battery swapping stations may be an alternative to charging at home or at public chargers. Battery swapping requires that all cars be built around compatible battery units so that the driver can drive to a swapping station and exchange a depleted battery for a charged one. The time requirement would be like pumping a full tank of gas, on the order of a few minutes. One disadvantage is that the overall design of the vehicle is more restrictive since different sizes and shapes of vehicles must be designed around a single battery configuration so that they will be compatible with the swapping station. On the other hand, the batteries could be leased from a battery provider, reducing the initial cost of the vehicle.

Even before a transition to a renewable-powered grid takes place, electric vehicle charging can be beneficial in the short run. As shown in Fig. 1 above, demand for electricity falls into a trough at night, so with "smart" charging where the electric grid operator controls the timing and rate of charging, electric vehicles could access unused generating capacity in the early hours of the morning. One possible challenge for widespread adoption of electric vehicles that charge at home is on the local distribution side: in some neighborhoods, adding many electric vehicles charging may overload the distribution system and require the utility to beef up lines to handle increased energy.

Since the year 2000, breakthroughs in battery technology have facilitated the growing penetration of battery-powered vehicles into the market that provide sufficient range without requiring the consumer to pay an exorbitant price. But there are diminishing returns to adding batteries: as the weight of the battery system grows, the car must carry the batteries around with it, reducing the effectiveness of adding more batteries. As an illustration, suppose we start with a representative electric vehicle that weighs 1,000 kilograms and has no batteries. It is assumed that the vehicle has typical performance in terms of aerodynamics and energy efficiency and uses lithium-ion batteries. Each kilogram of batteries can store a certain kWh of electricity, so as we add battery mass, the range increases. As shown in Fig. 6, with zero kilograms of batteries, the vehicle has no range, so when we add the first 250 kg of batteries, we get the largest incremental increase in range of 171 km. However, by the time we have added 750 kg of batteries, the vehicle now weighs 1,750 kg and is less energy efficient. Therefore, when we add another 250 kg (from 750 to 1000 kg), the range increases by only 57 km.

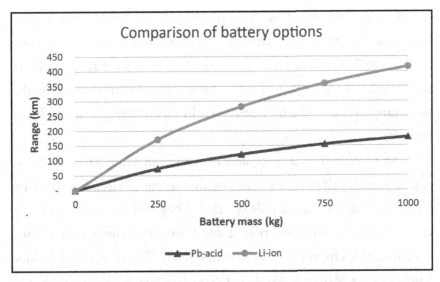

Figure 6 Range per full charge as a function of mass of batteries in the battery system for a representative electric vehicle, considering both lithium-ion ("Li") and lead-acid ("Pb") batteries.

The relationship between battery mass and range in Fig. 6 is simplified because it assumes that the weight of the balance-of-vehicle does not change as the batteries get heavier. In reality, an increasingly heavy battery system requires a stronger, heavier vehicle as well as heavier components so that the impact on diminishing returns will be even larger than what appears in the figure.

Figure 6 also shows the difference that the move from lead-acid to lithium-ion has made. The longest range for a lead-acid battery system shown is 179 km (about 112 miles) for a vehicle weighing 1,700 kg. The last increment of 250 kg of batteries (from 750 to 1,000 kg) adds only 25 km of range. Not only is the increase in range unsatisfactory, but the cost of adding more and more batteries is prohibitive. This hypothetical lead-acid EV at 1,500 kg and 121 km range resembles GM's Saturn EV-1 from the early 2000s, which weighed 1,350 kg, had about 12 km of range, and seated only two passengers. The lithium-ion battery has opened the market for either EVs with shorter range at lower cost, such as the Nissan Leaf, or luxury vehicles with longer range, such as the Tesla Model S with an 85-kWh battery that has approximately the same range value as the highest shown in Fig. 6 (359 km at 750 kg of batteries).

Compared to the energy content of gasoline that internal combustion engine vehicles (ICEVs) use, the energy content of electricity used by electric vehicles is less per mile traveled. They also have a lower energy cost per mile. As an illustration, Table 4 presents a comparison of two similar vehicles from the same maker, namely Nissan. Both are 5-door hatchbacks, and one is gasoline (Versa hatchback model) while the other is all-electric (Leaf). The combined fuel economy of the Versa is 30 miles per gallon, which translates to about 3,800 Btu per mile when considering the average energy content per gallon of gas.[48] The Leaf drives about 3 miles per kWh of electricity consumed, which converts to just 1,137 Btu per mile, a 70% reduction. As a result, the energy cost per mile is significantly lower at 4.7 cents per mile, compared to 10 cents for the Versa. The savings in energy cost per mile, along with the lower maintenance cost, can help to pay back the higher initial cost of an EV. Note that, to be conservative, the calculation assumes a relatively high price of electricity ($0.14/kWh) and that the price of gasoline is quite volatile, which might affect the comparison. Nevertheless, there is an opportunity for saving energy cost per mile for a wide range of plausible gasoline and electricity price combinations.

---

[48] Values used: 1 gal. gasoline = 115,400 Btu; 1 kWh = 3,412 Btu.

Element	Quantity	Units
2014 Nissan Versa Hatchback:		
Fuel economy	30	mpg
Energy/mile	3,847	Btu/mile
Gasoline cost	$ 3.00	per gallon
Cost/mile	$ 0.10	$/mile
2014 Nissan Leaf:		
Fuel economy	3	miles/kWh
	101.5	mpgge
Energy/mile	1137	Btu/mile
Electricity cost	$ 0.14	$/kWh
Cost/mile	$ 0.047	$/mile

Table 4 Comparison of energy consumption and cost per mile for Nissan Versa ICEV and Nissan Leaf EV.

One concern not addressed in Table 4 is the loss of fuel taxes to pay for infrastructure when an EV replaces a conventional light-duty vehicle that would otherwise regularly purchase gasoline. The price of electricity in the table is the retail price without any surcharge included to cover infrastructure cost. At present there is no mechanism in the U.S. to collect infrastructure fees from EV drivers when they purchase electricity. In the short run, this situation could be seen as an incentive to favor the economics of purchasing an EV when the technology is in a fledgling state. However, there will eventually need to be a system to pay for infrastructure wear and tear as EV penetration into the market increases.

On the question of "range anxiety," one option for addressing range limits in EVs is to provide a *plug-in hybrid electric vehicle* or PHEV, which initially runs on energy stored in the battery system and, if this source is depleted, switches to gasoline and an internal combustion engine (ICE) to continue driving. Since the PHEV can depend on the ICE for long-range travel (and since it also incurs this substantial additional cost beyond the batteries and motor), the all-electric range is typically less than that of a pure EV. For example, the Chevy Volt has a range of about 50 miles per full charge and an additional range of 370 miles on gasoline, according to the U.S. Environmental Protection Agency. Cumulative sales of both types of vehicles exceeded 1.4 million through 2019, including both EVs and PHEVs (Fig. 7).

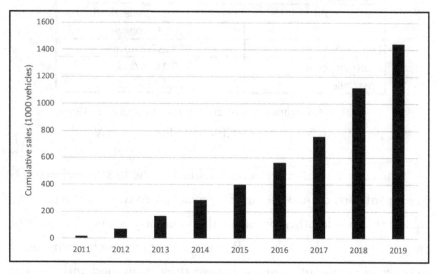

Figure 7 Cumulative sales of electric vehicles in the U.S., 2011 to 2019.
Source: Green Car Congress. Note: Includes both all-electric (EV) and plug-in hybrid-electric (PHEV) models.

While electric vehicle sales have been growing, both car makers and national governments have been expanding their commitments to phase in electrification. As of 2020, 14 countries have made commitments to phase out fossil fuel in cars between 2025 and 2050.[49] Volkswagen is committed to introducing its last generation of internal combustion engines in 2026 and to shifting to all-electric after that by replacing gasoline models with electric ones. As of 2019, Volvo is manufacturing

---

[49] List of countries: Canada, China, Costa Rica, France, Iceland, Ireland, Israel, Netherlands, Norway, Singapore, Slovenia, Sri Lanka, Sweden, and United Kingdom.

only hybrid-electric vehicles (HEVs, which include a battery powered not by a plug-in outlet but by the vehicle's internal combustion engines), PHEVs, or EVs, and has discontinued making pure ICEVs.

The evolution of the vehicle market can be seen in the sample list of vehicles marketed between 2001 and 2019 shown in Table 5. As a benchmark, the table starts with a compact ICEV sedan marketed in 2001, namely the Toyota Echo. The Echo is like the 2001 Toyota Prius HEV as both are five-passenger, four-door sedans. However, the Prius gets significantly better fuel economy despite being a heavier car thanks to the presence of the hybrid system in the drivetrain. The only EV marketed in the same timeframe is the Saturn EV-1, which was only produced in limited numbers and eventually withdrawn from the market, a development that generated controversy.[50] Although the two-passenger EV-1 has lower fuel economy (when electric consumption is converted to miles per gallon of gasoline equivalent, or mpgge) and less capacity than later EVs and PHEVs shown in the table, it helped to pave the way for the eventual return of a second generation of EVs, starting with the Nissan Leaf and 2011 Tesla Roadster. (The Roadster is not shown in the table.) The new generation, including PHEVs such as the Prius and Volt, or EVs such as the Leaf or the Tesla Model S, have larger passenger capacity and improved fuel economy compared to the EV-1. All vehicles shown from 2011 on are either four or five passenger models. The PHEV models achieve high fuel economy when running in all-electric mode, and they continue to consume gasoline efficiently thanks to their hybridized drivetrain when running on gasoline (although gasoline fuel economy is not shown). Also, the Tesla Model S luxury sedan achieves fuel economy only slightly lower than

---

[50] The controversy surrounding the rise and fall of the Saturn EV-1 is covered in the documentary film *Who Killed the Electric Car?* released by Sony Pictures in 2006.

the Nissan Leaf despite being heavier and built for performance driving thanks to the efficiency of the electric drivetrain.

Make / Model	Type	Weight (kg)	Fuel Economy (mpg)
2001 Toyota Echo	ICEV	927	32.6
2001 Toyota Prius	HEV	1259	49.7
2013 Toyota Prius	PHEV	1439	95.0
2019 Chevy Volt	PHEV	1264	106.0
2001 Saturn EV-1	EV	1350	60.0
2011 Nissan Leaf	EV	1521	99.0
2013 Tesla Model S	EV	2112	94.0

Table 5 Sample of vehicle makes, models, and model years to illustrate electrification of car market.

Note: For EV and PHEV models shown, fuel economy is miles per gallon of gasoline equivalent (mpgge), i.e., converting the energy content of electricity to equivalent energy per gallon of gasoline. For PHEV models, fuel economy figure is given for times when vehicle is operating on electric charge and does not consider contribution of driving on gasoline to overall fuel economy.

Looking to the future, it is interesting to consider how the competition between market share for EVs and PHEVs will play out. At present, car buyers have a choice between the two, and each has its appeal. For the driver who is certain they will not need the range-extending capacity of the gasoline drivetrain, there are a variety of all-electric vehicles available, with the possibility to pay more for an EV that goes farther on a full charge. The PHEV provides security that the vehicle can drive beyond the electric range. PHEVs also work well for long-distance travel, although this is increasingly possible with EVs as well, for example with the Tesla national network of fast charging points that make long-distance travel with occasional stops for fast charging possible. Eventually, the requirement for 100% carbon-free operation may push PHEVs out of the market, although such a transition does not seem imminent.

Electrification and Vehicle-to-Grid Systems

Electric vehicle charging is an ideal application of the smart grid discussed above. The EV is typically parked for long periods of time at night and plugged in for charging, meaning that the grid might accelerate charging when intermittent sources have increased output and decelerate charging when output slows. If charging facilities become broadly available in schools, office parks, and retail centers, EVs may have access to charging with real-time variable charging rate during the day as well as the night. An extension of this concept is the *vehicle-to-grid* system, or V2G, which not only permits variable one-way transmission of electricity from the grid to EVs during charging but also selling of electricity from vehicle batteries back to the grid when called upon by the smart grid control system. These power sales would be sized to help the vehicle owner pay for part of the cost of the vehicle but still make sure the battery retained sufficient charge for driving when the charging session finished. The V2G concept can be expanded to "V2X" systems, meaning that the charge in the battery could be used for other purposes, such as providing electricity to meet power demand inside the vehicle owner's residence if the system determines that the vehicle is sufficiently charged that it can part with some of its stored energy.

Figure 8 shows the function of the V2G system in detail. The ISO receives power produced by both intermittent sources such as solar and wind and by dispatchable conventional sources such as coal and natural gas (which over time would be replaced by carbon-free sources). The ISO then distributes the power to the various loads, represented by residences with charging stations in the upper right and workplaces with charging stations in the lower right. The workplace charging stations could represent any type of commercial or industrial location where commuters are likely to park their cars for an extended period. The bi-directional arrows show how the ISO can also call on the EVs that are parked and plugged in to charging stations to provide power back to the grid if and when it is needed.

Several physical and economic factors will motivate the development of V2G technology. First, a typical U.S. personal vehicle is being driven just 4% of the time in a 24-hour day and idle the other 96% of the time. This means that the battery system in an EV, which adds thousands of dollars to the cost, is both expensive and underutilized. Secondly, the total electric charge storage capacity in the batteries of a future fleet of tens of millions of EVs represents a physically large amount of storage capacity. The total storage capacity of these millions of battery systems would be larger than the current network of pumped hydro storage systems (see Table 1) and would have a maximum power output level that is significant, even in comparison to the total nameplate capacity of U.S. generation. For example, 1,000 power plants each with 1 GW of capacity represent 1,000 GW total, but 10 million electric vehicles each with 100 kW of capacity also represent 1,000 GW.

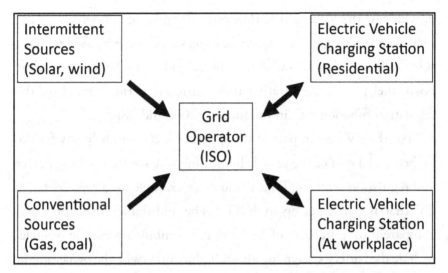

Figure 8 Schematic of vehicle-to-grid (V2G) system, showing relationship between intermittent and dispatchable energy sources, independent system operator, and V2G-enabled vehicles connected at charging facilities.

Note: ISO = Independent System Operator (see text).

For V2G to succeed, vehicle makers and grid component manufacturers will need to create charging infrastructure and controllers that will allow the vehicle owner to connect to the grid both at home at night and at their workplace during the day. The grid operator will then be able to store power from intermittent renewable resources in the batteries as it becomes available, or withdraw power, as needed. The charge control system can be designed to detect the amount of charge remaining in any given car's battery and make sure the driver retains enough charge for driving needs that remain until the vehicle parks for the night and can recharge fully. The grid operator, in turn, benefits from having thousands of distributed electricity reserves that can be called on to smooth demand from other types of electrical loads and respond to emergencies in the grid such as losses of generating plants or transmission lines. The grid operator also benefits from a service provided by the V2G vehicle fleet called "regulation", in which having many vehicles plugged in and available on standby can be used to make sure the AC oscillations and current in the grid are of the correct quality. Fossil fuel powered generation units currently perform much of the regulation function, but in the future V2G could assist.

For the EV owner, part of the appeal of V2G is to help pay for the higher initial cost of the vehicle by earning revenue from selling power and regulation services. Table 6 shows an example for a representative EV that is participating in V2G.[51] The additional costs for V2G, compared to purchase of an internal-combustion-engine vehicle, include the battery system for $10,000, since otherwise the owner might purchase an ICEV and avoid this cost. They also include the equipment to communicate with the ISO for $2,000, which with discounting annualizes to $325 per year. Assuming a lifetime of 130,000 cycles for the battery and a 10-year investment lifetime, the 13,000 cycles per year cost $0.125 per cycle to pay back the $10,000 battery system cost. The system must also purchase each incoming kWh of electricity for $0.10/kWh, so the combined cost is $0.225/kWh and $821 per year for current sold back to the grid, based on predicted energy supplied. The total cost is $1,147 per year.

The vehicle also earns $3,650 per year to be connected to the grid and to provide regulation services based on the connection available both at the residence at night and at the workplace during the day. It sells 3,650 kWh per year to the grid at $0.10 per kWh for an additional $365. After adding the combined revenue and subtracting total cost per year, a net revenue of $2,722 per year remains to pay for the $12,000 initial upcharge for an EV and for V2G participation.

---

[51] The figures in this example were adapted from an example in Kempton and Tomic (2005); the reader is referred to this source for an extended treatment of V2G.

Element	Time frame	Quantity
Capital Cost side		
Battery cost	Lifetime	$ 10,000
	Annual	$ 1,627
Cycles per year	Annual	13,000
Cycle cost/kWh	Per kWh	$ 0.125
Electricity cost	Per kWh	$ 0.100
Combined cost	Per kWh	$ 0.225
Roundtrip cost/yr	Annual	$ 821
V2G Equip Cost	Lifetime	$ 2,000
	Annual	$ 325
Total cost	Annual	$ 1,147
Revenue and net revenue side		
Total energy sold	kWh/yr	3650
Capacity revenue	Annual	$ 3,504
Energy revenue	Annual	$ 365
Gross revenue	Annual	$ 3,869
Total cost	Annual	$ 1,147
Net revenue	Annual	$ 2,722

Table 6 Summary of V2G calculations for a representative EV with annual V2G cost, V2G gross revenue, and net revenue.

Source: Adapted from an example in Kempton and Tomic (2005).

The example in Table 6 is intended only as one possible example, and there are many possible combinations of initial cost, frequency of V2G participation, and rate of revenues earned that would affect the outcome. Nevertheless, there appears to be a possibility of significant earnings if the system can be built out. Note that in this example most of the earnings come from the many hours today of connection to the grid and provision of regulation services, with only a small fraction coming from actually selling electricity. These revenues reflect what regulation is worth to the grid operator, so the economic opportunity is potentially large if the EV has access to grid-connected parking both day and night (the expectation is participation from 16 to 18 hours per day). Also, the figures shown allow plenty of battery system life for actually driving the vehicle. Of the 13,000 cycles (i.e., 1 kWh of electricity stored and discharged), 3,650 kWh are sold back to the grid, so more than 9,000 kWh are available to propel the vehicle.

As with the smart grid, cybersecurity poses a concern. Possible threats range from small-scale individual meddling with V2G-connected vehicles to use of the vehicles as a portal for causing a system-wide grid failure. This risk must be managed successfully if the public is to have confidence in V2G.

To sum up, the V2G concept illustrates the systems thinking principle of arriving at a better solution by solving two problems together rather than trying to solve them separately. The transportation sector needs to reduce CO_2 emissions and switch to renewable energy resources to propel vehicles. The electric utility sector needs to keep the grid stable and reliable and to incorporate renewable energy supplies from intermittent resources such as solar and wind. The two sectors converge on the technological concepts of smart grid, vehicle-to-grid transmission, and onboard electricity storage in EVs. In essence, they are sharing the "ownership" of the batteries: when the vehicle is moving down the road, the battery is a transportation asset, and when it is stationary and charging and discharging to and from the grid, it is a utility asset.

Other Transportation not Included in Light-Duty Electrification

The previous sections have shown how part of the challenge of carbon-free energy can be solved by taking two energy systems, namely the electricity grid and the light-duty energy supply, and combining them into a single system. Here another systems thinking principle can be applied, namely examining the redrawn boundaries to see what elements have been left out by the boundaries once redrawn. In the US, there are three major remaining elements: 1) long-distance trucking; 2) aviation; and 3) a "miscellaneous other" category that includes freight railroads, all types of ships, and remaining road-based public transportation systems.

The relative energy consumption of these three categories can be viewed in comparison to the size of energy consumption for light-duty passenger vehicles using 2019 data (Fig. 9). The four categories together consume about 26 Quads, or about one-fourth of all U.S. energy consumption. The category of "light-duty passenger vehicles" at 15.6 Quads represents the combined value for passenger vehicles and light trucks, most or all of which might be covered by electrification in the future, depending on whether the network of charging stations for fast charging of intercity EV travel succeeds in the future. The next largest category is heavy trucks at 6.2 Quads, which is significantly less than light-duty passenger vehicles, although large in absolute terms. The heavy truck category includes both single-body trucks and tractor-trailers used for moving freight. The third category of aviation at 2.3 Quads is still slightly larger than the sum of all remaining energy uses in the "All other" category at 2.2 Quads.

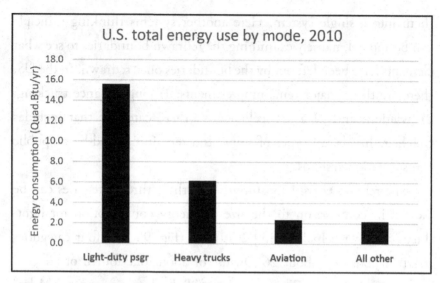

Figure 9 Comparison of four major categories of 2019
U.S. transportation energy use in Quadrillion Btus.

Source: U.S. Department of Energy, Oak Ridge
National Laboratories.

Starting with the smallest category in Fig. 9, we can consider how carbon-free energy might be brought to transportation applications within the "All other" category. Many of these modes already use electricity. The list includes urban subways, virtually all of which are powered by electricity for underground air quality reasons. It also includes classic electric streetcars that operate in street traffic, light-rail systems that run in both on-street and off-street conditions, commuter rail trains that run on electricity, and electrified long-distance travel including high-speed rail. Where the trains are already running on overhead electric wires (also known as "catenary"), the rail operator can shift to carbon-free electricity.

Rail operators can also electrify rail lines by adding catenary so that trains can run on electricity. For rail lines that do not have catenary, the conventional solution is the diesel-electric locomotive where the diesel internal combustion engine drives a generator that in turn powers electric motors that propel the train. Most locomotives use diesel-electric rather than pure diesel drivetrains because diesel-electric provides a more reliable way of transmitting the large quantities of power required for a train.[52] In any case, providing catenary and electric locomotives gives access to carbon-free electricity. As an example, the U.S. long-distance passenger rail operator Amtrak electrified the tracks on the northeast corridor between New Haven and Boston between 1994 and 2000, enabling emissions-free operation. For urban public buses, shifting from diesel propulsion to overhead wires in the form of trolleybuses or to battery-electric buses is another option. Battery-electric buses are increasingly popular in recent years thanks to lower weight and better performance of battery systems.

A third option is modal shifting from other modes to electrified rail. For example, a public transit operator might convert a busy urban bus line to electric light rail. Similarly, improving service speed and quality on electrified high-speed rail lines can win passengers from short-haul aviation, reducing emissions. In 2000 Amtrak introduced higher-quality electric "Acela" service on the Northeast Corridor between Washington, DC, and New York, and since that time, the share of the overall air-rail market served by rail has grown.[53]

---

[52] The only exception to the diesel-electric rule is for diesel locomotives in certain niche, light-duty applications where the maximum power required to move a small number of cars is small enough that a sufficiently strong mechanical drivetrain from internal combustion engine to wheels can be fabricated.

[53] This comparison looks only at the combination of rail and air service between DC and NY, considering these to be "high-quality" modes for which passengers are willing to pay a premium for higher linehaul speeds and avoiding congestion on major highways. Other modes, namely driving in a personal car or taking a public intercity bus are left out because they are not of the same quality and therefore not comparable.

Lastly, there may be some opportunities to replace shipping with land-based, electrified transportation. Both short- and long-distance ships typically use diesel in internal combustion engines as a propulsion source. There may be some limited opportunities to shift ship travel to electrified rail lines, for instance, if a rail bridge or tunnel opens in a metropolitan area and replaces a diesel-powered ferry service. Generally, though, ships operate on corridors for which they are uniquely suited such as long-distance travel on canals or across oceans. Biofuels or hydrogen, discussed below, are a more likely solution.

Heavy-Duty Trucks and Long-distance Trucking

Long-distance trucking in heavy-duty trucks poses a challenge for electrification because, unlike cars, trucks accumulate most of their vehicle-miles in long-distance movements between cities, as opposed to traveling short distances within cities. As a rough rule, the average U.S. passenger car drives four out of every five miles in routine daily short-distance driving and just one in five on long intercity trips (e.g., for business, vacations, etc.). For the U.S. trucking industry, the split is reversed: four out of every five miles driven are intercity miles. The expectation in trucking is that the vehicle can operate for distances of hundreds of miles between refueling stops, and that refueling happens swiftly so that the driver can return promptly to driving, if they are under time pressure to make a delivery. Not all truck operating patterns fit this description. Some trucks carry out a "milk run" in which each day they make a circular route of deliveries and pickups and return to the same base at night. This pattern lends itself better to electrification, and companies such as Tesla are developing battery-powered truck tractors that can fill this market.

Limited opportunities for electric trucks notwithstanding, the main options for transforming freight trucking are to improve the efficiency of trucks, shift more freight from truck to rail or shipping (which are more energy efficient), or use alternative fuels. Regarding efficiency, trucks are already relatively efficient compared to passenger cars: In a loaded trailer-truck, most of the weight is the freight, as opposed to the tare weight of the empty truck and trailer; in a car, most of the weight is the car, and not the passengers. As a result, U.S. freight vehicles move about the same total ton-miles of content as do passenger vehicles (i.e., the weight of either goods or people on board multiplied by the distance traveled) but use about a third of the energy.[54] Still, there are continuing opportunities to make truck bodies lighter and more aerodynamic and to improve fuel efficiency of engines. These measures might result in a 20% reduction in energy use if they fully penetrated the truck fleet, compared to a do-nothing scenario.

Even more energy and CO_2 savings are possible if we move more freight by modes other than trucks. Figure 10 shows how in recent years the truck mode has exhibited consistently higher energy intensity in moving freight. Freight energy intensity is measured as the average energy requirement per ton-mile of freight, estimated by dividing total energy attributed to a freight mode by total ton-miles moved by that mode. In the U.S., the truck mode has averaged significantly higher intensity, consuming between 2,000 and 2,500 Btus per ton-mile, while ship or rail use less than 500 Btus. These statistics must be interpreted carefully. They reflect the total energy consumed by a mode in a year divided by the total ton-miles moved. Railroads and ships move a significant quantity of bulk commodities that are dense and not time-sensitive,

---

[54] David Greene pointed out this fact in 1996 in the book *Transportation and Energy*. Based on freight tonnage and transportation energy consumption trends, it remains approximately true today.

allowing them to weight their average Btu/ton-miles toward the low end in a way not available to trucking, which carries a disproportionate share of high-value, rapidly shipped, and low-density consumer goods. Nevertheless, even after factoring out this influence, for comparable products, rail or marine are more energy efficient thanks to physical advantages over trucking. Shifting to railroads is especially attractive because rail can provide travel speed that rivals that of trucking, while still cutting energy use, by using shipping containers or truck trailers loaded directly onto trains. From an energy efficiency point of view, railroads have many advantages over trucks: a smoother rolling surface, more efficient propulsion in the form of a large locomotive instead of many smaller truck units, less aerodynamic drag in one train compared to many individual vehicles, and less stop-and-go operation during a trip. As a result, fuel economy for moving a tractor-trailer equivalent by container train is about twice as good as that of moving the same trailer-load by truck. Business has been booming for shipping containers by train: since the early 1980s, the container business for the major U.S. railroads (Burlington-Northern Santa Fe or BNSF, Union Pacific Southern Pacific or UPSP, and so on) has been a major growth driver of economic revenue for the overall railroad industry. Opportunities for shifting containers and other freight from truck to ships are more limited because ships travel more slowly and on a sparser network, but where these opportunities arise, they can save energy as well.

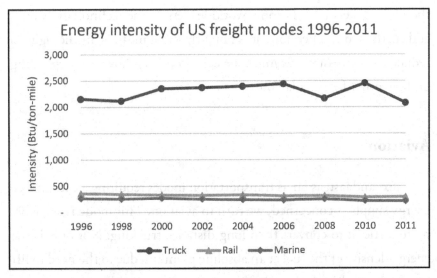

Figure 10 Freight energy intensity in Btu/ton-mile of U.S. Truck, Rail, and Marine modes 1996-2011.

Source: U.S. Department of Energy, Oak Ridge National Laboratories.

Transferring freight from trucks to trains in a big way would lop off much of the energy consumption currently attributed to the trucking industry, but as an additional measure, we might consider electrifying or re-electrifying some of the railroads so that they could have access to renewable electricity from the grid. This option is a further advantage of shifting freight to railroads since connecting locomotives to overhead wires is feasible for railroads but not for trucking. In the past, the U.S. used electrified rail systems more heavily, for example in the northeast where the Pennsylvania Railroad built an extensive network of electrified lines in the first half of the 20th century, and in the Pacific Northwest where the railroads used electricity to get trains through remote parts of the Cascade Mountains where it was difficult to supply fuel for diesel locomotives. Electrification is not cheap, however: not only are the wires expensive, but also the shift away from diesel locomotives (where the U.S. makers have become world leaders in the technology) would add further cost. Therefore, it is not a first-line measure in the fight to reduce CO_2 emissions. It might be called on later, however, depending on how other factors play out.

Aviation

Next and last, as far as transportation modes requiring a carbon-free energy supply is concerned, we turn to aviation. This mode is arguably more difficult to convert than long-distance trucking: Not only is the energy density of the fuel at an absolute premium due to the need to lift it to cruising altitude, but also low temperatures at those high altitudes affect how the fuels behave as they are stored in tanks and then burned in jet engines. In the interim, due to the challenges surrounding large-scale development of an alternative transportation fuel, the focus in aviation is on improving energy efficiency to squeeze as much utility out of each quantity of jet fuel consumed.

One area for improving efficiency is the use of lighter materials to reduce the tare weight of the aircraft, which does not include the passengers and their personal effects. A high-profile fatal crash of a passenger aircraft with wooden wings in 1931, which resulted in the death of the famous college football coach Knut Rockne, pushed the aviation industry in the direction of using aluminum instead of wood from the mid-20th century onward. In recent decades, the limits of lightening aluminum aircraft became apparent, and at the same time, carbon-fiber composite materials emerged that could meet the same strength requirements with even less weight. Jet engine technology has improved as well. For example, advanced ceramics allow jet engines to operate at higher maximum temperatures, improving efficiency.

Separate from advances in aircraft technology, airlines have developed operational best practices under the heading of "yield management" (also called "perishable asset review management" or PARM) that maximize the number of seats with paying customers in each scheduled flight. Yield management uses detailed knowledge of how customers respond to ticket prices to set prices that encourage travelers to buy tickets early if they know their travel plans so that part of the capacity fills up early. Then the rest of the seats are sold at higher prices on shorter notice, or in some cases, at the last minute at a deep discount. Since the marginal impact on energy use of adding a passenger to a plane that is already flying is small compared to the energy required for just the plane itself, yield management increases passenger-miles faster than energy consumption, and Btus per passenger mile decrease. Yield management has led to an increase in average U.S. occupancy of airliner seats from 49.7% in 1970 to 84.2% in 2019. Yield management can also be applied to other passenger modes such as long-distance rail travel, and where successful, it can reduce energy consumption per passenger by moving more passengers per fixed quantity of energy required to run a train.

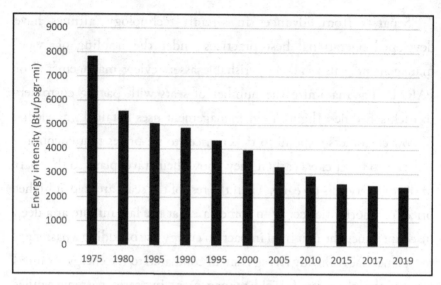

Figure 11 U.S. aviation average energy intensity in Btu per passenger-mile, 1975 to 2019.

Source: U.S. Department of Energy, Oak Ridge National Laboratories.

With the combination of improved technology and operations, U.S. average energy intensity for aviation decreased from 7,826 Btu per passenger-mile in 1975 to 2,444 Btu per passenger-mile in 2019 (Fig. 11). Current values are similar to delivered energy intensity of U.S. privately owned light-duty vehicles, even though aircraft are so much faster, because the occupancy of aircraft seats is so much higher. (The typical number of occupants of a car is between 1 and 2 people for a 5-passenger vehicle, and occupancy is around 25% of all available seats.) Going forward, there will be diminishing returns to efforts to further reduce aviation energy intensity. The change from 1975 to 2012 represents a 68% reduction in energy intensity. A further 68% reduction from the 2012 figure would leave intensity at about 800 Btu/passenger-mile, which would border on physically impossible. At some point, alternative fuels must come into play. This point brings us to the discussion of the first alternative fuel, namely biofuels.

First Alternative to Electrification: Biofuels

Bioenergy sources were already introduced in Chap. 7 as an energy source for electricity generation or heating, in the form of either dedicated bio-energy crops (e.g., wood pellets, dried grasses, etc.) or biological materials recovered from the waste stream. Simply put, a biofuel is a virgin or reclaimed bio-energy resource that is converted for use as a transportation energy source. The reason for the use of the prefix "bio" is that the plant or tree is using its internal biological process to capture energy from the sun and accumulate it internally in the form of seeds, oils, or woody materials.

In a context where society is trying to phase out GHG emissions from all types of energy use, the goal with biofuels is to minimize net GHG emissions from all stages of the supply chain and then to replace as much petroleum as possible. The emphasis on net emissions is important because in the short- to medium-term the overall supply chain may rely on fossil fuels as an energy source (e.g., transporting fuels by truck), so some amount of GHG emission will occur. Biofuels have some advantages as a petroleum substitute: they are liquids that can coexist alongside petroleum products (such as ethanol or biodiesel blends), and they would continue the use of dispensing stations that deliver liquid fuels and internal combustion engines in highway vehicles, all of which are familiar to drivers, mechanics, filling station owners, and so on.

On the downside, biofuels are more susceptible to storage and transportation problems than their fossil counterparts. Gasoline and petro-diesel are quite inert and can be stored for long periods of time without degrading, but ethanol and biodiesel must be used within a shorter timeframe.

Biofuels also have CO_2 emissions associated with their production life cycle (growing crops, processing into fuels, and transporting unprocessed crops and finished biofuels), which undercut the emissions reduction benefit of using agricultural commodities as feedstock. For example, biofuel crops may use fertilizers with fossil fuel inputs, or farm equipment may operate on fuels that are blends of petro- and biodiesel. Biofuels do have the potential to slow the rate of GHG accumulation in the atmosphere because, unlike petroleum-derived fuels, the carbon in the fuel initially comes from the atmosphere. Therefore, there is potential for a circular loop where carbon moves between fuel and atmosphere, without needing to extract fossil fuels. However, fossil fuels may be used in various ways during production, negating some of the savings. For example, in the distillation phase of corn ethanol production, crop sugars must be first fermented in a highly aqueous solution to make ethanol molecules (or else the fermentation process will not work), but then a large amount of energy must be expended to distill the ethanol fuel so that it is 99% or more pure ethanol. In the U.S., the energy for distillation usually comes from burning natural gas. In the long run, systems might be developed to use largely renewable energy during the life cycle. Transporting and processing raw materials and finished products could be electrified, and process heat for distillation could come from industrial heat pumps run on renewable electricity.

Considering all these factors, how can we be sure that biofuel use in any particular scenario will reduce greenhouse-gas emissions? Analysts use the metric of "net energy benefit" or "net energy benefit ratio" as an approximate indicator of how well a biofuel succeeds in avoiding environmental harm by maximizing the energy gained for one unit of energy input in the biofuel.[55] For a biofuel to have a positive impact, the NEB value must be positive, and the NEB ratio value must be greater than one.

Table 7 presents production of biodiesel from soybeans as an example of how the NEB ratio is calculated from agricultural- and industrial-processing energy inputs as well as the energy available in the fuel. A single gallon of biodiesel with energy content of 117,000 Btu/gallon is used as a basis. At first, energy must be expended on growing the soy crop and on fertilizer. During the industrial process of converting the soybean harvest to biodiesel, energy is expended on process heat as well and on transportation of raw materials and finished product. There is also embodied energy in the equipment used in the process. Finally, there are other small energy expenditures that would be broken out in a more detailed presentation but are captured here in an "All other" category. The total energy consumption is the sum of the six elements in the table at approximately 58,000 Btu, so for every 1 unit of energy input, approximately 2.02 units of energy are provided in the biodiesel. In this example, although the energy input into the process is significant, there is a substantial net energy gain in the resulting biodiesel.

---

[55] The difference between NEB and NEB ratio is as follows. Suppose a biofuel delivers 90,000 Btu of energy per unit for 30,000 Btu of energy input. Then there are 3 units of energy out for every 1 unit of input. The NEB would be 3 − 1 = 2, and the NEB ratio would be 3/1 = 3.

Element	Quantity	Units
Agricultural energy	17.46	Mbtu/gallon
Fertilizer	10.48	Mbtu/gallon
Process heat	13.74	Mbtu/gallon
Transportation	2.29	Mbtu/gallon
Embodied energy	8.07	Mbtu/gallon
All other	5.78	Mbtu/gallon
Total energy input	57.81	Mbtu/gallon
Biodiesel energy content	117.00	Mbtu/gallon
Net Energy Benefit (NEB)	1.02	--
Net Energy Benefit ratio	2.02	--

Table 7 Representative example of summary calculation of Net Energy Benefit (NEB) and NEB Ratio for biodiesel made from soybeans based on energy input and fuel content per gallon.

Note: 1 Mbtu = 1,000 Btu. Delivered values vary widely depending on local performance, weather conditions that vary by year, and other factors. See discussion in text.

The NEB ratio value suggests that shifting from conventional to biodiesel might reduce energy consumption by 50%, based on a value of approximately two to one. Estimating CO_2 reduction, however, is not as simple as assuming a one-to-one ratio between units of energy saved and emissions reduced. The energy inputs in Table 7 come from a variety of sources with different emissions rates. As an indication of the potential GHG reduction benefit, the National Biodiesel Board estimates a CO_2 reduction rate of 76.4% when shifting from petro-diesel to biodiesel and that the two emit 24.6 pounds and 5.8 pounds of CO_2 per gallon, respectively.

The figures in Table 7 are provided only as an example of how net energy benefit is calculated and to illustrate how biodiesel might save energy in some circumstances. Agricultural conditions, technical level of processes, and energy efficiency standards vary widely, and a different biodiesel process in a different location or year could have a different outcome. Also, the example does not represent other biofuels such as ethanol from corn. Regardless of the type of biofuel or the variation in possible NEB values, two points can be made regarding efficiency: 1) It is desirable in the short run to minimize energy required to maximize NEB and NEB ratio, and 2) If biofuels are to become truly sustainable in the long run, all energy inputs should be converted to carbon-neutral ones.

Along with energy efficiency, *productivity* of converting crops to biofuels can be a challenge. The difference between efficiency and productivity concerns the point at which transformation occurs. The process is inefficient if cropland makes available crops such as seeds or corn kernels, and then our various technologies only extract a small fraction of the energy available in the seeds or kernels. If, however, the crop volume coming from the land is small compared to the area under cultivation, then the process is unproductive, regardless of how good our technology is.

In the case of field crops, the fraction of solar energy arriving from the sun that is converted to grains or seeds that can be harvested is small, so that large amounts of land are required to make large amounts of bioenergy from crops. Compare a biofuel crop growing in a field to the same amount of space covered with solar PV panels. Whereas a field of panels in a solar farm might convert 10% of the incoming solar energy to electricity, less than 1% of that energy is made available in the seeds extracted (corn kernels or soybeans) for conversion into transportation fuels. As a result, the amount of land available around the world is insufficient to meet the global demand for transportation energy with biofuels from conventional crops, especially given the need to grow sufficient food for the world's population.

To illustrate, we might ask how much of these fuels we could produce if we pushed production to the limit using available technology.

For example, we use only a fraction of our corn and soy crops to make biofuels – but what if we could use all of them? In the case of corn, if we used the entire 2005 U.S. crop to make ethanol, we would have displaced just 12% of the gasoline consumption of 140 billion gallons in that year. The case of soy is even worse because, although the process of making biodiesel from soy is more energy efficient than that of corn to ethanol, energy yields per acre of soy are lower than those for corn. So, the entire 2005 soy crop would displace just 6% of the 2005 diesel demand of 38 billion gallons even though the total demand for diesel in gallons of fuel is less than that for gasoline. And, of course, it would not be practical to commit all these crops to biofuel production because they are vital as animal feeds and in the food processing industry, both domestically and as exports. It is surely possible to improve productivity of corn and soy production and thereby increase biofuel capacity, but when the starting point is 12% or 6%, these approaches by themselves clearly will not cover the entire demand for transportation fuel.

Another way to illustrate the limited productivity of corn ethanol and soy biodiesel is to compare energy content of the annual production to the total demand of transportation applications that might consume them (Fig. 12). In 2010, the energy content of U.S. ethanol was on the order of 1 Quad, and that of biodiesel was around 100 trillion Btu. In comparison, the consumption by heavy trucks, aviation, and marine applications are all larger than either one.

The intercity travel component of light-duty vehicle energy consumption is included in the figure as well, based on the estimated share of total light-duty vehicle energy use that is long-distance as opposed to short-range and urban and the possibility that in the future biofuels might power intercity light-duty vehicle movements in place of gasoline. In fact, the sum of all the applications including rail is almost

13 Quads, which is more than an order of magnitude larger than that of combined ethanol and biodiesel.

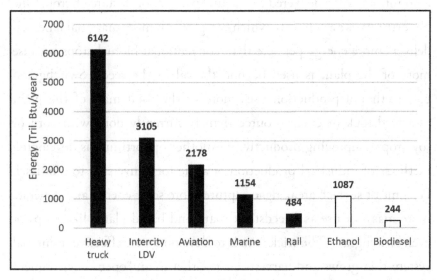

Figure 12 Comparison of biofuel energy content to U.S. transportation energy demand for applications suitable for biofuels in 2016 in trillion Btu.
Source: U.S. Department of Energy.

In the worst case, the large land take for biofuels can lead to policy failures in which measures intended to develop greener fuel alternatives make the situation worse. In the 2000s, heavy reliance on imports pressed European countries to develop new resources so that they could supply a larger share of transportation energy from biofuels. Some turned to overseas plantations to grow palm oil for the biofuel, and this led to the clearing of rain forests to grow palm oil plantations. Not only was the loss of biodiversity objectionable, but the process of planting the palms lead to tillage and other practices that released large amounts of CO_2 bound up in the soil and trees into the atmosphere. Instead of decreasing, net CO_2 emissions went up.

In the case of biomass and biofuels, here are on the horizon some technologies that may partly address the problem of relatively low amount of energy delivered in the fuel per acre or hectare of crop. One opportunity is switchgrass, which can grow on more marginal land and delivers more energy per acre than conventional biofuel crops because more of the plant is used beyond the oil in the seeds. Switchgrass-based ethanol production uses more of the total mass of the plant as a feedstock or energy source than is currently done with corn or soy crops, improving productivity. Another opportunity is developing methods of industrial production of algae for conversion to biodiesel. Per unit of surface area, algae capture more solar energy and generate more mass for use as a feedstock than land-based plants like crops or even switchgrass. The trick here is to develop a cost-effective industrial system that grows and harvests algae either in an "open" environment (e.g., some sort of natural lagoon) or a "closed" one (a purpose-built industrial pool or tank).

In the short- to medium-term, heavy trucks and commercial aviation remain two areas where biofuels are especially of interest. For trucks, a more abundant feedstock for making biodiesel could increase the share of the energy supplied by biofuels, displacing petro-diesel. On the aviation side, operators have made some inroads on using mixtures of petroleum-derived jet fuel and biofuel. Virgin Airlines claims to be the first to have flown a commercial flight using a biofuel mixture, a flight from London to Amsterdam in February 2008 with one of four tanks containing 20% coconut and babassu oil. Boeing and Honeywell have developed a fuel called Bio-SPK (synthetic paraffinic kerosene, produced from a variety of biologically-derived oils), first announced at the Paris Air Show in June 2009. According to this joint venture, Bio-SPK has been found to perform as well as or better than standard jet fuel. The challenge with Bio-SPK will be to create a sustainable supply chain based on a feedstock that does not threaten food security and that does not have other major adverse environmental side effects.

Second Alternative to Electrification: Hydrogen

As a transportation energy source, hydrogen has much in common with electrification but also some key differences. Fueling of a hydrogen vehicle resembles that of a hydrocarbon-driven one, with hydrogen dispensed into a tank on board the vehicle. To store sufficient hydrogen so that the vehicle can travel meaningful distances between refueling, the hydrogen is at present typically stored at high pressures of 5,000 or 10,000 psi (pounds per square inch). Another option, although less common, is to cool the hydrogen to a very low temperature so that it becomes liquid, again so that it can be stored compactly on board the vehicle. When consumed as an energy source to propel the vehicle, the hydrogen supply creates a voltage drop on a circuit to power an electric motor, at which point the function is identical to that of an EV.

At the heart of a hydrogen-powered vehicle is the *hydrogen fuel cell*, which converts the hydrogen fuel to an electric current (Fig. 13). Hydrogen arrives from the hydrogen tank under pressure to the anode side of the fuel cell, where a membrane allows protons to pass but not electrons. A surplus of electrons between the anode and the cathode on the other side of the membrane results in a voltage difference that can be applied to the vehicle motor for propulsion. As electrons pass through the motor and arrive at the anode, they recombine with the protons to form hydrogen molecules again, which combine with oxygen molecules in the air as they exit from the fuel cell to form water molecules. Formation of water from hydrogen and oxygen happens naturally because hydrogen as an element does not remain isolated in ambient conditions.

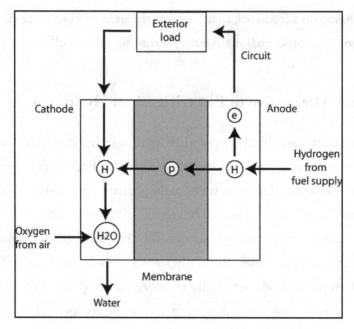

Figure 13 Components of a hydrogen fuel cell, including hydrogen supply and exhaust system.

An individual fuel cell generates a voltage difference of about 1 Volt in practice. This amount is not sufficient to perform significant work such as powering a vehicle, so fuel cells are arranged in series into a *fuel cell stack* that provides sufficient voltage and power for vehicle propulsion. Fuel cell stacks used in limited-production hydrogen-fuel-cell vehicles, or HFCVs, from makers such as Toyota or General Motors, have a maximum power output on the order of 100 kW. This amount is equivalent to about 135 horsepower, which is similar in size to a small car engine, although both hydrogen and battery-electric vehicles can achieve similar performance to an ICEV with lower maximum power.

Hydrogen emerged as a transportation fuel at a time when automakers and governments were looking for a long-term alternative to petroleum-based fuels, and breakthroughs in battery technology had not yet happened. An industrial capacity to extract pure hydrogen for chemical refining already existed, and although it would be complex to expand the infrastructure to include the transportation energy supply, there was a promise of abundant fuel for cars and trucks, and possibly other modes of transportation. The feedstock would be abundant for making the hydrogen, either from natural gas in the short run or eventually from water to be 100% carbon free.

Today, many of the advantages of hydrogen remain. Hydrogen combusted in a fuel cell results only in water emitted from the tailpipe. The energy for converting water to hydrogen is also abundant, provided we build the infrastructure. Any type of renewable resource or nuclear energy could be used to make electricity that would then drive electrolysis, resulting in hydrogen that could be distributed and byproduct oxygen that could be vented to the atmosphere. Heat from renewable or nuclear energy sources might eventually be used to directly separate hydrogen from oxygen in water, without the intermediate step of generating electricity.

Industry does not currently extract hydrogen using carbon-free energy sources. Instead, most industrial hydrogen is extracted using steam reforming of methane from natural gas, which also results in CO_2 emissions as the carbon in the methane combines with atmospheric oxygen. But this temporary stepping-stone could be overlooked, because if the hydrogen vehicles and their dispensing station network took off, hydrogen providers could in the future switch from non-renewable natural gas to renewable energy to make the hydrogen.

As the first decade of the 21st century progressed, optimism about the promise of hydrogen gave way to growing concerns about its difficulties. Some of these were technical: building an efficient, reliable fuel cell or a compact and safe storage system that is also cost-effective proved to be an elusive target. Consider just one of these challenges, namely storage on board the vehicle: storing enough hydrogen in a passenger car requires either cooling it down to cryogenic temperatures or compressing it to 5,000 or 10,000 psi. For reasons of energy losses and cost, high pressure has been the most favored option recently, but even this solution adds substantially to vehicle cost compared to an ICEV that simply stores gasoline at normal pressure in a gas tank.

The second set of problems came from infrastructure, where the concept of hydrogen as a transportation fuel began to face growing competition from an emerging force, namely the EV. The emergence of EVs from Tesla, Nissan, and other makes built on the success of gasoline-powered hybrid vehicles by connecting them to grid-supplied electricity, sometimes in the case of PHEVs used in tandem with gasoline as an energy source. Compared to the situation with electrification, hydrogen vehicles were at a disadvantage because there was not an infrastructure system for dispensing hydrogen ready to go. The industrial hydrogen infrastructure did not have nearly the capacity it would need in the long run to power the entire transportation system. Also, there was no capacity to deliver hydrogen long distances via pipeline or filling station equipment for the national fleet of hydrogen vehicles that would presumably emerge.

A pathway did exist for growing hydrogen deliveries, in which at first hydrogen filling stations could take delivery from hydrogen plants by tractor-trailer or make hydrogen on-site using small-scale electrolysis machines. As the use of hydrogen grew, a network of underground pipelines could replace over-the-road delivery or decentralized electrolysis as central manufacturing would presumably be the cheapest and most energy-efficient way to produce hydrogen in large quantities.

Compared to electric vehicles, however, too few of the infrastructure pieces were in place. As the electrification of light-duty vehicles took root in the period 2011-2019, there was no opportunity for hydrogen infrastructure to catch up. Electric charging is now a mature technology, and in some cases has advantages over refilling a gasoline tank; for example, for many vehicle owners, recharging at home is a practical possibility. And of course, where the "hydrogen network" is, as yet, non-existent for transportation, the electric grid is already ubiquitous. In May 2009, the Obama administration terminated federal support for research into hydrogen as a light-duty transportation fuel.

Electric vehicles may have eclipsed hydrogen in the light-duty vehicle market, but in the meantime the auto industry, led by Toyota, General Motors, Hyundai, and other automakers, has developed a hydrogen fuel cell vehicle with reliable fuel cell stacks and on-board high-pressure hydrogen storage. The obstacles are that they are expensive to build and do not have a hydrogen fueling network. However, there may eventually be niche applications for hydrogen. For certain larger light-duty vehicles that typically travel long distances each day, such as large SUVs, it may eventually make more sense to replace petroleum with hydrogen rather than electricity.

Long-distance energy consumption in heavy trucks provides an especially favorable application for hydrogen fuel cells. It may be possible to store energy in a trailer-truck with greater energy density, and therefore less weight, using high-pressure hydrogen rather than an equivalent lithium-ion battery system. Also, long-distance trucks might refuel in the future with hydrogen at a truck stop along interstate highways similarly to how they refuel with diesel now, loading a large quantity of energy into the truck much faster than they could charge an equivalent amount into a battery system in an all-electric truck. Even if there were a cost premium compared to using diesel and internal combustion engines, the operation may be able to absorb the cost because trucking is such a vital form of freight for high-value finished goods.

Lastly, concepts exist for hydrogen in commercial aircraft as a substitute for hydrocarbon jet fuel. This solution is technically very challenging. In 2019, a start-up company called ZeroAvia began flying a hydrogen-powered regional aircraft with six seats and a range of 500 miles. However, there are currently physical limits on both the range and maximum payload of the airborne hydrogen drivetrain and there is no timeline for when a prototype full-size hydrogen jet liner might appear.

Integrating the Energy System While Re-evaluating Our Relationship with Energy Demand

We can summarize this chapter on systems integration with three key observations. First, energy systems that were previously in separate silos are converging toward one, with a central theme of electrification. With electricity penetrating the light-duty vehicle fleet and other modes, the petroleum-based transportation energy supply that was previously separate is becoming part of the electrified energy supply. With the influx of heat pumps for space heating and process heat applications in industry (see Chapter 7), a third system, namely the infrastructure for providing heat currently supported by natural gas, may be joining as well. So, in the end, a single electricity grid powered by renewables may support a wide range of applications: lighting and electronics, pumping, air conditioning, transportation, and heating. For the time being some transportation applications (such as aviation and long-distance marine transport) do not fall easily inside the boundaries of this system, so alternative carriers besides electricity are still in the running.

Second, the need for many of the technologies discussed in this chapter results from the challenges posed by the intermittency and seasonality of renewables. The integrated energy system of the future might incorporate a mixture of increased storage capacity and long-distance transmission, smart grid technology, distributed generation in electricity microgrids, and vehicle-to-grid enabled light-duty vehicles. Taken together, these elements can store and release electricity more effectively, and they can also smooth out overall demand so it more closely matches available generation.

And third, the transition to a renewably powered energy system of the future provides a juncture to ask the more fundamental question of "how much energy do we really need to consume?" The solutions proposed in this chapter are complex, require significant capital investment (even though they can pay for themselves by avoiding severe environmental damage), and require a long time to complete. Individuals and society collectively have opportunities to choose different levels of simplicity or complexity. The challenge of reducing GHG emissions from aviation is a prime example. We could invest large sums of money in expensive carbon-free solutions for flying – or we could shift to more business meetings in virtual space that allow participants to communicate without leaving the location where they live and work, through Skype, Zoom, and so on. We can rethink our whole relationship with energy and energy consumption. As Bill McKibben writes in the book *Deep Economy*, the fossil energy systems of the past were good servants that did whatever we asked them to do. The renewable energy systems of the future are more like partners; we need to work together, considering our needs but also renewables' capabilities.

Speaking of renewable energy, the contents of Chaps. 5 to 8 have been predicated on the assumption that the energy system would be built on renewable energy sources. We have, however, already described how nuclear energy or fossil fuel with carbon sequestration might also contribute to a carbon-free energy supply. These two sources deserve a closer look, so they are the focus of the next chapter.

CHAPTER 9

Other Options – Nuclear and Sequestration

Up to this point, the focus has been on renewable energy as the carbon-free source of energy that can eliminate the emissions of carbon to the atmosphere from energy use. However, this goal could also be achieved in the future using nuclear energy. Nuclear fuels are not based on carbon, so when they are consumed in a nuclear plants, they do not emit CO_2 or other GHGs as a byproduct. The life cycle of nuclear power, including building plants, transporting fuel, and other stages, have some amount of climate impact, but these contributions are similar to those for any energy source. It is also possible in concept to continue to burn fossil fuels for energy without impacting the climate if carbon capture and sequestration (CCS) can be developed successfully. Using CCS, byproduct CO_2 from the combustion of fossil fuels is diverted from being released to the atmosphere and instead is captured and placed into long-term storage, for example by injection into underground geologic formations. Fossil fuels are nonrenewable resources and will eventually run out if we continue to use them, but in the meantime they could be rendered carbon-neutral if CCS is successful.

Currently, the main alternative energy strategy in use around the world is to expand renewables, not nuclear or CCS. While advanced nuclear or CCS technologies have made relatively little progress in the last two or three decades, renewable technologies such as solar PV or wind progressed rapidly and are expanding year after year. Solar PV panels or utility-scale wind turbines are by now "commercial off the shelf," or COTS, technologies, and many countries are regularly adding solar and wind capacity, driven by both policies and market demand. By contrast, nuclear and CCS are not being expanded at this time, except for a small number of conventional large nuclear power plants, including a single plant in the U.S. (the Vogtle plant in the state of Georgia) and several plants in China and South Korea; CCS is being pursued in a limited number of pilot projects. Lack of a mature, proven next-generation nuclear or CCS technology prevents the uptake of these options. (The difference between conventional and next-generation nuclear is explained below.)

On the other hand, renewables may be growing, but their inroads into changing the world's mix of primary energy supply has been modest to date. In 1980, world total primary energy demand was 283 Quads, of which 85% came from fossil sources. In 2019, the total had risen to 600 Quads, of which 84% came from fossil fuels, according to the U.S. Energy Information Administration. This change represents a mixed result. The non-fossil portion grew by ~54 Quads, or 126%, over this period, and since nuclear grew only modestly, most of this growth was in the renewable sector. But because the overall growth of 317 Quads (112% increase) was so large, non-fossil sources were only barely keeping pace and increased by just one percentage point. Despite great interest among many countries to reduce environmental impact, the fact that the share for fossil fuels decreased so little in 39 years shows how challenging it will be going forward to replace fossil fuels. This process will likely play out over a time period on the order of decades. Therefore, there is time for breakthroughs in either nuclear or CCS to emerge that might change the course away from renewables and toward one of these other two sources.

If either nuclear or fossil fuels with CCS were to become a major non-carbon emitting source of the future, many of the downstream transitions described in Chap. 8 would remain the same. Electrification would still be central to the sustainable energy system, to avoid carbon emissions to the atmosphere. Battery-electric vehicles or electrified rail systems would come to dominate the transportation market. Heat pumps powered by electricity from nuclear power or fossil fuel plants with CCS would replace conventional fossil fuel plants to avoid carbon emissions.

Nuclear Energy

The status of the world nuclear energy industry as an option for carbon-free energy is mixed. On the one hand, a fleet of reactors located largely in wealthier countries continues to generate emissions-free energy, in some countries meeting a significant fraction of total demand. On the other hand, only a few new plants are being added. Aging plants are retiring as they reach the end of their life cycle, and new technologies that could address challenges of safety, high initial cost, and long-term waste storage are slow to emerge. Of particular interest is the question of whether nuclear energy could overcome its current challenges and become a major contributor to solving the climate problem, so the latter part of this section of the chapter will delve into these longer-term questions.

Table 1 shows world electricity output from nuclear power plants in 2006 and 2014, including individual national production for seven leading generating countries. The U.S. is consistently the largest producer of nuclear power from year to year while France has the largest share of total electricity generated by nuclear, at ~77% in 2014. The countries broken out in the table generate most of the world's nuclear power; at 1.7 trillion out of 2.4 trillion kWh in 2014, their share amounts to 73% of the total. World production from nuclear declined from 2006 to 2014, from 2.66 to 2.36 trillion kWh, according to the table. This decline occurred despite the ongoing political pressure to reduce CO_2 emissions. Policy decisions in Japan largely precipitated this fall-off in world output as Japan took all nuclear power plants off-line after the 2011 Fukushima nuclear plant accident, in which a strong undersea earthquake (the Great Tohoku Earthquake of 2011) triggered a tsunami that flooded and destroyed the plant, which is located along the northern Pacific coast of Japan. As a result of the shutdown, output fell from 292 billion kWh to zero. If output in Japan had remained constant, the world total would have been approximately the same from 2006 to 2014. At the same time, world total electricity output grew by 18% from 16 trillion to 20 trillion kWh, so nuclear would have still lost a share of the total. Note that China, the world's largest consumer of primary energy, is not among the highlighted countries on the list because its share of electricity from nuclear is still relatively small. Current activity to add new nuclear power plants is limited to a few countries including China, Korea, and the United States (in a limited way).

Country	2006 Output [bil.kWh]	Share (%)	2014 Output [bil.kWh]	Share (%)
United States	787.2	19.4	798.6	19.5
France	428.7	78.1	418	76.9
Russia	144.3	15.9	169.1	18.6
Korea	141.2	38.6	149.2	30.4
Japan	291.5	30	0	0
Germany	158.7	31.8	91.8	15.8
Canada	92.4	15.8	98.6	16.8
Subtotal	2044	n/a	1725.3	n/a
Other	617	n/a	638.7	n/a
Total	2661	16.0	2364	12.0
Subtotal share	77%		73%	

Table 1 Output of nuclear electricity for the world and for selected leading countries in billion kWh along with share of total electricity market, 2006 and 2014. Source: U.S. Nuclear Energy Institute.

Expansion of nuclear power both in the U.S. and around the world faces several obstacles. The Fukushima accident in Japan has been a blow to confidence in the technology. The tsunami from the Tohoku Earthquake crippled the plant's control system, leading to an explosion of the plant's nuclear reactor that destroyed the generating system and also contaminated surrounding towns and agricultural land. Not only did investors lose their investment as the plant was destroyed and could no longer generate financial revenue, but the negative impact on electricity availability for the whole of Japan and the displacement of the population from around the reactor proved traumatic and created a strong political backlash. The industry had been in the midst of a "nuclear renaissance" since the early 2000s after being dormant in the U.S. following the accident at Three Mile Island near Harrisburg, PA, in 1978. The Fukushima accident reduced confidence in the safety of nuclear technology.

In addition, nuclear power in some countries faces stiffer economic competition from growing sources including wind, solar, and natural gas. Natural gas is an especially potent competitor for nuclear because it is possible to build large, centralized gas-fired plants capable of replacing the output of an entire nuclear power plant. Natural gas is of course not carbon-free, but it reduces smokestack CO_2 emissions per unit of electricity compared to coal as well as toxic compounds found in coal that are emitted as byproducts, such as mercury. To keep nuclear power plants solvent, some regions in the US are increasing fees on electricity ratepayers. Other regions are not intervening and instead are allowing them to go out of business.

In terms of types of nuclear plants, boiling water reactors (BWRs) and pressure water reactors (PWRs) dominate the world's fleet (Table 2). The two designs differ in that water passing through the reactor core in the BWR feeds directly to the steam turbine whereas in the PWR the water passing through the reactor heats a separate loop of water that passes to the turbine, via a heat exchanger. In the U.K., a number of gas-cooled (as opposed to liquid-cooled) reactors were built in the past although their numbers are in decline as older reactors are decommissioned at the end of their useful lives and not replaced. One other design is the "heavy water" reactor that uses water comprised of hydrogen atoms with one neutron (deuterium) rather than the common "light water" that contains water with hydrogen containing no neutrons (protium), which is by far the most common isotope of hydrogen. The first four types of reactors in the table comprise most of the world's nuclear power plants, and they rely in various forms on a "regular fission" reaction that splits the U-235 isotope of uranium to release energy. The small number of breeder reactors in the table use "fast fission" as an alternative reaction and are not limited to splitting U-235; this process is discussed below.

Reactor type	Main countries	Number	
		2004	2015
PWR	CN, FR, JP, KR, US	252	229
BWR	JP, KR, US	93	77
Gas-cooled	UK	34	15
Heavy water	AR, CD, CN, KR	33	49
Breeder*	JP, FR, RU	3	4
Other*	Various	14	69
TOTAL		429	443

Table 2 Distribution of world nuclear reactor types by country, 2004 and 2015.

Source: U.S. Nuclear Energy Institute. Abbreviations: PWR = Pressure Water Reactor, BWR = Boiling Water Reactor. Abbreviated countries in alphabetical order: Argentina, Canada, China, France, Japan, Korea, Russia, United States.

In the U.S., activity to add new plants is limited to the southeast of the country. Two plants under construction in South Carolina were recently forced to discontinue work and file for bankruptcy due to cost overruns and intensifying competition from other energy sources. Meanwhile, in Tennessee the Watts Bar 2 plant was completed, bringing a new plant on line for the first time in decades. At the same location, the Watts Bar 1 plant came on line back in the 1970s, but the adjacent Watts Bar 2 was left unfinished after the accident at Three Mile Island in 1979. There remains just one new plant under construction in 2019, the Vogtle plant in Georgia.

In the short- to medium-term, there is a possible role for nuclear power plants to continue operating, thereby avoiding CO_2 emissions that might otherwise be released by generating the same electricity using fossil fuels. Nuclear plants generate radioactive waste, and its safe disposal and management remains an ongoing concern. If nuclear power does not expand by orders of magnitude in the future, the nature of the waste problem will not change materially if activity continues at its current pace for two or three decades. Thereafter, a phase-out of nuclear power might come about due to some combination of the world's reactors reaching the end of their useful lives, a lack of investment in new reactors, and eventual scarcity of fuel for conventional reactors. Protecting sites that house high-level nuclear waste for the long term and preventing accidents would remain an important responsibility. However, for nuclear energy to make a major contribution to climate protection, it would need to become much more of a dominant carbon-free energy source in the future. The next section considers challenges that would need to be overcome for that to happen.

Prospects for a Robust Nuclear Future

A "robust nuclear future" can be defined as a situation where over a long period of time most of the world's primary energy comes from nuclear power. For example, nuclear might replace all current fossil fuel use, while the share for renewables stays the same, so that we arrive at shares of around 90% for nuclear and 10% for renewables. Furthermore, the world economy would sustain this arrangement for a long period of time, on the order of centuries at a minimum. The challenges to this arrangement are at least three: easily accessible nuclear fuel, technical challenges to the development of new designs that can overcome lack of fuel, and the challenge of high-level radioactive waste.[56] All of this assumes that designs in use in the future are safe on a day-to-day basis.

---

[56] "High-level" nuclear waste consists of highly radioactive materials typically in spent nuclear fuel that are both highly hazardous and very long-lived. The opposite of high-level waste is "low-level waste," such as physical items that become radioactive at a low level from contact with nuclear power generation. Low-level waste is larger in volume but is not as pressing a concern because it does not pose the same acute threat to living beings.

Fuel Availability

Table 3 shows estimated tonnage of uranium by country for the world, including both uranium ores that are relatively cost-effective to mine, and those that are more difficult to extract. The figure of 9.1 million metric tonnes total includes mostly the Uranium 238 isotope, and just 1-2% Uranium 235, which is the isotope useful for conventional reactor designs. In fact, nuclear fuel must be "enriched" by removing some of the U-238 so that the concentration of U-235 reaches the 3-3.5% range for the fuel to be used effectively in a nuclear reaction. Raw uranium when it is first mined is a blend of the two isotopes, mostly U-238 with some U-235 in the mixture. The uranium enrichment process moves some of the U-235 into a portion of the uranium ore so that its U-235 concentration increases. The process leaves byproduct "depleted" uranium, with an even lower concentration of U-235, which can then be used for other purposes such as munitions. Suppose that conventional nuclear power was to persist up to the point that fuel scarcity became a constraint, and that the mining sector was able to provide only 1% of the total in Table 2 in U-235, due to obstacles in extracting all 9 million tonnes of uranium. This quantity could support the existing nuclear power industry for several decades or perhaps to the end of the 21st century, possibly with the addition of some new reactors, depending on how the economics play out. *Nuclear reprocessing*, or the process of extracting still usable quantities of unreacted elements from spent nuclear fuel to be returned to reactors, can extend this timeline. However, a robust future implies expansion of the worldwide generation of electricity from nuclear energy to 20 or 30 times the current rate, based on both increasing market share for nuclear and large overall growth in world energy demand as emerging economies grow wealthy. Available U-235 would be insufficient, so a different technology would be needed.

Country	1000 MMT
Australia	2234
Brazil	190
Canada	824
Kazakhstan	911
Niger	259
Russia	738
United States	1642
All other	2312
Total	9110

Table 3 Available world uranium reserves by country in 1,000 metric tonnes.

Source: U.S. Nuclear Energy Institute.

One solution would be to use the U-238 isotope instead of U-235 as fuel, by building a reactor around the "fast fission" or "breeder" reaction. This reaction is allowed to occur at a much faster rate, so that U-238 is converted into plutonium in large quantities. The plutonium can then be split by neutrons released from the ongoing reactions, releasing energy. In this way, the U-238 becomes a useful fuel for generating energy; the process of generating or "breeding" plutonium fuel from U-238 inspires the name. By exploiting the full quantity of uranium in the mined ore instead of just the 1-2% that is U-235, the lifetime of nuclear fission as an energy source could be greatly extended. However, this design is also more technically complex because the faster reaction rate implies more sophisticated controls and more complicated safety systems. Therefore, the nuclear industry has not yet developed it into a mature technology that is commercially available. If breeder reactors were to succeed commercially, they would have the potential to power robust nuclear for a period of hundreds of years, thanks to the much larger fuel volume involved. In the current climate, however, where few new conventional nuclear reactors are being built, it is difficult to see how the necessary R&D would obtain funding in the short to medium term.

Another concept for extending the life of nuclear energy generated from uranium is to accumulate trace amounts of uranium found in the oceans. Although the concentration of uranium in the ocean is very low, the total amount of uranium is large because the volume of the ocean is so vast. Taken together, if this resource could be accessed, it would greatly add to the total fuel availability. However, the problem is again one of insufficient motivation and public support to carry out the needed R&D.

Waste Disposal

Whether the isotope used is U-235 or U-238, a major challenge for all types of nuclear energy based on the fission of uranium is the long-term management of high-level nuclear waste. As mentioned above, the world has already created a quantity of high-level waste that will remain radioactive and hazardous for thousands of years. Taken as a whole, its volume is small. If it were all accumulated in solid form in one place on the planet, it would occupy a tennis court about 10 feet deep, hence the adage in the industry that "we already have a nuclear waste challenge, so operating existing reactors for a few more decades won't change the nature of the problem." One could envision the volume growing to a tennis court 20 feet deep, at which point either all available U-235 will have been consumed, the reactor fleet will have reached the end of its useful life, or both. However, if the volume grows to be 100 times this amount under a robust nuclear future scenario based on breeder reactors, the challenge of managing nuclear waste would grow to a new level.

One of the challenges with high-level nuclear waste is the lack of a permanent disposal plan that can put waste out of reach so that it cannot accidentally contact living beings (human and non-human) nor escape into the environment – literally for thousands of years, since this is the lifetime of the threat. At present, this waste is stored primarily on-site at operating or decommissioned nuclear plants, and occasionally at other temporary locations. The U.S. government spent billions of dollars to design and build a permanent storage facility at Yucca Mountain in Nevada, yet in 2017 this project was indefinitely suspended due to local opposition. Given this experience, it is not surprising that countries are reluctant to expand nuclear power generation as a carbon-free energy source if they have doubts about what will happen to the high-level waste.

Nuclear Fusion

Another pathway to a robust nuclear future, and the one that perhaps generates the most interest as an R&D opportunity, is nuclear fusion. Fusion operates at the opposite end of the atomic spectrum. Instead of breaking apart a heavy atom like uranium, it fuses light isotopes of hydrogen into helium, releasing energy. If it could be commercially developed, fusion would avoid the problem of high-level waste because it does not generate long-lived radioactive elements. The largest challenge for fusion is how to contain the intense temperatures of the reaction on an ongoing basis and at a large enough scale to be able to generate power continuously. Taking the perspective of the solar industry, solar energy proponents say that "we already have nuclear fusion – the reactor is located safely 93 million miles away in the sun." In other words, if we are willing to adapt to the intermittency of nuclear fusion energy arriving from the sun in the form of solar energy, we can in a sense develop nuclear fusion using solar panels. However, if we were able to develop the structures to harness the nuclear fusion reaction on our own planet, it would open up many advantages as a dispatchable resource.

The extent of the technical challenge notwithstanding, R&D continues because fusion holds the possibility of a much larger fuel source than U-235 and avoids the high-level waste problem. For decades, governments have been collaborating through the development of the International Thermonuclear Experimental Reactor, or ITER. Construction is under way in France but will take decades longer to complete and test. Recently, the private sector has also begun to invest in fusion, hoping that the more agile and nimble pace of privately funded R&D might lead to breakthroughs sooner.

Carbon Capture and Sequestration (CCS)

The concept and process of carbon capture and sequestration, or CCS, means intercepting streams of CO_2 after they have been generated, but before they accumulate in the atmosphere, and then storing the CO_2. It is essential to perform both parts of the process. Industry has already developed a process to extract CO_2, for example at power plants where a fraction of the exhaust CO_2 is diverted from the smokestack into reservoirs to be distributed to the carbonated beverage industry. Of course, this carbon source eventually ends up in the atmosphere after consumption. The challenge is to accumulate it in some form or medium where it will stay for the long term, on the order of centuries if not indefinitely.

Direct Carbon Capture

This section focuses in particular on mechanical or "direct" carbon capture, using some manufactured device or system that either works at the point of generation (e.g., a fossil-fuel fired power plant) or at a location where CO_2 is extracted directly from the atmosphere.

"Indirect" carbon capture, such as planting forests that then accumulate carbon in trees and underlying soil, is a worthwhile pursuit not only for sequestration but also other ecological and social benefits, but is outside the scope of this chapter.

Conceptually, CCS could capture most or even all CO_2 generated at large electricity generation stations, and it could also remove significant amounts of carbon from the atmosphere to slow or even reverse the increasing concentration in parts per million. If power plants with CCS became the dominant world primary energy source, the rest of the evolutionary path would be the same as described above for nuclear: decarbonization of the grid, electrification of transportation, and transition of heating applications to heat pumps. However, the necessary technology is not available currently in a commercially viable form.

Some power plants operate CCS systems on a small scale in Europe, China, and Canada (Table 4). Only the Boundary Dam plant in Saskatchewan, Canada, has diverted the entire carbon stream from a single turbine system from atmospheric emission to capture and sequestration. The others divert part of the carbon stream as it passes from the facility, with the goal of slowing the carbon emissions rate but not stopping it completely. This step aligns with the short-run goal of partially reducing GHG emissions common to many policies across industry, transportation, and built environment sectors. Nevertheless, it does not represent a complete transition to fossil fuel use without emissions. Challenges facing CCS at power plants include high capital cost, large parasitic energy losses to operate the carbon capture system, large water requirements, and resulting large increases in the levelized cost per kWh of electricity produced at the plant.

Plant name	Country	Sequestration rate	Start year
		1000 tonnes/yr	
Brindisi Pilot project	Italy	8	2011
Porto Tolle	Italy	<1,000	2015
Belchatow	Poland	100	2015
Vattenfall	Germany	<600	2014
Luzhou*	China	60	2011
Boundary Dam, SK	Canada	1000	2014

Table 4 Early examples of carbon capture and sequestration (CCS) in selected countries.

*CO_2 diverted at this plant is used for industrial purposes rather than sequestered.

Concepts for systems that capture and sequester 100% of the CO_2 from the combustion of fossil fuels are emerging although they are currently in an embryonic form. Figure 1 shows a possible scheme to take a fossil fuel as an input (coal in this case) along with oxygen and produce energy products (electric power and also pure hydrogen) while diverting CO_2 so that it is not emitted to the atmosphere. Thus the system generates power from coal, as in a conventional power plant, but is capable of removing the CO_2 for sequestration. In the first step, the incoming coal is pulverized, and oxygen is extracted from the air in a separate system. The pulverized coal and oxygen are then combined and converted to gaseous carbon monoxide (CO). Although the source is not shown in the diagram, water is provided next and reacted with the CO gas, releasing hydrogen (H_2 molecules) and CO_2. The CO_2 is then cooled in a heat exchanger, which also preheats the oxygen upstream from the coal gasification step, and then channeled to some form of long-term sequestration (described next). The resulting hydrogen is useful as an energy source or as a feedstock for industry. It is either reacted in a fuel cell downstream from the hydrogen/CO_2 separation system to make electricity for the grid, resulting in water as a byproduct that can be recycled to the gas separation step. Alternatively, the hydrogen can be diverted and transported off-site for other uses.

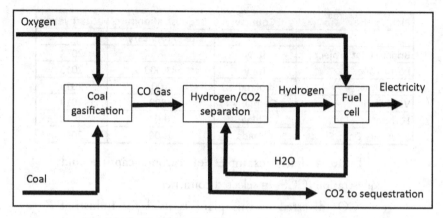

Figure 1 Concept for generating electric power and industrial hydrogen from coal, water, and oxygen, with CO_2 diverted to sequestration.

Carbon Sequestration

As represented in a limited way in Table 4, schemes for sequestering CO_2 underground involve either constructing the carbon-diverting power plant (or other carbon-emitting source) directly on top of the underground reservoir or piping the CO_2 from elsewhere (Fig.2). A potential sequestration site includes an underground "caprock" layer that keeps the CO_2 in place once it has been injected. There are different possible end states for the carbon. It might become hydrodynamically trapped in the rock strata under the caprock, thus remaining as a mass of CO_2 but unable to escape. There are also large saline aquifers in many locations, i.e. underground water reservoirs that contain some amount of salt and are therefore not useful for agriculture or other human purposes. The CO_2 might also dissolve in these aquifers. Either end state has the capacity to sequester large amounts of carbon worldwide, and any increase in pressure on the surrounding geologic formations due to the accumulating carbon would be small enough that it could not escape back to the surface and atmosphere in any significant quantity. (According to sequestration research, some trace amount of escaping CO_2 is tolerable as long it does not significantly undercut efforts to reduce emissions to the atmosphere.)

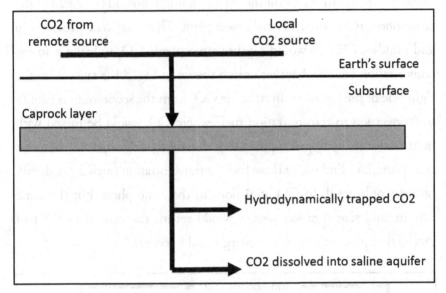

Figure 2 Two options for underground injection of CO_2 as part of a CCS system: Hydrodynamic entrapment or dissolution in saline aquifer

Figure 3 shows how we might create a system over a larger geographic region that extracts fossil fuels and then generates energy that can both power stationary energy uses (e.g., electricity for homes) and mobile uses (e.g., transportation by highways or railroads) and power a system to capture and recycle or sequester carbon. The system in Fig. 3 incorporates both electricity generation facilities (Fig. 1) and underground sequestration sites (Fig. 2) to use fossil fuels as an energy source without a net increase in CO_2 atmospheric concentration. The lines in the diagram show the basic process (left side) from extracting fossil fuels, to conversion to energy, to the byproduct CO_2 either released to the atmosphere or captured and passed to a separate facility (center) for carbon injection underground. This process is similar to the example in Fig. 2 where the CO_2 is diverted in a separate location and then travels by surface pipeline to the injection site. In Fig. 3, two pathways for CO_2 are kept open: CO_2 might be captured at the "fossil fuel combustion" plant shown, but it might instead be vented to the atmosphere as in a conventional power plant. Then a separate process (top and middle of Fig. 3) would capture atmospheric CO_2 to bring it to the sequestration facility. Another option shown in Fig. 3 is a system on the right side of the figure to divert some CO_2 from the sequestration facility to "conversion to transportation fuel" where CO_2 would be mixed with industrial-scale hydrogen supplies (not shown) to create hydrocarbons for transportation. End use of these fuels in transportation (such as road, rail, or air) would result in CO_2 emissions to the atmosphere, but the same capture and sequestration system would return the carbon to the fuel production process, or else to underground injection.

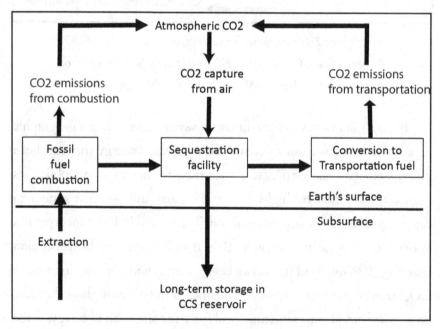

Figure 3 Concept for carbon and CO_2 cycle with extraction, conversion to energy and fuel, carbon capture from the atmosphere, carbon capture and sequestration (CCS) facility, and underground injection.

The goal of this system is net carbon neutrality. Electric power from the fossil fuel combustion plant on the left would contribute to the electricity supply needed to power the sequestration and transportation fuel facilities, supported by carbon-free renewable or nuclear power as needed to make the system net carbon neutral. Also, the amount of carbon injected in the center would balance the carbon extracted on the left to balance atmospheric CO_2 concentration at the top of the figure. Small steps have begun toward building such a system. As of 2022, some enterprises have started to operate these airborne CO_2 capture systems on a small scale, such as Climeworks of Rotterdam, Netherlands.

A Future Role for Nuclear and CCS as Firm Low-Carbon Energy Sources

As the world moves towards deep reductions in carbon emissions, there may be a special role for nuclear energy and fossil energy with CCS to provide "firm" low-carbon energy. Firm low-carbon resources are those that do not emit carbon and are also dispatchable. They are distinct from intermittent low-carbon sources such as solar and wind because they do not rely on a system of storage, additional distribution, or smart-grid controls to contribute to a reliable energy supply.

The list of firm low-carbon sources also includes hydropower and biomass energy. Hydro and biomass are, however, limited by their geographic footprint, as discussed in previous chapters. There are simply not locations on the planet to dramatically increase total worldwide hydropower output, nor to grow additional crops or forests to increase biomass energy by an order of magnitude or more. Nuclear and CCS, on the other hand, do not have such a large land footprint, so they could contribute much more to the firm low-carbon energy supply.

At present, as a society we do not acutely feel the need for firm low-carbon energy because the conventional energy supply can easily complement the intermittency of our growing solar and wind generation. As the energy supply reaches around 80% renewable, however, the need will grow more pressing. Beyond this milestone and as we approach 100% carbon-free, the complexity of smoothing out intermittency may dictate that it is easier to complement intermittent renewables with firm low-carbon sources, rather than attempting to develop sufficient storage and redistribution, a process that grows exponentially more complex and expensive (Sepulvida et al, 2018).

There are many ways in which total reliance on renewables can raise challenges. For example, in a mature renewable energy economy, devices would continuously cycle through a lifetime of use, decommissioning, and replacement. Materials from end-of-life devices would need to be recycled, or else new raw materials would need to be mined. The energy transmission and distribution system would change to reflect the distribution of renewables such as solar, wind, and hydro, and this development would impact the environment. Also, the distribution of new hydropower plants, wind farms, solar panels, and new distribution and storage would have a much larger footprint on the landscape. People would see it everywhere and sense its aesthetic impact. Other challenges arise with heavy reliance on renewables because of the decline of alternatives. If the current fossil fuel infrastructure is being phased out as a backup for renewables, intermittency may be more of a challenge.

Unfortunately for nuclear and CCS, based on the present status of the technology, the same challenges that we have today with these two options would apply in the future at the point where most of the world primary energy supply has been converted to renewables.

For nuclear power, even though it avoids CO_2 emissions, there is still impact from mining of uranium or other resources for fuel. (Note that this impact is not as large as that of fossil fuels because the energy yield per kilogram of nuclear fuel is so much larger: the energy released from 1 kilogram of U-235 is approximately 2 million times larger than the energy obtained from 1 kilogram of coal.) There is also the risk from accidents at nuclear power plants, which, although a very low probability, can lead to major contamination of the surrounding area and financial loss if they occur, with accompanying risk of death and illness as well as harm to plants and animals. Lastly, there is the question of management of high-level radioactive waste over very long periods of time. Unless we can create a commercially viable technology for using nuclear fusion as an energy source, or for converting high-level waste into some other material that has a shorter radioactive half-life, a robust nuclear future commits society to managing this waste for millennia.

Turning to CCS, even if this technology stems the rise of atmospheric concentration of CO_2, there is still the problem of extracting the energy resource that releases that carbon. Drilling for oil and gas or mining coal has a large impact on the land compared to using nuclear or renewable energy. Over time, as the easiest to reach fossil fuel resources are extracted, the more difficult to obtain resources are extracted, increasing the burden on the land. Oil spills, gas leaks, and contamination from the coal waste stream are all possibilities.

It will be many years, of course, before we see how the end-game of the transition to carbon-free energy plays out. The potential future demand for firm low-carbon energy is, however, one reason why we should keep an eye on progress in nuclear and CCS technology and not dismiss them out of hand because they are not growing vigorously at present.

To conclude, we are left with two possible end states for the future: one powered entirely by renewables and one with a continuing supporting role for nuclear and CCS due to the challenges around powering the final increment of the energy supply with renewables. Both end states currently have technical challenges that are not resolved, so we can be open to either one. What remains in the next and final chapter of the book is to tie together advances in energy efficiency and sustainable energy supply with some overarching observations and directions for the future, which will apply regardless of what final energy mix emerges.

CHAPTER 10

Conclusion – Delivering Sustainable Energy for All

This concluding chapter offers three discussions for a deeper understanding of energy literacy. The first part reviews some of the overarching and system-wide questions from the previous chapters. The second presents an "energy transition pathway" toward sustainable energy that brings technologies and trends together into a vision of how the movement toward new energy sources might play out. And the third is a discussion of specific concluding topics, some raised by the transition pathway in particular and others by the subject of energy literacy in general.

Some Key Concepts from Previous Chapters

After an introduction to the book in Chapter 1, in Chapter 2 we encountered the "scale-up problem," namely that once we have identified technologies that solve the problem of sustainable energy, time is required to phase them into place in the global energy supply. Many factors affect the pace of scaling up, including resources to build devices, skill in the labor force, funds to invest, and locations to deploy devices.

Chapter 3 explored the way fossil fuels have shaped our relationship with energy in the last two centuries. Since the dawn of the industrial revolution, coal, petroleum, and natural gas have become the dominant resources for the world economy. These resources are relatively energy dense and can be conveniently transported and stored, which causes us to expect that all energy resources, including renewables, will be similarly available and inexpensive.

In Chapter 4, improving the efficiency of how energy is used emerged as a starting point for transitioning to a sustainable energy system. Efficiency both reduces emissions in the short to medium term and decreases the total amount of carbon-free energy generation infrastructure that will be required in the long run. Improving efficiency alone cannot get us all the way to a sustainable level of greenhouse gas (GHG) emissions, but it can make an important contribution.

The treatment of renewable energy generation began in Chapter 5 with the subject of solar energy, the most ubiquitous, and globally the largest, of all renewable sources. Solar works especially well in locations in the tropics and in sunny and dry climates, but it can also work adequately in less ideal locations at higher latitudes or where cloudy weather is more prevalent.

Chapter 6 showed how wind energy is the other large renewable resource alongside solar. Like solar, wind is a vast resource – there is a larger total amount of wind energy available in nature than the total human energy consumption of the planet. Wind is also complementary to solar, in the sense that it blows at night when sun is not available, and it often (though not always) peaks in winter when available solar energy ebbs.

Solar and wind may be the largest renewable sources available around the world, but other renewables are significant as well. Chapter 7 covered these "supporting renewable resources," including hydro, biomass, geothermal, wave, and tidal energy. These renewable sources are sometimes concentrated in specific locations, and some also provide dispatchability as a complement to the intermittency of solar and wind.

Separate from the generation of renewable energy from different sources, "systems integration" was given its own treatment in Chapter 8. This topic includes new ways of storing energy, expanding distribution networks, controlling the demand side of the energy system with smart grid technology, and transforming the transportation energy supply.

Finally, nuclear power and carbon capture and sequestration (CCS) are presented in Chapter 9. These resources are not moving forward as quickly at present as renewable energy, so this chapter explained why this is the case, why these alternatives face significant challenges in the short to medium term, and why they might return to a more prominent role in the future.

An Energy Transition Pathway to Protect the Climate

Energy literacy entails not just observing how energy systems function but also exploring what it would take to achieve climate protection by transforming our energy system. Therefore, the next several sections present and interpret an "energy transition pathway" for the world community of nations to change its energy supply to achieve climate protection objectives while still meeting demand for energy.

For any person interested in acting on climate change, understanding the transition pathway is valuable because it goes beyond merely saying that another system is possible. The pathway aims to understand how we will travel from where we are now to where we want to be. Otherwise, there is a risk that our leaders can set targets for goals that we will achieve many years from now without being challenged on steps we need to take right now to get started. Armed with this information on the path we need to travel, the climate activist can push even harder for government and the private sector to become serious about traveling down that road.

The concept of energy pathway planning is not new. Energy experts use this technique extensively to create future scenarios at the national and global level. The pathway presented here has been developed from publicly available figures, and although the resulting numbers are original, the underlying technique builds on the practice in the energy field. The pathway is used to study what a transition to 80% less CO_2 by the year 2050 (the stated goal of many governments) would imply in terms of rate of renewables deployment, changing use of fossil fuels, and year-on-year CO_2 emissions.

A transition pathway can be contrasted with a "comparative static" analysis of energy use before and after a transition where we look at the current allocation of energy by source and GHG emissions level and compare it to some state in the future with zero emissions, i.e., a state in which 100% of energy comes from carbon-free sources. The transition pathway goes beyond the comparative static transition by quantifying how energy and demand will change in each interim year, thereby creating a visual illustration of the energy supply changing that can improve understanding. The pathway presented here is at a basic level, but even a simple pathway is a useful first step toward planning for a global energy transition.

Certain elements that underlie the pathway are known at present. Because they have inertia and cannot change radically from year to year, they can be projected into the future using basic assumptions. For example, world population is regularly estimated by organizations such as the United Nations Development Program (UNDP) and tends to either grow or decline smoothly in different countries, depending on circumstances. Furthermore, peoples' day-to-day consumption habits change gradually as well so that energy per capita changes gradually, leading to an overall world energy demand curve that varies only moderately from year to year. And while the health of the world economy has an impact on energy, as increased growth in GDP puts upward pressure on energy use and vice versa, the changes are not dramatic: annual change from the previous year might range from 3-4% in the years of the greatest growth, to negative 1-2% in periods such as the Great Recession 2008-2009. Lastly, energy infrastructure requires much planning and investment and therefore changes slowly as well so that the mix of energy sources can change only gradually.

The possible pathway for a transition to sustainable energy is therefore dependent on the pathways for world population, energy demand, and the mix of energy resources (e.g., fossil, renewable, or nuclear). Since these latter three are constrained in how quickly they can change, the pathway for sustainable energy is also constrained. It is therefore more plausible to create a basic pathway from some simple assumptions. Relatively stable metrics such as global population or energy demand are in this way different from a notable other metric that is both important to many people's day-to-day existence and sometimes volatile, namely the value of the stock market (e.g., Dow Jones Industrial Average in New York, Financial Times Stock Exchange (FTSE) in London, Hang Seng in Hong Kong, etc.). Since stock valuations are financial and not physical quantities, it is possible for them to change dramatically. When investors took money out of U.S. stocks in the Great Recession between 2007 and 2009, the total valuation declined between 30% and 40% in two years. This kind of change is possible in stock values because they are symbolic values; reduced confidence can profoundly affect them. However, it is not possible for a metric such as global population to change so dramatically in such a short time, despite any world disaster that we can anticipate, no matter how catastrophic. Even during the global disaster of World War II, world population declined by 100 million from 2.3 billion to 2.2 billion between 1940 and 1945; although this event represents an apocalypse in terms of sheer magnitude of human suffering, the decrease was less than 5%. (The only exception is an all-out nuclear world war where most of the human population perishes, but at that point the question of a sustainable energy supply would of course be moot, so we do not consider it further here.)

Pathway Characteristics

The pathway has the following four characteristics:

1. *Global commitment to phase out net emissions of GHGs to the atmosphere*: To achieve the goal of stabilizing atmospheric GHG levels, all countries with significant levels of emissions must participate in an action plan to phase out net emissions, not just a subset of the countries. The focus on "net emissions" allows for the possibility of offsetting emissions in one location with reductions in another: If the goal is net one unit reduced, then increasing them by one unit in Location A but reducing them by two units in Location B suffices. In the pathway it is assumed that countries meet their individual targets so that global emissions stay on track. Note that the 2015 Paris Climate Accord is a step in this direction, but it does not fully meet agreed-upon goals. The nations within the accord have committed to holding temperature rise below 2° centigrade but have not yet committed to sufficient emissions reductions to meet this target.

2. *Acceleration of the annual rate of emissions reductions*: While many countries have stepped up their rate of improving efficiency or

phasing in renewables compared to 10 or 15 years ago, the overall net rate of change worldwide is not yet commensurate with the targets that have been set for atmospheric CO_2 and other GHGs at key milestone years in the future. Therefore, the community of nations must mobilize the global convention established in the previous Point 1 ("global commitment") to accelerate the transition rate. Greatly accelerating the rate at which renewables are installed will push the world onto a trajectory toward the 2050 emissions target.

3. *Maintenance of consistent performance from year to year*: As part of accelerating the rate of transition, the community of nations should take steps to ensure that once a rapid pace of transition is established, the rate should be sustained from year to year, rather than varying widely, as it has done up until now. Continuity and consistency keep emissions reductions on target for the 2050 goal.

4. *Pathway timetable that can be moved or compressed*: For convenience, the pathway uses the year 2020 as a starting point and 2050 as an ending point so that it is easy to track a 30-year period in terms of its enactment and execution. However, the start year of 2020 has already passed, and global energy consumption is not yet on the pathway described. Therefore, the specific milestones should be seen as representative of a way to achieve climate protection goals. The steps taken could be compressed to reach the 2050 goals. For example, if the transition started in 2030, the steps would need to be taken in 20 instead of 30 years. Alternatively, the pathway might be moved back by one decade, thereby lasting from 2030 to 2060, although this adjustment would have negative consequences for total GHG emissions.

Quantitative Rollout and Pathway Endpoint

Building on the characteristics in the previous section, this section presents the transition pathway that achieves an 80% reduction in CO_2 emissions from the use of fossil fuels for energy, including annual energy consumption, share of primary energy sources, and resulting emissions along the way. This new pathway maintains a mid-range energy growth pathway developed by the IEA (International Energy Agency) for annual energy consumption between 2020 and 2050. It also projects continued steady population growth from a projected 7.8 billion in 2020 to 9 billion in 2050.[57] However, the pathway shifts much more rapidly to renewable energy than the pace observed in the years leading up to 2019, which makes the 80% reduction by 2050 possible. Based on the IEA energy pathway, world energy demand rises at a linear rate of 6.95 Quads/year from 583 Quads in 2020 to 792 Quads in 2050. The pathway begins with projected global CO_2 emissions of 36.5 billion U.S. tons/year in 2020.

To meet the CO_2 reduction target, all new energy generation (including electricity and also other forms such as non-electric transportation fuels) is assumed to be renewable after 2020. Nuclear is assumed to stay at the present level of 35 Quads/year worldwide throughout the transition so that its share of total primary energy decreases as global energy demand grows. Once the quantities of renewables and nuclear are known in each year, the remaining primary energy supply is obtained from fossil fuels. Figure 1 shows the quantity of renewable, nuclear, and fossil primary energy supplied each year.

---

[57] Throughout the presentation about the energy transition pathway, projected values for 2020 are used because the transition needs to begin at a future date for which energy, population, and emissions can be forecast but are of course not known exactly.

At first fossil fuel consumption declines slowly, but gradually the rate increases until it reaches a maximum rate in 2030 of -15.0 Quads/year, which it maintains as a constant value for the remainder of the pathway.

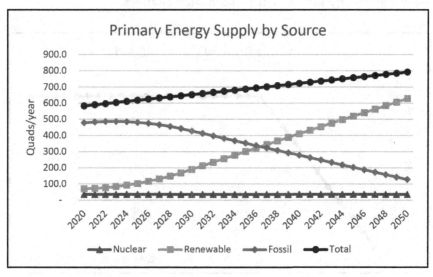

Figure 1 Energy generated from fossil, nuclear, and renewable energy, and total energy supplied, for the 2020-2050 transition pathway.

Consistent with the expected path of typical industry growth, renewable energy market penetration is divided into two phases for the period 2020-2050 (Fig.2). In the first "ramp-up" phase from 2020 to 2030, the rate of renewables penetration is accelerating. Then in the second full-scale phase from 2030 to 2050, primary energy production from renewables grows by a constant amount each year and at a sufficient rate to achieve the 2050 target. During the ramp-up phase, the world starts by increasing renewable production by 2.2 Quads/year in 2021, and then increasing the rate by 2.2 Quads/year in each subsequent year, thus 4.4 Quads/year in 2022, 6.6 Quads/year in 2023, and so on. Then, when the rate of 22 Quads/year added is reached in the year 2030, this rate is maintained as a constant in subsequent years. At the same time, the emissions rate from the remaining use of fossil fuels falls from 76.3 million tons per Quad in 2020 to 60.0 million tons per Quad in 2050 thanks to the transition from coal to natural gas, improvements in the fossil fuel energy supply chain, and related changes.

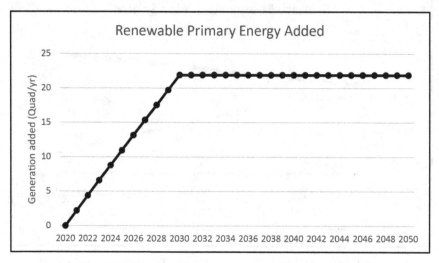

Figure 2 Renewable primary energy generation added in Quads per year during transition pathway in Quads/year, 2021-2050.

The result is that in 2050 emissions have fallen 80% compared to the peak value in 2020 (Fig. 3), meeting the 2050 reduction target that numerous studies and reports have advocated (e.g., California Air Resources Board, 2019). After 2050, the world energy sector might continue to reduce CO_2 at a constant rate so that 100% of emissions would be eliminated by 2060. On the other hand, the rate of emissions reduction might slow after 2050; it is often the case that the final stages of the penetration of a new technology are the slowest because the last increment of transition is the most difficult to achieve. This problem goes back to the "scale-up" problem and Figure 11 in Chap. 2: at the end of the transition process, the "stragglers" are the hardest customers to reach, and in the same way, the final 20% of carbon emissions are the hardest applications to decarbonize.

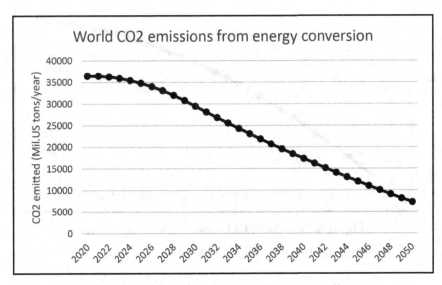

Figure 3 Annual global CO_2 emissions in million U.S. tons per year during transition pathway 2020-2050.

Lastly, the changing energy mix of the transition pathway impacts cumulative CO_2 emissions (Fig. 4). Cumulative emissions are the sum of annual emissions from Fig. 2 up to a given year. These emissions surpass 700 billion tons by 2050. Although they are continuing to climb even at the end of the pathway in 2050, the rate of increase has greatly slowed by then. The direction of the curve suggests that with continued effort emissions would be phased out completely before reaching 800 billion cumulative tons.

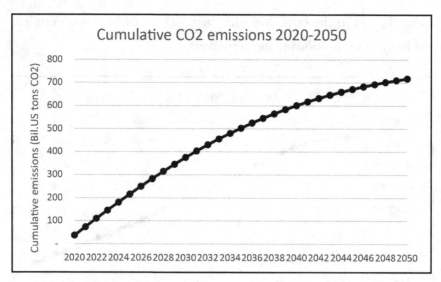

Figure 4 Cumulative CO_2 emissions in energy transition pathway 2020-2050 in billion U.S. tons.

Next, we translate the increasing renewable energy generation in Figs. 1 and 3 into the requirements for physical installation of generating devices and accompanying monetary value of investment. Growing renewable output implies new installed devices, measured in nameplate capacity (i.e., in units of MW or GW). To keep the analysis transparent and simple, we make the following assumptions:

■ *Widespread electrification as a substitute for diverse energy supplies:* Current world primary energy supplies are characterized by a diverse range of energy supplies, dominated by three types: electricity from the electric grid, liquid fuels for transportation, and natural gas from the natural gas grid. To simplify the analysis, we assume the quantities of primary energy in the previous section are maintained, but they are provided entirely by electricity. This outcome is plausible since electrification may eventually dominate world energy production. For example, surface transportation might transition to electrified cars, trucks, and locomotives, and space heating and cooling might transition to various types of geothermal, air-source, and water-source heat pumps that use electricity to power pumps and compressors. (Alternatively, some global energy demand for process heat or living space heating might be met directly with solar thermal energy, rather than using solar-generated electricity as an intermediate carrier. However, this level of specificity is beyond the scope of the presentation of the pathway.)

■ *A mix of solar and wind as a proxy for a full range of renewables:* The eventual renewable energy system would likely involve the full range of resources, including solar, wind, hydro, geothermal, biomass, and so on. To simplify the presentation, we consider the two resources that will likely dominate the system due to the potential size and geographic spread of their availability, namely solar and wind, as explained in Chapters 4 and 5. Furthermore, we assume they will be installed in quantities such that they each meet 50% of the new need, considering the different contribution that they make by season and also on a diurnal/nocturnal basis. In the actual deployment of renewables in the future, some demand would be met by resources other than solar and wind. However, other renewable resources (e.g., surface geothermal, biomass, hydropower, wave, or tidal) have limited global capacity compared to world energy demand. Therefore, because these other resources can only provide a minority fraction of world energy, it is a reasonable simplification to adopt the capacity and cost of solar and wind as a representation of all types of renewables.

■ *Uniform capacity factors for all renewable energy devices:* As another simplification, solar and wind devices are assumed to produce at an average capacity factor value in all regions, rather than attempting to assign different capacity factors in different regions. The same values introduced above of 16.7% and 33%, respectively, are applied. These values are of course only approximate since we do not know where solar and wind will eventually be deployed, but they reflect a sampling of existing facilities around the world.

- *Constant cost per unit of wind and solar in real economic terms:* It is assumed that the cost per kW of capacity for solar or wind will grow with the world average rate of inflation. Therefore, although prices in current dollars in the future will rise sooner or later, these devices will cost the same as they do now in constant 2019 dollars.

Summary statistics for solar and wind are shown per GW of capacity in Table 1. Capacity in GW has been converted to annual output in GWh/year using the capacity factor shown. Energy in units of TWh (Terawatt-hour) are then converted to trillion Btu to make comparisons to the pathway of the energy transition from Fig. 3 above. For example, from 2030 to 2031, the pathway expects an increase of 21.9 Quads per year in primary energy provided by renewable energy. This amount is equivalent to 6,421 TWh/year, which is divided equally between solar and wind, dictating the number of GW of capacity that must be added. Thus 50% of the total, or 3,210 TWh/year, must come from solar, so 2,195 GW of solar PV capacity must be added in 2031 to meet this goal. Repeating the calculation for wind energy shows that 1,111 GW of wind capacity must be added; the difference is due to the higher capacity factor for wind.

Resource	CF	GWh/yr	Tril.Btu/yr	Cost (Bil.$)
Solar	16.7%	1463	4.99	1
Wind	33.0%	2891	9.86	1.6

Table 1 Annual output in PJ and TWh, assumed capacity factor, and installed cost per 1 GW of capacity for solar and wind used in the renewable energy transition scenario. Example of GWh per year calculation: 1 GW of solar PV delivers (8760h/year) x (0.167) x (1 GW) = 1,463 GWh/year.

Table 2 summarizes the quantity of added capacity and added output in each year during the linear growth phase 2030-2050. During this phase, the transition is happening at full speed to rapidly reduce emissions from energy conversion, with combined solar and wind generation added each year totaling 6.4 million GWh/year or 21.9 Quads/year (also shown in Fig.1). The 2050 fossil energy generation value is a projected 128 Quads/year, resulting in CO_2 emissions of 7.3 billion U.S. tons, or 80% less than 2020.

Resource	Added Cap.	Added output		Cap. Cost
	(GW)	(Mil.GWh/yr)	(Quad/yr)	(Tril.$)
Solar	2,195	3.21	10.96	$ 2.19
Wind	1,111	3.21	10.96	$ 1.78
Combined	n/a	6.42	21.91	$ 3.97

Table 2 Annual capacity and generation added and annual capital cost during 2030-2050 phase of transition pathway. Conversion: 1 million GWh = ~3.412 Quads of energy.

As may be surmised by looking at the ramping up of renewables installation in Fig. 2, the annual capacity and output added in Table 2 is vast by historical standards. From 2016 to 2017, the global wind industry added 51 GW, so the figure of 1,111 GW added per year is 22 times as fast. For solar PV, the ratio is similar: the world added 98 GW of solar PV capacity from 2016 to 2017, so the ratio is also 22 times as fast, if 2,195 GW per year is to be achieved.[58] How might such a large quantity be achieved? Could the ratio be lowered somehow? Questions like these naturally lead to the discussion in the next section.

Interpreting the Energy Transition Pathway

One benefit of the pathway is that it helps us to visualize what it would take to achieve a transition to a carbon-free energy system, not just a vision for what a world that eventually runs completely on renewable energy might look like. The first takeaway point is that regardless of how adjusting assumptions might change the total investment required, we need to move much, much faster than at present. Some countries are better positioned for the transition and moving faster, but climate change is clearly a global problem, and if only some of the countries make a transition, the climate change problem will continue to intensify. Conversely, suppose that installations of renewable infrastructure continue at the rate of ~50 GW of wind and ~100 GW of solar added per year, as quoted earlier. Growing to ~800 Quads/year of global energy supply all from renewables would take hundreds of years.

Also, the fact that the energy industry cannot instantly achieve the maximum sustained output, and cannot accelerate indefinitely but must at some point reach a plateau lengthens the time required. In the example, the "ramp-up" phase took 10 years to reach the steady-state rate of 22 Quads of additional output per year. Each of these years of growth is faster than any that have been achieved as of 2019. It would

---

[58] Data sources: for wind, Global Wind Energy Alliance; for solar PV, Yale University School of Forestry and Environmental Studies.

be convenient if the industry could keep accelerating installations after 2020 to reach 80% reductions faster. However, as it is, the 20 years from 2030 to 2050 of finding sites and building sufficient devices and infrastructure will put great strain on the energy sector.

On a more favorable note, if we arrange the physical supply chain to rapidly grow renewables according to the pathway, then the financial dimension is within the bounds of global GDP (although large by historical standards). Table 2 presents a financial investment of $4 trillion per year for PV arrays and wind turbines during the full-scale transition phase from 2020 to 2030, based on current installed cost values. We do not know what panels and turbines will cost in 2030, nor the value of GDP in that year. However, in 2018, GDP was $85 trillion according to the International Monetary Fund, so the investment would be 5% of world GDP if we were to invest in solar and wind at this scale today. This figure should not be interpreted as purely a burden on the world economy: such activity creates sales opportunities for businesses, employment for the workforce, and possible returns for investors. Additional costs for adaptations such as transmission, storage, smart grid, and vehicle charging assets are not included in the $4 trillion/year figure because these are more difficult to quantify. However, the world energy sector is already large, constituting trillions of dollars of GDP per year. During the transition pathway, expenditures currently related to conventional energy would divert to sustainable energy infrastructure like smart grid and storage. Overall, the fraction of GDP dedicated to energy, even including infrastructure changes, would be expected to increase, but the increase is not outlandish.

The required rate of renewables influx could of course be changed by greatly reducing the future energy requirement, but the amount of renewable energy capacity installed each year would still be a very large number. For example, Ernst von Weiszacker popularized the concept of

"Factor Four," or the goal of doubling wealth and quality of life while at the same time cutting resource use in half (von Weiszacker et al, 1997). What if the 2050 world energy requirement could be cut in half (from ~800 to ~400 Quads/year) as part of reaching the goals of Factor Four? The renewables transition in Fig. 2 would also be cut approximately in half, but the rate of installation of solar and wind would remain ten times as fast as in recent years. Furthermore, Factor Four would require an accelerated transition in much of our built environment, including factories, buildings, and transportation systems, to make them much more efficient. We might simply exchange one massive investment in transforming technological infrastructure for another.

Lastly, the investment in energy infrastructure would not disappear after the transition was complete in 2050. By that year, the earliest wave of renewable devices would be wearing out, requiring a new generation to be installed in its place. In fact, the replacement would continue at approximately the same pace as the initial installation, and it would be required indefinitely as long as a world energy system based on renewable energy continued.

Limitations of the Energy Transition Pathway Model

We now turn to some of the limitations in the model used to create the pathway. First, the pathway describes a physical pathway in terms of how much new capacity is required and roughly what it might cost, but it does not include any policy prescriptions that could bring it about. To address this need, analysts use mathematical models solved on computers to explore the impact of policies on changing the trajectory of energy use and GHG emissions. Within this field, "integrated assessment models" incorporate both physical models of the global climate system and socioeconomic models of human economic activity and behavior.

Adding the policy dimension, as is done in integrated assessment models, is complicated. First, the model must include enough granular detail to capture the dynamics of economic interactions. It must then be "calibrated," i.e., adjusted so that it reproduces observed historical behavior to give assurance that it could accurately be extrapolated into the future. Setting up, running, and explaining the model to the general public takes extensive training. Another challenge is the lengthy time horizon for modeling policies leading to an 80% reduction in world CO_2. Any major policy including a carbon tax, cap-and-trade system, or renewable portfolio standard could be modeled, but typical past examples of modeling have focused more on the short to medium term, and not on the entire pathway leading to such large reductions, in part because it is difficult to predict how the world will respond to policies far into the future.

The pathway also overlooks potential inherent energy savings from switching from fossil fuels to renewables. Often when coal or petroleum products are combusted in a power plant or internal combustion engine, a significant fraction of the chemical energy in the fuel is lost due to inherent physical limits on the process.[59] For a power plant with an overall efficiency from fuel to electric current of between 40% and 60%, much of the loss of 40% to 60% can be attributed to this physical limit. When a solar panel or wind turbine generates electricity, there are losses in transferring the electric current to the location where it is used or stored, but they are not nearly of this magnitude. To be conservative, the pathway has used the IEA midrange energy pathway regardless, but

---

[59] The physical limit is called the "Carnot Limit" after Sadie Carnot, a French thermodynamicist of the 19th century, who observed that the maximum possible efficiency was the ratio of change in temperature to starting temperature.

some significant savings could be expected from the transition from fossil fuels to renewables.

The pathway does not include renewable energy sources other than solar and wind. Even if they were included, solar and wind would still likely provide the majority of primary energy because globally they are much more widely available. However, explicitly including other sources in the mix such as hydropower or biomass would be more realistic since the full range of sources would play a role in the actual transition to renewable energy. This change to the pathway would help to quantify the potential role for the other renewable sources covered in Chapter 6, and the pathways for solar and wind would be adjusted accordingly since their contribution to energy generation would change.

Similarly, nuclear energy is treated with a very basic assumption, namely that plants retired at the end of their useful lives are replaced so that global output remains constant, but net capacity does not increase. For reasons discussed in Chapter 8, the pathway sees nuclear power as not being able to move into a position of playing a significant role, and its share actually declines from 6% to 4%. It is possible that nuclear instead might grow to maintain its 6% share, or at the other extreme, be completely phased out (market share of 0%) by 2050. For any share value between 0% and 6% that might be used in the pathway, the impact on the need to rapidly increase renewables would be minimal – ambitious installation of renewable capacity is required regardless.

Lastly, the pathway considers only one trajectory for how the output of renewable and fossil fuel energy changes year by year. Multiple pathways are possible. For example, there is a strong possibility that the community of nations will not generate the rapid pace of renewables penetration mapped out in the pathway, and CO_2 emissions therefore decline more slowly. Different pathways could be added with slower renewables growth and hence greater cumulative emissions than shown in Fig. 4. Such a pathway would reduce the stress on the economy from needing to rapidly shift energy sources, but it would also increase stress from destructive impacts of more rapid climate change.

Overarching Energy Literacy Issues

The preceding energy pathway lays out a way forward on energy that meets demand while reducing emissions and in turn suggests the rate at which new energy systems must be deployed to reach those targets. However, many questions raised about the pathway's consequences are not explicitly incorporated in the calculations that result in the types of energy systems that are available year-on-year, the energy they deliver, and the CO_2 they emit. Therefore, in this section we raise these issues on a qualitative level, knowing that they are not easily solved, but must be considered carefully at the outset.

Sustainable Energy and Material Resource Management: A Calculated Risk

The first point raised considers material resources as opposed to energy. We know that there is sufficient physical energy available in nature from sun, wind, water, and other sources to generate enough energy from renewable resources to meet global needs. Whether demand is ~500 Quads/year currently or ~800 Quads/year in the future, it is possible to generate this energy without burning fossil fuels and emitting CO_2 to the atmosphere – if we deploy enough devices.

Transitioning to this new energy system would solve the GHG emissions problem, but it would also create a whole new material resource management challenge. A new and much larger generation of solar panels, wind turbines, and other renewable energy devices would need to be built, requiring the extraction of raw materials. This commitment would be continual: since the devices themselves last 30 to 50 years, there would be turnover each year of worn-out devices replaced by new ones. Storage systems, including large-scale stationary electricity storage centers and lithium-ion battery systems in electric vehicles, would contribute to the increased flow of raw materials and end-of-life components needing management. In the case of electric vehicles, life cycles would likely be shorter, perhaps on the order of 10 to 15 years. To reduce the burden to landfill materials, the global energy industry would need to recycle as much material as possible. Certain components of solar panels, turbines, and battery systems may contain toxic materials or rare earth metals, requiring special care.

It is not a foregone conclusion that this materials management task will be easy or work adequately. Instead, if as a society we choose to go down the road of shifting to renewables (as we appear to be doing in the decade of the 2020s), then we are taking a calculated risk. We are using renewable energy to address the clear and present danger from runaway, radical climate change, under the assumption that we will be able to manage the materials burden.

Put another way, Chapter 8 considered nuclear and CCS as alternatives to renewables and concluded that the latter were the most likely to succeed going forward from this point. However, this comparison does not prove that renewables will succeed in the long run. They might eventually succeed in phasing out emissions, only to create a materials management crisis that leads to their demise.

Deep-Ecologic Critique of Renewable Energy Adoption by the Mainstream

Although the mainstream of society appears to support increasing the rate of materials consumption and recycling to reduce GHG emissions, there may be a small minority, sometimes under the label of "deep ecologists," who advocate for de-industrializing global society starting now. From this perspective, the goal is to dismantle large-scale energy grids, move to a more agrarian lifestyle, and greatly shrink the human population on the globe. Such a shift might solve both energy and materials problems, but it would be very disruptive. Consider the simple fact that there are nearly 8 billion people on the planet, of which half live in urban areas, a fraction that is growing. These individuals cannot abruptly change from participating in the industrial and service economy one day to subsistence farming the next. As Jim Plummer, dean of the Stanford University College of Engineering, said in a speech in 2004, the only alternative to solving the sustainable energy problem is to "shut down our economy in 25 years."[60]

Comparing the Position of Industrialized and Emerging Countries

In this section we break down global energy consumption, whether ~500 Quads/year in 2020 or ~800 Quads/year in 2050, between industrialized and emerging countries of the world. The industrialized countries include the traditional industrial powers already extant in the 1960s and 1970s, such as Europe, North America, Japan, Australia, and New Zealand. The emerging countries include all other countries of the world, from middle-income countries such as China and Russia to countries with low GDP and energy use per capita in Africa, Asia, or Latin America. The term "emerging" implies that all countries desire to move toward participation in the global economy and raising standards of living, and they are in various stages of moving toward that goal.

---

[60] Jim Plummer, speech given at Stanford University, Palo Alto, CA, 2004.

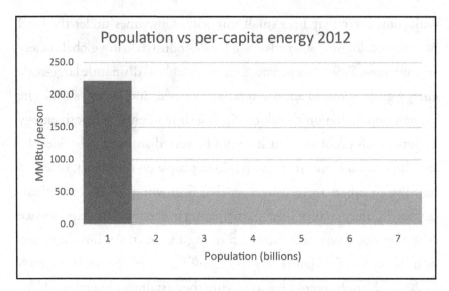

Figure 5 Population versus energy per capita for industrialized (dark grey bar) and emerging (light grey bar) countries, 2012.

Source for underlying data: U.S Energy Information Administration.

The world energy consumption in 2012 divides as follows, based on adding up population data from the United Nations and energy consumption by country from the U.S. Energy Information Administration (Fig. 5). Total population in 2012 is 7.2 billion people. The industrialized countries account for about 1 billion people and have an average of 221.1 million Btu per person (MMBtu/person). (For comparison, U.S. energy per capita was 312 MMBtu/person in that year.) The remaining 6.2 billion people consume an average of 48.4 MMBtu/person. The total consumed by each of the two groups is the product of population and energy per capita, so the area covered by each in Fig. 5 visually represents the size of their energy use. The emerging countries consume 299 Quads/year, and the industrialized countries consume the remaining 225 Quads/year. The contrast is stark: The emerging countries consume somewhat more energy than the industrialized, but the amounts are close compared to the population ratio where the former have six times the population of the latter.

Note that in the group of emerging countries, some countries may have started with low energy use per capita in the 1960s but today are on a par with European countries in terms of per person GDP or energy use. The "Asian Tigers" provide an example of this trend: the countries of South Korea, Taiwan, Hong Kong, and Singapore are today similar in standard of living to those of the European Union. However, they remain in the group of emerging countries because they represent the outer edge of the envelope for how emerging countries might advance economically and therefore demand more energy per capita. In any case, whether these four countries appear in the emerging or industrialized block in Fig. 5 would not qualitatively change the shape of the figure because these countries together represent under 100 million in population, versus over 6 billion total in the emerging block.

Among the largest consumers of energy in the world, there has also been a major transition in the top countries on the list. Table 3 shows the top-eight consumers of energy in 1980 and 2012, along with energy consumption for the remaining countries and the world total. With globalization and economic advancement in the emerging countries, new major economic powers have emerged, pushing some of the smaller energy users in 1980 off the top-eight list. The BRIC countries (Brazil, Russia, India, and China) introduced in Chapter 1 are now all in the top eight, and with their rise, France and the U.K. have been pushed off the list. In 2012, Russia has replaced the former Soviet Union, and China has surpassed the U.S. to become the world's largest energy user. Remaining industrialized countries still on the list, including Japan, Germany (replacing West Germany of 1980 after absorbing East Germany), Canada, as well as the U.S., grew more slowly than the world average, so they have all moved down the list in terms of rank. Overall, world energy consumption nearly doubled in 32 years.

Rank	Year 1980		Year 2012	
	Country	Quads/yr	Country	Quads/yr
1	USA	78.07	China	105.88
2	USSR	46.74	USA	95.06
3	China	17.29	Russia	31.52
4	Japan	15.20	India	23.92
5	West Germany	11.27	Japan	20.31
6	Canada	9.80	Germany	13.47
7	UK	8.84	Canada	13.35
8	France	8.39	Brazil	12.10
ROW	n/a	87.57	n/a	208.48
World	n/a	283.15	n/a	524.08

Table 3 World top eight countries ranked in order of energy consumption, in units of Quadrillion Btu, 1980 and 2012. Source: U.S. Energy Information Administration.

The rapid growth in energy consumption in BRIC countries points to one of the main drivers of future global growth in energy consumption. These four countries in Table 3 represent more than 2 billion of population in 2012, versus approximately 500 million for the other four countries. The BRIC countries have a growing middle class and with it potential for sustained long-term growth in energy demand. The "emerging country" block in Fig. 5 includes the BRIC countries and many other emerging and middle-income countries outside of BRIC with a growing middle class. What might the effect be of so many people moving into a middle-class lifestyle? The impact can be visualized using a second population versus energy/capita diagram with projected values for the year 2050. Suppose the population in industrialized countries remains at 1 billion, due to a mix of countries with both rising population (e.g., U.S.) and falling population (e.g., Japan and some countries in the European Union). The remaining 8 billion of a projected U.N. total population of 9 billion in 2050 would be in the emerging countries. The industrialized countries tend toward reducing per-capita energy consumption over time, and the emerging ones tend toward increasing consumption. Therefore, to arrive at ~800 Quads/year in 2050, one possible allocation is 150 MMBtu/person in industrialized countries, and 81 MMBtu/person in emerging countries. This allocation shows how even with robust growth in world access to energy, there would remain a substantial gap between the two groups in terms of per-capita energy use, implying limits on improving standard of living for some of the population in the emerging countries. This observation leads to a deeper exploration of the question of "how much is enough?" in the next section.

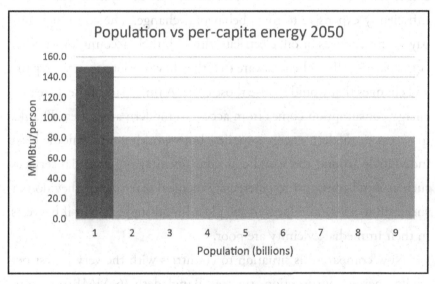

Figure 6 Population and energy/person scenario in the year 2050 for industrialized (dark grey bar) and emerging (light grey bar) countries, such that total world energy equals ~800 Quads/year.

Francis M. Vanek

How Much Energy per Person is Enough?

At first glance, wealth is the primary reason why some countries have much higher energy intensity per capita than others – residents purchase more energy because they can afford it. Delving more deeply, some of the increase in energy per person comes from consumer choices where the individual makes purchases of higher value beyond the bare essentials. For example, they might purchase a larger home or car where a smaller one would be sufficient or travel on vacation to a distant foreign country when they could have vacationed nearby, increasing energy use. Another component of increased energy consumption comes from inefficiency and waste hidden in the system that is not sufficiently expensive to force behavioral change. The consumer may pay for heating gas or oil, electricity through their account, or gasoline at the pump without being aware that they have options to make repairs and changes that would reduce those costs. A third part of the increased energy consumption comes from access to modern amenities. Thanks to access to modern energy supplies, both working- and middle-class individuals around the world can take advantage of essential services such as rapid transport to emergency medical care so that they do not succumb to an acute illness or the global food supply chain if harvests in their immediate vicinity are poor.

Now compare this situation to countries with the very lowest per capita energy consumption, such as Bangladesh (6 MMBtu/person) or Zimbabwe (13 MMBtu/person), versus 312 MMBtu/person for the U.S. mentioned above. Many residents of these low energy per capita countries do not have access to any of the three types of energy consumption just mentioned, including the most basic lifesaving and life-extending access to emergency medical care and basic nutrition. Suppose as a thought exercise, we take as a representative figure

10 MMBtu/person for a low energy country and use this figure as a benchmark for global energy consumption. If the world countries could achieve this low value planet wide by 2050 for a population of 9 billion people, energy consumption would decline to 90 Quads/year compared to ~500 Quads/year currently, and if CO_2 emissions were directly proportional to energy use in both years, we would achieve the goal of at least 80% reduction. However, such a low level would cause severe deprivation in human development, since all three factors that cause higher energy use per capita would disappear (not only choice and hidden waste, but subsistence necessity). Society would not tolerate such a radical shift: both individuals and governments would prefer to take on greater risks from climate change in return for the diverse benefits that come from higher per capita energy use.

The answer to the question of how much is enough then comes down to the choices we make. Some fraction of the energy we consume is essential for living in a modern industrial society and is therefore not a choice. This amount is more than 10 MMBtu per person per year. Beyond that, there are different combinations of access to amenities and levels of investment in carbon-free energy possible, and any of them can accelerate the reduction in GHG emissions. We can work hard to change our choices to lower our energy footprint. We can also work harder to transform the energy system more quickly to reduce emissions per unit of energy used. In any case, we need to reduce emissions to make room for the very poorest countries to grow their access to energy. We should not constrain these countries from growing their energy use per capita so that they can have access to basic energy services that citizens of middle- and high-income countries take for granted.

Francis M. Vanek

The Climate Challenge in Historical Context

Our grappling with climate change is part of a larger historical transition in which humanity comes to terms with being at the limits of the carrying capacity of the planet. It is both urgent on an everyday basis and one of the great long-term transitions in all human history. It is an ecological revolution, alongside which there are two others of equal significance, namely the agricultural (Neolithic) revolution around 6,000 BCE and the industrial revolution starting around the year 1800. Systems philosopher Joanna Macy has coined the term "The Great Turning" for this period: a great turning away from increasing conflict with the natural world and toward greater harmony.[61]

As part of the great turning, individuals will need to take on a new role in protecting the environment. In the first part of the industrial revolution, most of society was part of the labor force (as opposed to members of the upper classes that controlled the means of production). Their primary role was that of producers since they had not yet accumulated sufficient wealth to impact the function of the economy with their spending habits. However, this shifted in the second part of the industrial revolution: In more recent times, countries such as the U.S. moved to "service economies" where most employment was in services rather than manufacturing, and consumer spending became the main driver of the economy (68% of the U.S. economy in 2019).[62] Although services became dominant, the number of workers employed in manufacturing is still significant and will continue to be so. A third role for the population will need to grow in importance alongside

---

[61] Joanna Macy, comments made during public presentation at First Presbyterian Church of Ithaca, NY, Fall 2009.

[62] U.S. Bureau of Economic Analysis, "Report on U.S. Economic Indicators," June 25, 2019.

"consumers" and (for some) "producers", namely that of "environmental protectors." This function is too important to be left to a small group of specialists, hidden from public view. Everyone who participates in the economy, benefits from its wealth, and contributes to its environmental impact will need to play a role, and this commitment will need to continue for the foreseeable future. The role of environmental protector includes both individual choices and joining collective action to bring about positive change. Signs that this is already happening can be seen everywhere, so the transition is already underway.

Another challenge of the great turning is that much needs to be changed in a short amount of time. If the time seems short, it is instructive to think how past changes might have seemed rapid at the time if the leaders of the day could have been told in advance of how events would unfold. Imagine that you were able to travel back in time to the year 1879 and met Thomas Edison in his laboratory in Menlo Park, New Jersey, where he had just successfully tested the first electric light bulb. Knowing exactly what would transpire from 1879 to the early 21st century, you could have predicted hydropower at Niagara Falls starting in just 22 years, with a 10-MW hydroelectric plant opening there in 1901 that provided enough power for 100,000 lightbulbs. You could have also predicted the first power plant coming online in 70 years that was capable of powering 10 *million* lightbulbs (equivalent to 1,000 MW of power, at Avon Lake, OH, in 1949). Just seven years after that, and 76 years after Edison's first bulb, the first nuclear power plant in the U.S. would come online at Shippingsport, PA, harnessing the energy inside the nucleus of the atom to generate electricity. You could have even predicted the reach of electricity beyond the limits of earth: only 90 years after that first lightbulb, astronauts would carry electricity with them and travel 240,000 miles to set foot on the surface of the moon in 1969. You could predict that electricity would control the space craft, light it, heat it, and even allow wireless communication between the earth and the moon.

If we come back from the past and the year 1879 to today and look forward in time, the situation is, of course, very different. Edison and his contemporaries as they looked forward to the future focused primarily on opportunities that new inventions would create, and they were not as concerned about moving away from the status quo. In our case, our motivation is to move away as quickly as possible from the current conundrum of excessive GHG emissions. Also, the time scales are different. World energy consumption has increased by about 500 Quads/year since 1879, a timespan of 140 years. If the pathway in Fig. 2 were to be followed, however, we would have 30 years to add 560 Quads/year of renewable energy generation, and not 140 years. There are similarities as well between the situation in the late 1800s and that of now. Just like inventors of Edison's day, we cannot predict precisely how technology will evolve and advance, and therefore we cannot know with certainty the path to a carbon-free energy future even though we understand the imperative to travel that path. It is also difficult to predict which inventions will have the most impact. There are millions of innovators all over the world working on the climate challenge, and yet we cannot identify the eventual leaders who will solve many of the remaining problems. As an example, the electric private car seemed like it had a dim future as recently as the year 2005, and yet with breakthroughs in lithium battery technology and improved drivetrains, the EV's future now seems solid.

Finally, because the climate challenge is so complex and daunting, a note of caution is in order as we move toward the future. Progress will not move forward in a linear, orderly fashion, and there will be setbacks along the way. The final section below considers how as a society we might find resilience to keep going.

Parting Thought: The Storm and the Ship

At the beginning of this book, we started out with the premise that sustainable energy begins with the personal energy of making a commitment to support change and move forward. Here at the end, we return to this premise.

If the global quest for phasing out GHG emissions began in 1992 with the Rio de Janeiro Earth Summit, then we have clearly fallen short of a trajectory for reaching that goal. It can also be said that collective failure often stems from personal failure. Leaders fail to act resolutely; individual consumers continue in old habitual ways, and businesses and governments choose the harmful path. A political leader may fail to stand up for climate action, prioritizing other goals instead. Individual consumers make choices that are harmful to the environment. Businesses develop and promote products and services that generate excessive carbon emissions. The pattern is repeated over and over so frequently that it is difficult to know where to start making changes.

If the problems start with personal failures, then the challenge of the times presents an opportunity for personal growth, to be strong where we were formerly weak. Joanna Macy likens the situation to being on a path forward. On one side of the path is falling off into despair, retreating into giving up hope, and living in a state of paralysis. On the other side is blaming and lashing out, also giving up on forward progress but directing our anger and frustration at others. We must not fall off the path on either side, but keep moving straight ahead, toward the end goal of the Great Turning.

Our situation in relation to the path forward could be likened to a ship on the ocean where a great storm lies somewhere ahead on its course. Those on the ship wish they could avoid the storm. If they had changed course earlier, they might have gone around it. But it is too late for that: The storm is moving at a certain pace on its path, and the ship can only sail so fast. No matter what direction the crew chooses, the ship will go through the storm.

The storm is no ordinary storm. In the history of ships, it is the strongest storm that has ever formed. It wreaks its destruction in many forms: powerful wind, enormous waves, and twisting currents, all capable of inflicting grave damage on the ship. It is also a storm with vast longevity, capable of going on and on.

The storm may be the strongest in history, but the ship is also the toughest and most resilient ship ever built. Perhaps at first glance it seems fractious onboard, with the crew arguing about their current situation and how to proceed. On a deeper level, though, the structure is strong. It is made strong by the vast network of individuals and organizations in the crew dedicated to keeping it afloat. The skills of this crew include R&D skills, the ability to explore and detect, skills for caring for both the natural environment and for others in human society, skills in the areas of transportation and communication, and the ability to fabricate and repair. The outer edges of the storm are already testing the ship, and so far, whenever some part of the ship is damaged, the crew steps up to make the necessary repairs. The more difficult the challenges, the more heroic and creative the response. The ship has the unusual feature, for a ship, that decisions made on board can lessen or increase the severity of the storm – anthropogenic causes are major contributors to climate change. Even here, though, the ship's strength comes through in the ability to model and anticipate how policies can hurt or help the impact of climate change. The ship's crew understands its relationship with the storm.

Will the ship survive the storm? No one can predict the exact future either of how the storm will unfold or how the ship will fare. It is possible that our upsetting of the climate system with our industrial society has already set in motion the eventual destruction of that society, the very thing that, as was argued above, should be avoided because of all the additional problems it would create. But the ship has every chance of succeeding, of remaining afloat and not sinking. Furthermore, its prospects can only be helped by approaching the situation with a positive attitude. If we decide as a society to strive for the most effective climate solution we can create, it can surely make a difference. Those who have the good fortune to have access to modern amenities and enjoy relative comfort owe it to the less fortunate, to future generations, and to all the non-human living beings on the planet to try.

ABOUT THE AUTHOR

Francis Vanek grew up in Ithaca, NY, was a Rotary Exchange student in Japan from 1985 to 1986, and graduated from Cornell University in 1991 with a Bachelor of Science degree in Mechanical Engineering and a Bachelor of Arts degree in Asian Studies. After working with the Nissan Motor organization he returned to graduate school and earned a doctorate in Systems Engineering from the University of Pennsylvania in 1998. He taught at Heriot-Watt University in Edinburgh, Scotland, from 1998 to 2001, and then returned to Cornell University to join the faculty, where he is currently Senior Lecture in Civil and Environmental Engineering. His teaching and research focuses on renewable energy, sustainable transportation, and green building, and he is the lead author of the textbooks *Energy Systems Engineering: Evaluation and Implementation* (editions released in 2008, 2012, 2016, and 2021) and *Sustainable Transportation Systems Engineering*, both from McGraw-Hill. Since 2002 he has been a resident with his family of the Ecovillage at Ithaca cohousing community, which pursues energy efficiency and renewable energy as part of its sustainability mission.

REFERENCES AND FURTHER READING

Chapter 2

Cambridge Energy Research Associates. (2006) Press release 60907-9. Cambridge Energy Research Associates, Cambridge, MA.

European Photovoltaic Industry Association (2018). Global Market Outlook 2018-2022. EPIA, Paris.

Global Wind Energy Council. (2018) Global Wind Report 2018. GWEC, Hamburg.

Intergovernmental Panel on Climate Change. (2018) Summary for policymakers of IPCC special report on global warming of 1.5 Degrees C. IPCC, Geneva.

International Council on Systems Engineering. (2006) Systems Engineering Handbook: A guide for system life cycle process and activities. INCOSE, Seattle.

International Energy Agency. (2018) World Energy Outlook 2018. IEA, Paris.

Lorenzo, E. (1994) Solar Electricity: Engineering of Photovoltaic Systems, PROGENSA, Seville, Spain.

Sperling, D, and D Gordon. (2009) Two billion cars: Driving toward sustainability. Oxford University Press, New York.

U.S. Energy Information Administration. (2018) Annual Energy Outlook 2018 with Projections to 2050. USEIA, Washington, DC.

Chapter 3

Bartlett, A. (2000). "An Analysis of US and World Oil Production Patterns Using Hubbert-Style Curves." Mathematical Geology, Vol. 32, Num. 1, pp. 1–17.

Cambridge Energy Research Associates. (2006) Press release 60907-9. Cambridge Energy Research Associates, Cambridge, MA.

Howarth, A., R. Santoro, and A. Ingraffea (2011). "Methane and the greenhouse-gas footprint of natural gas from shale formations: A letter." Climatic Change, online journal, April 12, 2011, edition. Accessed April 21, 2011.

Hubbert, M. K. (1956). Nuclear Energy and the Fossil Fuels. American Petroleum Institute, Drilling and Production Practices, pp. 7–25.

International Energy Agency. (2018) World Energy Outlook 2018. IEA, Paris.

U.S. Energy Information Administration. (2018) Annual Energy Outlook 2018 with Projections to 2050. USEIA, Washington, DC.

Chapter 4

Krigger, J, and C Dorsi. (2008) The Homeowner's Handbook to Energy Efficiency: A Guide to Big and Small Improvements. Saturn Resource Management, Helena, MT.

Mackay, D. (2009) Sustainable Energy: Without the Hot Air. UIT Cambridge Limited, Cambridge.

Randolph, J., and G. Masters (2008). Energy for Sustainability: Technology, Planning, Policy. Island Press, Washington, DC.

Von Weizsacker, E. (1998) Factor Four: Doubling Wealth, Halving Resource Use. Earthscan, London.

Wulfinghoff, D. (1999) Energy Efficiency Manual. Energy Institute Press, Wheaton, MD.

Chapter 5

Earthscan Publishing. (2008) Planning and installing solar photovoltaics: Second edition. Earthscan, London.

Moore, H, and L Post. (2007) Five years of operating experience at the Springerville solar PV plant. Technical report, Sandia National Labs, Albuquerque, NM.

Solar Energy Industries Association (SEIA). (2017) Solar Market Insight Report 2017 Q2. SEIA, Washington, DC.

Weisman, A. (1998) Gaviotas: A Village to Reinvent the World. Chelsea Green Publishers, White River Junction, VT.

Chapter 6

American Society of Heating, Refrigeration and Air-conditioning Engineers (ASHRAE). (2001) Handbook of Fundamentals. ASHRAE, Atlanta, GA.

Lu, X, M McElroy, and J Kiviluoma. (2009) Global potential for wind-generated electricity. Proceedings of the National Academy of Sciences, Washington, DC.

Manwell, J. F., J. G. McGowan, and A. L. Rogers (2010). Wind Energy Explained: Theory, Design, and Application, 2nd Edition. Wiley, Chichester, West Sussex.

US Department of Energy. (2009) 20% Wind by 2030: Increasing Wind Energy's Contribution to US Electricity Supply. National Renewable Energy Laboratories, Golden, CO.

Vanek, F, L Albright, and L Angenent. (2016) Energy Systems Engineering: Evaluation and Implementation. Third Edition. McGraw-Hill, New York.

Wan, Y. (2012) Long-term wind power variability. Technical report, National Renewable Energy Laboratories, Golden, CO.

Chapter 7

Berge, R and J Zerbe. (2004) Primer on wood biomass for energy. Technical report, USDA Forest Services, Forest Products Laboratory, Madison, WI.

Campbell, R. (2010) "Small hydro and low-head hydro power technologies and prospects." Technical report, Congressional Research Service, Washington, DC.

Jeyapandian, L, A Makmoen, G Quist, and D Tao. (2017) "Hydropower on Sixmile Creek: A Feasibility Study." Final report, Master of Engineering Management Project, Cornell University, May 2017. Available online at www.lightlink.com/francis/.

Loucks, D.P., and Van Beek, E. (2005) Water Resources Systems Planning and Management: An Introduction to Methods, Models, and Applications. United Nations Education, Scientific, and Cultural Organization (UNESCO), New York.

McPhee, J. (1971) Encounters with the Archdruid. Farrar, Strauss, and Giroux, New York.

Revelle, C et al. (1997) *Civil & Environmental Infrastructure Systems*. Prentice-Hall, New York.

Sorensen, B. (1992) Renewable Energy: Physics, Engineering, Environmental Impacts, Economics, and Planning. Elsevier, London.

U.S. Department of Energy. (2010) Hydro potential. On-line resource, Office of Energy Efficiency and Renewable Energy, USDOE, Golden, CO.

U.S. Department of Energy. (2015) 2014 Hydropower Market Report. USDOE, Office of Energy Efficiency and Renewable Energy, Wind and Water Technologies Office, Golden, CO.

Chapter 8

Davies, J, M Grant, J Venezia, J Amador (2007). "Greenhouse gas emissions of the US transport sector: trends, uncertainties, and methodological improvements", Transportation Research Record Number 2017, pp. 41-46.

Greene, D. (1996) Transportation and Energy. Eno Transportation Foundation, Lansdowne, VA.

McKibben, Bill. (2008) Deep Economy: The Wealth of Communities and the Durable Future. St. Martins Griffin, New York.

National Biodiesel Board. (2019) Emissions calculator. On-line resource, available at www.nbb.org. National Biodiesel Board, Washington, DC.

Sony Pictures. (2006) Who Killed the Electric Car? Documentary Film. Directed by Chris Paine. Sony Pictures, Los Angeles, CA.

Sony Pictures. (2011) Revenge of the Electric Car. Documentary Film. Directed by Chris Paine. Sony Pictures, Los Angeles, CA.

Kempton, W. and J. Tomic (2005). "Vehicle-to-Grid Power Fundamentals: Calculating Capacity and Net Revenue." *Journal of Power Systems* 144, 268–279.

U.S.-Canada Power System Outage Task Force (2004). Final Report on the August 14, 2003 Blackout in the United States and Canada: Causes and Recommendations. U.S. Department of Energy, Washington, DC.

U.S. Energy Information Administration. (2013) Pumped storage provides grid reliability even with net generation loss. Report, July 8, 2013. USEIA, Washington, DC.

Wald, M. (2008) "Wind energy bumps into power grid's limits." New York Times, August 26, 2008.

Wood-Mackenzie. (2019) Power & Renewables Report. Wood-Mackenzie, Washington, DC.

Chapter 9

Beck, P. (1999). "Nuclear Energy in the Twenty-First Century: Examination of a Contentious Subject." Annual Review of Energy & Environment, Vol. 24, pp. 113–137.

International Energy Agency. (2013) World Energy Outlook 2013. IEA, London.

Lackner, K., C. Wendt, D. Butt, et al. (1995). "Carbon Dioxide Disposal in Carbonate Materials." Energy, Vol. 20, No. 11, pp. 1153–1170.

Nuclear Regulatory Commission (2011). Recommendations for Enhancing Reactor Safety in the 21st Century: The Near-term Task Force Review of Insights from the Fukushima Dai-ichi Accident. Technical report, NRC, Washington, DC.

Sepulvida, N, J Jenkins, and R Lester. (2018) "The Role of Firm Low-Carbon Electricity Resources in Deep Decarbonization of Power Generation." Joule, Vol.2, N.11, pp.2403-2420.

White, C., B. Strazisar, and E. Granite. (2003). "Separation and Capture of CO2 from Large Stationary Sources and Sequestration in Geological Formations—Coalbeds and Deep Saline Aquifers." Journal of the Air & Waste Management Association, Vol. 53, pp. 645–713.

Chapter 10

California Air Resources Board. (2019) California Scenarios to 80% CO_2 Reduction by 2050. CARB, Diamond Bar, CA.

Macy, J. and C. Johnstone. (2011) Active hope: How to face the mess we're in without going crazy. New World Library, Novato, CA.

Rockstrom, J, W. Steffen, and K. Noone. (2009). "A Safe Operating Space for Humans." Nature, 461, pp. 472–475.

Von Weiszacker, U., A. Lovins, and H. Lovins (1997). Factor Four: Doubling Wealth, Halving Resource Use. Earthscan, London.

Yergin, D. (2012). The Quest: Energy, Security, and the Remaking of the Modern World. Penguin, London

INDEX

material resource management 361

Mayacamas Mountains 229

McKibben, Bill xxvii, 317, 383

Melbourne 148

Menlo Park 371

methane 46, 62, 219, 225, 275,
　313, 380

Michigan 255

microgrid 269, 270, 271, 272, 273, 317

micro-hydropower 22, 201

microturbine 76, 92, 219, 220,
　221, 223

Mildura 151

mini-grid 270

Minneapolis 103

Minnesota 181

mitigation 71

motorcycle 277

mountain-top removal 52

Mount Signal 123, 263

Muehlhausen 123

multi-megawatt solar 131, 266

Munich 232

municipal solid waste 219, 224, 244

N

nacelle 153, 154, 156, 157, 166, 176

nameplate capacity 6, 99, 124,
　168, 186, 216, 229, 257, 271,
　288, 352

nanogrid 270

Nantucket Sound 191

National Biodiesel Board 306, 383

National Grid Great Britain 249

National Oceanic and Atmospheric
　Administration 11

National Renewable Energy
　Laboratories 102, 104, 106, 107,
　381, 382

natural gas xxvi, xxxii, xxxv, 10, 19-20,
　23-24, 35, 46, 49-52, 55-64, 75,
　77, 91, 94, 134-136, 178, 215-
　216, 226, 238, 248, 261-262,
　287, 304, 313, 316, 323, 324,
　342, 350, 352, 380

neolithic 370

Netherlands 112, 241, 284, 337

net metering 79, 112, 117, 118, 119,
　120, 133, 134

Nevada 124, 196, 330

New Haven 295

New Mexico 98, 104, 124

New York State xxviii, 34, 103, 110,
　125, 182, 188, 245

New York State Electric & Gas 245

New Zealand 363

Niagara Falls 194, 198, 202, 371

nonconventional fossil fuels 12

nonrenewable resources 319

Normandy 210

North America 15, 149, 162, 232,
　240, 363

North Carolina 9

North Dakota 67

Northeast blackout 248

Northeast Corridor 295

Northern Ireland 210, 249

North Korea 269

North Sea 169, 191

not-in-my-back-yard 190

Vogtle plant 320, 325

Volkswagen xxv, 284

Volvo 284

W

Wales 249

Washington state 105, 197, 200, 264

waste stream 193, 212, 218, 220, 225, 226, 239, 244, 303, 339

waste-to-energy conversion 219, 224

wastewater 218, 219, 220, 221, 222, 224, 239, 240, 244, 271, 273

wastewater treatment plant 219, 220, 239, 271, 273

Watts Bar 2 325

wave energy station 211

waves 8, 25, 150, 193, 209, 211, 243, 343, 353, 358, 374

weir 201

Weiszacker, Ernst von 357

Wind xxv, xxviii, 8, 11, 21-22, 25, 27, 34-40, 42, 44, 50, 53-54, 57, 62-63, 72-73, 76, 90, 97, 102, 136, 149-194, 196, 202-203, 206-207, 210, 217, 236, 243-247, 252-253, 260-266, 268, 287,
292, 320, 323, 337-338, 342-343, 353-361, 374, 379, 381-384

wind farm xxviii, 11, 22, 34, 54, 76, 151-160, 169, 171, 175, 177-188, 191, 196, 236, 252, 260-262, 266, 338

windmill 154

wind rose 171, 172

wood-burning stove 214

Wood Mackenzie 258

World Bank 200

World War II 18, 346

worldwide agreement 8

Wyoming 182

Y

Yale University 356

Yangtze River 197

yaw 154, 177

yield management 301

Yucca Mountain 330

Z

ZeroAvia 316

Zimbabwe 368

Zoom 317

Printed in the United States
by Baker & Taylor Publisher Services